# ROSS.
## In the Twelfth Century.

after Robert Bain
Dingwall, 1899

ARMS OF THE CHIEFS OF CLAN ROSS OF BALNAGOWAN

The

# Great Clan Ross

## WITH HIGHLAND NOTES
## and
## GENEALOGIES OF THE CADET BRANCHES
## IN SCOTLAND AND THE NEW WORLD

JOHN ROBERT ROSS, M.D., B.SC.

*in collaboration with*

Sheriff Charles Campbell Ross, Q.C.
and
A. C. Gordon Ross, MB., Ch.B.

PRINTED AND BOUND IN CANADA
BY
JOHN DEYELL LIMITED/LINDSAY

# FOREWORD

I have followed with great interest the preparation of this book of the Clan Ross, its families and personalities. It might be argued that such a book, inspired by our pride and interest in the long and, for the most part, honourable history of our clan, traced back to the twelfth century, is an anachronism today. Moreover, it might be argued that the families of whom this book treats are not the whole clan; but they are the lines of bright colour in the sett of the tartan. The Rosses remained on their same lands for many generations and intermarried locally, or with families along the shores of the Moray Firth. Their good and bad fortunes, their politics and their lawsuits, affected the lives of their tenants and retainers. The younger sons went out to seek their fortunes in Sweden and Russia, in India, the United States, and Canada; as professional men, merchants and planters. Some engaged in the service of the East India Company and fought with the forces of the Crown. A few returned with fortunes to enrich their family estates, many more died abroad, young and unmarried, in the eighteenth and nineteenth centuries. In this twentieth century, the great dispersion of the Scots continues. Surely the ties of interest, love, and pride, serve to bind these scattered generations of Scots to Scotland, and bind the Ross clansmen to their homeland and to their present Chief, Miss Rosa Ross of Pitcalnie. These ties will continue to weave a strong web of friendship across the world.

Charles Ross of that Ilk, Younger
Chief Designate Clan Ross

Dellachapple,
Garmouth,
by Fochabers, Moray.
January 23rd, 1966.

# QUOTATION FROM SIR GEORGE W. ROSS,

PREMIER OF ONTARIO AND PRESIDENT OF THE CLAN ROSS IN AMERICA

"The patriotic spirit which the Scottish race exhibits in all parts of the world, comes, in my opinion, from the traditional feeling that no matter where they reside, they are still clansmen, and feel in their veins the emotions of devotion to each other which were necessary in the early history of the race. To be a clansman in the true sense of the word means a sense of brotherhood, ready in any emergency to repell an invader, to protect the weak and assist a fellow clansman in adversity or need. This feeling of brotherhood is an inheritance to be prized and is a never failing fountain of loyalty which is calculated to promote unity in national affairs and a spirit of kindness and citizenship in all its forms and duties. In bringing together the members of the Clan Ross you are promoting this unity and connecting a new land with the traditions of a race whose skill in arms and art and song have given them a place in the history of the world, of which our fellow clansmen, I am sure, are proud. In this history the Clan Ross has played its part. What has made Scotland great will make your country and my country great. Energy of character, integrity of purpose, nobility of ideals and a conscience void of offense before God and man, are qualifications for the citizenship which is our desire to cultivate."

Office of the Premier.

George W. Ross, K.B., LL.D.,
Pres. Clan Ross in America 1913

# PREFACE

The Clan Ross has played a proud part in the pageant of Scottish history, and has produced many members of the early highland aristocracy.

Euphemia, Countess of Ross married Richard II of Scotland and became Queen of Scots in 1371. There were ten Earls of Ross, two dukes of Ross and thirteen chiefs at Balnagowan castle, the hereditary seat of the clan.

A short summary of the highlights in the history of this great Clan will acquaint the reader with some of the more important details of its history, and with the sequence of events occurring in Ross-shire after the early years of the thirteenth Century.

The history of Clan Ross dates from Farquhar who was created first Earl of Ross by King Alexander II of Scotland in 1234. Thus the origins of Clan Ross are antecedent to those of many of the other clans of the Highlands. Earl Farquhar was a trusted supporter of his king. He defended the royal standards in battle as early as the year 1215, and his military prowess was a deciding factor in protecting the western shores of Scotland from the Norse invaders. For his loyal support, Earl Farquhar was given extensive lands which became known as the Earldom of Ross (later Ross-shire) over which he held complete control.

This illustrious soldier, and hereditary priest, lived in the ancient pictish village of Applecross which is situated on the west coast of Scotland. From here his influence and that of the succeeding Earls of Ross spread through the highlands, and the descendants of this family owned a number of castles and strongholds as well as vast estates in Ross-shire. One of these descendants, William, third Earl of Ross fought at Bannockburn, where his younger son Sir Walter de Ros was killed. Sir Walter was one of the few Scottish nobles who fell in this battle. Many of the later Earls of Ross and the Rosses of Balnagowan followed the noble precepts of the first Earl, Farquhar; but some Clan chiefs became too satiated with power, and came to consider themselves superior to royalty, an attitude which had repercussions decidedly to their disadvantage.

One of these was Earl John, tenth and last Earl of Ross and last Lord of the Isles. He was a lawless and unscrupulous man who made a determined stand against the King and Court of Scotland. After contracting a treasonable alliance with the English king he was finally apprehended and brought to justice. He was then deprived of his title to the Earldom and to the Lordship of the Isles by James IV and the Earldom of Ross reverted to the crown.

Hugh of Rarichies, being a son of the fourth Earl of Ross, became first of the Rosses of Balnagowan, and first Chief of Clan Ross. Hugh obtained a charter of the lands of Balnagowan in 1374 and for over three centuries the Rosses of Balnagowan remained the principal family of the Clan, and its members were staunch supporters of law and order in the Highlands.

David, twelfth Chief and laird of Balnagowan, was a brave soldier and loyal royalist. He raised a regiment of 800 Ross-shire highlanders at his own expense and marched with the Scottish Army to the fatal battle of Worcester, where he and most of his men were taken prisoner by Cromwell's army. A number of these men and their families, who belonged to the Balblair branch of Clan Ross, were sent to New England as colonists. Their names are found in the early records of the Massachusetts Bay colony.

After the death of his son David Ross, thirteenth laird of Balnagowan in 1711 the title and estates were usurped first by a family of Stewarts and later by an urelated family of Rosses of Hawkhead. The rightful heir at this time was Malcom Ross, fifth of the cadet branch of Pitcalnie. However Malcolm and his heirs were unsuccessful in gaining possession of the Balnagowan estates, or the title of Chief, until the early years of the twentieth century when Sarah Williamson Ross of the house of Pitcalnie established her claim and finally became Chief of Clan Ross. Miss Rosa Williamson Ross, a sister of Sarah was chief of Clan until her recent death in March 1968 at the age of ninety years. She was the last surviving member of the Rosses of Pitcalnie.

The chiefship was to have passed to Chief Designate Charles Campbell Ross of that Ilk Younger, of the Cadet house of Shandwick who matriculated arms in 1961. Recently however, the members of the clan were saddened by the death of the Chief Designate, who died in 1966 after a lingering illness. David Campbell Ross his son is now chief of Clan Ross.

One of the notable Chiefs of Clan Ross in recent years was Sir Charles Lockhart Ross ninth Baronet of Nova Scotia who resided at Balnagowan

Castle. Sir Charles, a fine sportsman, invented and perfected the famous Ross Rifle which was used by the Canadian troops in the first World War.

Another outstanding member of the Clan was Sir Ronald Ross. This great soldier and surgeon while serving in India in the later years of the nineteenth Century discovered the causative factors of malaria, and this dread disease was brought under control. For this important work he was awarded the Nobel prize in 1902 as well as many other honorary degrees. The Ross Institute at Putney, England bears his name.

Many of the Rosses who have emigrated to different parts of the world have reflected great credit on the country of their origin. A number of members of the clan have made outstanding contributions in the sciences, in literature, in exploration, and in the fields of medicine, government, astronomy, and railroad building. Brief accounts of some of their accomplishments are included.

The myths, legends, and early Scottish ballads were an important part of the life of the Gael and reference is made to these, as well as to the early history of clanship in the Highlands.

# TABLE OF CONTENTS

| | Page |
|---|---|
| CHAPTER 1 / Early History of Ross-Shire | 1 |
| Origins and growth of Clan Ross | 1 |
| Septs of Clan Ross | 3 |
| Lands and Clans of Ross-shire and Clanship in the highlands | 4 |
| Castles and Strongholds | 10 |
| Religion in the Highlands | 15 |
| Ancient Abbeys and Chapels in Ross-shire | 18 |
| Brochs, Inscribed Stones, and Vitrified Forts | 19 |
| Legends and Ballads of Ross-shire | 20 |
| CHAPTER 2 / The Earls of Ross | 36 |
| The Original Line of succession | 36 |
| Farquhar first Earl of Ross | 38 |
| William second Earl of Ross | 40 |
| William third Earl of Ross | 41 |
| Hugh fourth Earl of Ross | 43 |
| William fifth Earl of Ross | 44 |
| The Leslie Line of succession | 46 |
| Sir Walter Leslie sixth Earl | 46 |
| Alexander Leslie seventh Earl | 49 |
| Sir John Stewart eighth Earl of Ross | 49 |
| The Lords of the Isles | 49 |
| John (Eoin) of Islay, first Lord | 50 |
| Donald, second Lord | 51 |
| Alexander, third Lord of the Isles and ninth Earl of Ross | 54 |
| John, Earl of Ross and fourth Lord of the Isles | 55 |

Claimants for the Earldom of Ross and Lordship of the Isles 58

CHAPTER 3 / Chiefs of Clan Ross of Balnagowan 60

Hugh of Rarichies 60
William Ross of Balnagowan 61
Clan Ross of Balnagowan and Cadet branches 62
Walter Ross third Baron of Balnagowan 64
Hugh Ross fourth chief of Clan 64
John Ross fifth Laird 65
Alexander Ross sixth Laird 65
Sir David Ross Chief of Clan 67
Walter eighth Laird 67
Alexander Ross ninth Chief 67
George Ross tenth Chief of Balnagowan 70
David Ross eleventh Chief of Clan 72
David Ross twelfth Chief 73
David Ross thirteenth Chief of Balnagowan 75
Disputes for the succession; Lady Ross, the Earl of Moray, and Francis Stewart 76
The new line of succession of Balnagowan 77
The Lord Rosses of Hawkhead 80
Lt. Gen. Charles Ross 80
Col. Charles Ross 81
The Lockhart Rosses of Balnagowan 82
The Balnagowan and Tain Historical Documents 88

CHAPTER 4 / Cadet Branches of Clan Ross 90

The Rosses of Pitcalnie 90
The Rosses of Shandwick 96
Matriculation of Arms of Chief Designate Charles Campbell Ross 109

CHAPTER 5 / Clan Ross in the New World 113

Failure in Nova Scotia 113
The Rosses in New England 114
The Rosses of Balblair, early American Colonists 116
Betsy Ross and the American Flag 120
The Rosses of Bladensburg 121
Early Colonization in Canada 122
Scots Settlements at Pictou, Antigonish, and Prince Edward Island 124
The Glengarry Settlement 127
The Red River Settlement 129

Rosses in the Hudson's Bay Company 132
Clan Ross Society in America 133

CHAPTER 6 / Outstanding Members of Clan Ross 143

In Britain 143
In the Tropics 151
Australia and New Zealand 154
At the Poles 155

APPENDIX I / Cadet Branches of Clan Ross 159

The Rosses of Invercharron 159
The Rosses of Braelangwell, Easter Fearn and Ankerville 161
The Rosses of Achnacloich 163
The Rosses of Kindeace 165
The Rosses of Invercastley 167
The Rosses of Calrossie 169
The Rosses of Aldie 170
The Rosses of Pitkerrie and Cromarty 171

APPENDIX II /

King Robert Stewart II of Scotland and the Clan Ross 176

APPENDIX III /

The Seven Euphemias 180

APPENDIX IV /

Genealogy of the Twelfth Lord Ross of Hawkhead 184

This history of the Clan Ross is dedicated to
my father and mother
William John Ross and Margaret Helena (Shields) Ross

and to

The Right Honourable William Ross M.A., M.B.E.
Secretary of State for Scotland

and

Col. the Honourable Frank M. Ross C.M.G., M.C., L.L.D.
Former Lieutenant Governor of British Columbia

# ACKNOWLEDGEMENTS

The author wishes to express his sincere gratitude to the late Chief designate Charles Campbell Ross and to Dr. A. C. Gordon Ross. Their generous collaboration in supplying many details of clan history and their assistance in the editing of this book are greatly appreciated.

The expert guidance proffered by Major J. J. Ross, president of the Clan Ross Association of Canada has been invaluable in preparing this clan history for publication.

Much of the historic background and clan genealogies have been derived from "The History of the Clan Ross" by the late Alexander M. Ross of Dingwall, published in 1932. Appreciation is acknowledged for the information derived from this important source.

Many other standard works relating to early Scottish History and Literature have been consulted. Particular acknowledgement is made to the following:—

1. The Clan Ross by Donald Mackinnon
   W. and A. K. Johnston and G. W. Bacon Ltd.
   Edinburgh and London, 1957
2. Scottish Highlands, Highland Clans and Regiments
   by J. S. Keltie F.S.A.
   Five Vols. William Mackenzie, London, 1868
3. Scottish History and Literature by John M. Ross. LL.D., Glasgow, 1884 James Maclehose & Sons
4. Castles and Keeps of Scotland by F. R. Fraprie, L.C. Page & Co. Boston, 1907
5. Old Ross-shire and Scotland as seen in the Tain and Balnagowan Documents
   by W. Macgill, Inverness, 1909
   The Northern Counties Newspaper and Publishing Co.

6. Ballads and Songs of Scotland by J. C. Murray, Toronto, 1874
7. Scottish Historical and Romantic Ballads by John Finlay, Edinburgh, 1808, James Ballantyne and Co.
8. Scotland and the Scots by Peter Ross, Scottish American Office, New York, 1899
9. A History of the Highlands and Highland Clans by James Brown, Edinburgh, 1854. A. Fullerton and Co.
10. Dingwall's Story of A Thousand Years, by Norman Macrae, The North Star Proprietors, Dingwall, 1923
11. History of the Ancient Province of Ross From the Earliest to the Present Time by Robert Bain
Pefferside Press Ltd., Dingwall, 1899
12. The Coldstream Guards, 1914-18
by Lieutenant-Colonel Sir John Ross-of-Bladensburg, K.C.B., K.C.V.O. Oxford University Press, London. Humphrey Milford, 1928
13. Heroic Gaelic Ballads collected in Scotland from 1512-1871 by J. F. Campbell. Spottiswoode and Co., New St. Square, 1872
14. The Romantic Settlement of Lord Selkirk's Colonists
Dr. Geo. Bryce
Musson Book Co., Toronto, 1909
15. Ancient Monuments in Scotland
Great Britain Ministry of Works, 1955
16. History of County of Pictou, Nova Scotia
Rev. George Patterson D.D., 1877
17. Scots in Canada. J. M. Gibson. Kegan, Trench, Tubnez & Co.
Driden House, London
18. The Scotsburn Congregation, Pictou County by John Murray D.D.
News Publishing Co., Truro N.S., 1925
19. The Book of Highland Minstrelsy
D. Ogilvy, Richard Griffin and Co.
Glasgow, 1860

The authors are indebted to Agness Mure Mackenzie, C.B.E., LL.D., M.A., D.Litt., for making plain several parts in her book, "The Rise of the Stewarts", and to Professor J. D. Mackie for his "History of Scotland".

Finally the authors are most grateful to Eila Isobel Ross for the artistic illustrations and reproductions found throughout the book.

# 1. THE EARLY HISTORY OF ROSS-SHIRE

## THE ORIGINS AND GROWTH OF CLAN ROSS

Clan Ross, or, as it is known in the Gaelic, Clann Rois or Clann Aindreis (Anrias), arose originally from the Celtic O'Beolain Earls of Ross, but the surname of Ross was not taken by this family until 1357, when Hugh of Rarichies adopted the name from the County of Ross where he held his estates. Hugh Ross' ancestors were the powerful and influential Earls of Ross.

The Rosses as a family, or clan, can be traced back for more than seven hundred years under the name of the Earls of Ross. Ross County is mentioned in the North Sagas along with the districts such as Moray, which were ruled by the Mormaers who preceded the Earls. Finleigh was one of the early Mormaers of Ross. He was assassinated in 1020 in a feud with Maolbride, the Mormaer of Moray. Severe punishment and retaliation were considered right and just at this time in Highland history. It is not unusual then to find that twelve years later, in revenge for Finleigh's murder, Maolbride with fifty of his men were locked up and burned within their own castle by the men of Ross.

Skene, in his *Highlanders of Scotland,* writes as follows: "It is well known that the surname of Ross has always been rendered in Gaelic, Clann Aindrias or Clan Gille Aindrias, and that the Rosses appear under the former of these appellations in all the early Acts of Parliament; there is also an unvarying tradition in the Highlands that on the death of William, last Earl of Ross of the original family in 1372, a certain Paul MacTire was for some time Chief of the clan, and this tradition is corroborated by the fact that there is a charter by this William, Earl of Ross, to this very Paul MacTire, in which he styles him his cousin. There appears, however, among the numerous clans designated in the manuscript of 1450, one termed Clan Gilleanrias[1], which commences with Paul MacTire, so that there can be little doubt that this clan is the same with that of the Rosses, and in this manuscript they are traced upwards in a direct line to a certain 'Gilleon na h'Airde' or Collin of Aird, who lived in the tenth century."

In 1463 Alexander MacKenzie of Kintail "Alasdair the Upright" received from John, Earl of Ross, the lands of Strathgarvie. The MacKenzie Chiefs were originally dependents of the Earls of Ross, but after the forfeiture to the crown of his lands in Ross-shire by John, Earl of Ross in 1476, they became completely independent. From that time onward the MacKenzie clan spread themselves over a large portion of Wester Ross, including Applecross, Goul, Delvin, Assint, and other counties. According to Simbert, a large number of families who belonged originally to Clan Ross were absorbed by the MacKenzies, and having adopted the name, the numbers of Clan Ross were greatly depleted.

In an Act of Parliament, passed in 1587, the names of all the Highland Clans are specified, among them Clan Aindreis or the Rosses. By that year the Rosses were the most numerous of the family names in the Highlands and outnumbered all the other clans. The majority of the population of the county of Ross at that time considered themselves as belonging to the family of Rosses of Balnagowan, descendants of the ancient Earls of Ross.

During the seventeenth century, the growth of Clan Ross was not as rapid as that of the MacLeods and the MacKenzies. Of the Highland clansmen that were raised for King James' army in 1704, the Rosses of Balnagowan were credited with 200 men, the MacLeods having 700, and the MacKenzies (including Macraes) having raised 700. In the 1715 (Jacobite) Rebellion, the Rosses and Munros together sent 700 men to fight for His Majesty's cause. They were joined in this resistance with the men of Argyll, Lord Sutherland's, Lord Lovat's Frasers, the Grants, and the Forbes Clan. The MacKenzies, with 3000, were the most numerour clan, and along with the Macdonalds, MacLeods, Camerons, Chisholms, and Macintoshes, they took the side of the "rebels".

Clan Ross continued to increase in numbers but at a slower rate than previously. In the 1845 *Statistical Account* we read, under the heading of "Tain", "Most of the landowners, and in truth most of the people, bore the name of Ross; or, to speak more correctly, almost everybody possesses two surnames, by one of which (in general a patronymic beginning with *Mac*) he was universally known in conversation, though he deemed himself called upon to change it to Ross, or sometimes to

[1] The Clan Gilleanrias, descended from Clan Aindreis, are claimed by Donald Mackinnon to be a separate and distinct clan from the Rosses.

Munro, whenever he acquired any status in society, or became able to write his name. . . . When the by-names of those who had risen in society had been forgotten, it became absolutely necessary to invent others to distinguish the multitudes of Rosses and Munros."

During the nineteenth century the Rosses were somewhat fewer in number than the MacKenzies, but were more numerous than the Munros, Macraes, MacLeods, Urquharts, and other principal surnames of the country; all of them (if we include the Lewis MacLeods) claiming Ross-shire as their original home. In the Scottish census of 1861, the Ross surnames numbered 18,254, as compared with 23,272 MacKenzies, 15,571 MacLeods, and 10,098 Munros.

In spite of the evictions of many families of Rosses during the "clearances", and the emigration over the years of many more families of Rosses to America, Australia, New Zealand, and elsewhere, there are still more persons bearing the name of Ross at the present time in the old clan territory than there are persons of any other name.

### *Septs of Clan Ross*

Like all other Highland clans, the Rosses have several septs and dependents*. The full list, as commonly allowed, is as follows:

| | | |
|---|---|---|
| Corbett | MacCulloch | Mitchell |
| Denoon | Maclulich | Taggart |
| Dingwall | MacTaggart | Tarrell |
| Fearn | MacTear | Vass |
| Gillanders | MacTyre | Wass |

Of these the Dingwalls, the MacCullochs, and the Vasses were at times associated with other clans, but chiefly with the Munros, taking part with them in several of their feuds in earlier days. The Vasses, or Wasses who held Lockslyn Castle, joined the Rosses in their ancient clan feuds. In 1487, the chief of the clan Ross, Alexander Ross of Balnagowan, led his men into battle against the combined forces of the Sutherlands and Mackays. The Rosses suffered a severe defeat at Alt a'Charrais and many of the name of Vass (given as Waus) were slain fighting on the side of the Rosses. In the same conflict, Angus MacCulloch of Tarrell, "one of the gentlemen of Ross of Balnagowan," was listed among those slain. In 1647 the Lyon King of Arms matriculates the coat of armour of Sir Hugh MacCulloch as "being descended of the family of Cadboll in Ross."

The Dingwalls, Gillanders, MacAndrews, and MacTaggarts had associations with the Rosses at various dates. The Gillanders have never

*Persons with these names belong to the Clan Ross.

been a numerous clan, but they have had a family history as respectable as it is ancient. The 1450 genealogical manuscript of the Mathesons states that the Ross portions of North Argyll were in the hands of several Ross-shire clans, the Gillanders being mentioned along with the Mathesons and the MacKenzies. They are referred to by a later chronicler, who, quotes the same manuscript and refers to the Gillanders as "Rosses". During the thirteenth, fourteenth, and fifteenth centuries the Gillanders were in Gairloch before the MacKenzies, who at that period lived in Kintail, their chief domicile.

Some historians include the Andrews and the Andersons as members of Clan Ross but the late Donald Mackinnon, in his excellent book *The Clan Ross,* does not allow this. He states that "although Clan Ross is frequently referred to as *Clann Aindreis* or *Siol Aindreis* (the offspring of Andrew) this is incorrect. . . . Referring to the 1467 Manuscript it is shown that *Clann Aindreis* descended from Gillanders as a distinct clan, and was not connected with Clan Ross."

## THE LANDS AND CLANS OF ROSS-SHIRE AND CLANSHIP IN THE HIGHLANDS

The earliest historical reference to the area of the Highlands which now comprises the County of Ross and Cromarty was said to be made by Ptolemy of Alexandria, the famous Greek geographer, writing about 130 A.D. He gave the names of three tribes occupying this area: the Smerti, who lived in the valleys of the Oykel and Carron rivers and around the Dornoch Firth; the Dekantar tribe on the east coast from the Beauly River northward; and the Karnonaki tribe on the west coast. These and other tribes occupied the territories of Caledonia, and each tribe had a chief at its head. The Caledonians were the progenitors of the Highlanders, and were of Celtic extraction.

The Scots were originally inhabitants of northern Ireland (Dalriada) and after many raids on the southwest coast of Scotland, they finally established themselves in Argyll, Islay, and Jura. The principal obstacle to the Scottish establishment was the opposition of the Picts, who held possession of the entire central and northern sections of Scotland. The kingdoms of the Picts and the Scots were finally united under Kenneth MacAlpin in 844 A.D.

The names of the rivers, towns, and villages in the county of Ross and Cromarty are derived from the Pictish, Gaelic, Norse, and English language depending on the period of history in which they became inhabited. The Picts, spoke a Celtic language more akin to Welsh than Gaelic. They are the earliest inhabitants of whom we have any contemporary written record. The Picts were called Picti by the Romans, Pettr by the Norse, and Cruithne by the Gaelic-speaking Scots. During the eighth, ninth, and tenth centuries the native Picts were continuously harassed by the Norse pirates, who left evidences of their presence in northern Scotland in place names such as Dingwall and Tain.

The original County of Ross formed at that time part of the great province of Moray, but when the rule of the Celtic Mormaers ceased, as a result of the settlement of the district by people from other parts (as ordered by David I, who was anxious to break the power of the Celts), the boundaries of Moray were contracted, and the Earldom of Ross was formed in the early thirteenth century.

At first, Ross proper included only the territory adjoining the Moray and Dornoch Firths, but later it extended from the Black Isle on the East, to Skye and Lewis on the west (see early map of Ross, front cover).

Hector Boece in 1527 describes in some detail the territories of Ross: "Beyound the watter of Spanye[1] Lyis Ros, rising with strait narow hals[2], and thaireftir in cassin furth, with mair braid lesuris[3], valis, and montanis; circulit, baith on the ta syde and the tothir, with the occeane. This cuntre guhair it lyis maist approchand to Ireland seis, hes richt difficill passage and ganis mair[4] for store of bestiall[5] than any habitatioun of man. In Ros ar sundry lochis, bot Lochbroun[6] is maist. Many rivers are in Ros, full of fische. In Ros is Cromarte, an firth and sicker[7] port to all shippis, to saif thame fra danger of tempest, namit be[8] the peple the Heil of Schipmen. In Ros is the town of Thane[9] guhair the blissit banis[10] of Sanct Dutho[11] restis in gret veneratioun of peple."

The County of Ross was constituted in 1661, and that of Cromarty in 1685, both being consolidated into the present County of Ross and Cromarty in 1889. English was probably introduced into the County of Ross in the twelfth century by the sons and grandsons of the Saxon Princess Margaret, wife of Malcolm III, and from that time onward the English language has been gradually supplanting the Gaelic. The Gaelic has remained longer in the islands of the outer Hebrides than in other parts of Scotland, and in parts of Lewis and Skye it may be heard to the present day.

John M. Ross, LL.D., the Scottish historian, writes in 1884: "Amidst all the momentous changes that Scotland witnessed during the twelfth and thirteenth centuries, between the deaths of the Celtic King, Malcolm Canmore (1057-1093) and Alexander the Third (crowned in 1249), noth-

[1] Spey River
[2] hills
[3] open country
[4] is better fitted
[5] for keeping wild beasts
[6] Loch Broom
[7] succour
[8] named by
[9] Tain
[10] Bans
[11] Saint Duthac

ing is more certain than this, that as Scotland increased in political power, subduing internal revolts of disaffected chiefs, now in Galloway, now in Moray and Ross; and wresting from the obstinate hold of Norsemen the Earldom of Caithness and the Lordship of the Isles, her national spirit and pride also increased. The great struggle for independence, which began with the night assault on the English garrison at Lanark and ended with the crowning victory at Bannockburn, planted in the heart of every genuine Scot an undying love of his country and an invincible determination to defend its liberties."

In the sixteenth century the sense of nationality received a fresh and powerful impetus from the religious reformation, in the change from catholicism to presbyterianism, which bound the community together in new bonds of faith and doctrine. Still later, the grand insurrection of the kingdom in defence of its Scottish Presbyterian Church further influenced the character and culture of the people. It is impossible to say at what date, Gaelic, the language of the Gael (originally derived from the Irish), came to be spoken first in Ross, but from the evidence of the Norsemen, the Scots Gael were in possession of at least the west coast of Ross by the end of the eighth century (about 795). Norse settlements were formed in various parts of the western seaboard of Ross and the island of Lewis in the ninth century, and many place names in this area are Norse. The Norse occupation lasted over four hundred and fifty years and ended in 1266, when Magnus IV, successor to King Haakon of Norway, ceded all the Scottish islands except Orkney and Shetland to the Scottish king.

The people of the Hebrides and the adjacent coastal areas of the mainland were a mixture of Celtic and Scandinavian blood, but the Celtic predominated. At the end of the eleventh century Gaelic was the language of Scotland, and was even spoken in the north of England. In the reign of King William the Lion, 1165 to 1214, the Highland mormaers, or chiefs, began to assume the title of earl, in deference to the new Saxon innovations, but the customs of the people remained Gaelic. The lowlands then adopted the Anglo-Saxon language, but the Highlands above the Grampians clung to the Gaelic.

By this time, the division of the population into clans was beginning, a clan being a number of families of the same name, governed by the lineal male descendant of the chief of the original family. Gradually, there arose the institution of clan chiefs, who naturally became the judges and arbiters in the quarrels of their clansmen and followers. They were devoted to the defence of their rights, their property, and their power, and eventually established within their own territories a system of jurisdiction as it existed in other parts of the country. In clanship the people followed their chief as the head of their race, the representative of their common ancestor; they owed him military service for their respective portions of the lands assigned to them. One of the first duties of a new chief was to "ride the marches". He and the men of his clan would follow in procession around the boundaries of his property and in this way establish the claim to his heritable lands. The Highland Chief was the hereditary lord of all who belonged to his clan, wherever they dwelt or whatever lands they occupied. The clan system was well adapted to a people inhabiting a country like the Highlands of Scotland, which, from its peculiar nature and conformation, not only hindered the adoption of other modes of government, but because of the difficulties of travel and communication, may be said to have contributed to the division of the people into separate families or clans. Each clan became divided into branches of the main stock, having individual chieftains. These were known as cadet branches.

The Highlanders esteemed it the sublime degree of virtue to love their chief, and pay him blind obedience, even if it were in opposition to the royal power. Next to this love of their chief was loyalty to the particular branch from whence they sprang, and in the third degree, to that of the whole clan or name; these they would assist, rightly or wrongly, against any other clan with which they might be at variance.

The Highlanders also adhered to one another as Highlanders, in opposition to the people of the Low Country, whom they regarded as inferior to themselves in courage. They believed, therefore, that they had the right to plunder the lowland territories which, according to tradition, were the possessions of their ancestors.

A fifteenth century historian states: "All of these Islanders and lykways the Heilanders are by nature most bent and prone to adventure themselves, their lyffs, and all they have, for their masters and lords, yea beyond all other people. . . ."

Nothing could shake the fidelity of the people to their chiefs, nor induce them to compromise anything they believed to be for the honour of, and in the interest of their clan. The authority of the sovereign, if nominally recognized, was usually unfelt and inoperative. The king's mandates could neither stop the feuds between different clans nor allay their hereditary hostilities. From opposing interests or wounded pride, deadly feuds frequently arose between the chiefs. These were warmly supported by the members of the respective clans, and were often transmitted, with aggravated animosity, from one generation to another.

Bonds of friendship, or *manrent*, were also frequently formed between neighbouring clans. By such bonds, the clan members came under an obligation to assist one another, and thus strengthen themselves against the attacks and encroachments of their enemies. Smaller clans which were unable to defend themselves, as well as clans which had lost their chieftains, found these bonds of manrent very satisfactory for their protection. The smaller clan was obliged to follow the fortunes, engage in the quarrels, and fight under the chief of the larger clan.

The succession to the chiefship and its usual prerogatives was termed the law of *Tanistry*, and the law of succession to the land and estates themselves was called *Gavel*. In later years, however, the law of *Tanistry* became the law of succession to the property as well as to the chiefship. The Tanist was the successor to the chief. In the Highlands, this law applied to males only; females could succeed neither to the chiefship nor to the property. In more recent times, the law of *Tanistry* has applied also to the female lineage, but only following the death of all males. The chief retained a sort of superiority over the whole possessions of the clan, and received from his cadets and tenants a portion of the produce of the land as an acknowledgement of his chiefship; in turn he dispensed hospitality to the members of his clan. The underlying principle of this system was the military advantage which accrued from its adoption. Mutual protection and assistance in combat were all-important in the clan system. To avenge the death of a relative in a clan feud, or to wipe away the stigma of a defeat were considered by the Highlanders to be sacred and paramount duties. If, because of the weakness of the clan, or the minority of the Chief, or for any other cause, the day of deadly reckoning was delayed, the feelings which prompted revenge were never dormant, and the earliest opportunity to vindicate the honour of the clan was seized upon.

Next in importance to the chief or laird and his immediate family were the cadets of his family, or gentlemen of the clan, who paid a nominal rent to the chief for their farms. The rent of these *tacksmen* usually took the form of produce from the farms, and much of the rent was later consumed in feasts given by the laird for the entertainment of his clansmen. Many of the tacksmen from Ross-shire in later years became pioneers in the Canadian northwest, as officers of the Hudson's Bay Company. According to ancient custom the tenants and subtenants, or cottars, were of the name and clan of the proprietor. If they were not really so, the chief obliged them to assume the clan name, and they were glad to do so in order to procure his protection and favour.

Each clan had a stated place of rendezvous, where they met at the call of their chief. When an emergency ceilidh was called as a result of the incursions of a hostile clan, the fiery-cross or *tarie* was immediately dispatched through the territories of the clan. Two clansmen, each with the burning cross in his hand, were dispatched by the chief in different directions. They ran with great speed, shouting as they went the war cry of the clan and the place of rendezvous. The cross was delivered from hand to hand, and, since each fresh bearer ran at full speed, the clan assembled with great celerity.

In later years, the Clan system was thought to be a menace to government jurisdiction and the maintenance of law and order in the Highlands, and, as a consequence, the well known Disarming Acts were passed. The first Disarming Act was passed by the British Parliament in 1716. By its terms, the Highland clans were to deliver up their personal arms to the tax collectors, who were empowered, as government officers, to collect them. These measures were taken to repress the disorders so prevalent in the north at that time, and to render the Highlanders less capable of entering into rebellion.

The Disarming Act was so poorly enforced, however, that a number of clans in the interior of the Highlands remained for some years better armed than before. Summonses were sent accordingly to the clan chiefs to bring or send in all their arms and war-like weapons to various re-receiving points. Detachments of troops were sent to receive them, at such places as Brahan Castle, Ruthven Castle in Badenoch, Castle Duart, and the Barrack of Bernera, the last two being the collecting depots for the Isles of Mull and Skye. When the English troops were sent to the Highlands to carry out the orders for disarming, one division which arrived at Kintyre, "was obliged speedily to retrace its steps, amid the jeers and laughter of the Highlanders." This episode is described by Balfour in vivid terms: "Glengarry stood out, and in effecte the heighlandmen forced them home againe to the lowlands; some with faire wordes; others stoode to their defence; and the Inglishe finding nothing amongest them save hunger and strokes, were glad, (their bisquet and cheesse being all spent, and their clothes worne, with their horsses out-tired) to returne, cursing the heighlandes, to their winter quarters. So, weill laughin at by the heighlanders, they were forced to returne with penurey aneuche, werey glade all of them that ther lives were saved."

After the Royal edict prohibiting the wearing of highland dress was issued, many of the Highlanders were imprisoned for this offence. A Sheriff's warrant issued in 1751 states ". . . that whereupon information Wm. Ross Son of Alexr. Ross in Dalnacleragh, now prisoner in the Tolbooth of Tain, has been taken up and incarcerate for wearing and using the Highland dress and arms . . . contrar to and in defiance of the Act of Parliament . . . summoned Hugh Rose, teacher of the grammar school at Kilmuir Easter, and Donald Ross, Roderick Ross and Alexr. Mackenzie, students at the said school . . . to bear leal and soothfast witness as they shall be spured at. . . ."

The final Disarming Act was more vigorously enforced and resulted in great discontent throughout the highlands.

## HIGHLAND CASTLES AND STRONGHOLDS

Many of the castles of northern Scotland played a major role in the historic background, first of the Lords of the Isles, later of the Earls of Ross, and finally of the Clan Ross. Succeeding generations of the Earls and the Rosses of Balnagowan held lordship rites over extensive lands, as well as many castles and strongholds in the Highlands. Dingwall Castle and later Balnagowan Castle were the chief headquarters of the Clan Ross. At different periods of history the Clan Ross also held possession of Castle Swin, Ardtornish, Urquhart, Balconie, Inverness Castle, Ruthven, Loch-an-Eilan, Delney, Avoch, and Dundonald Castles. Five of Ross-shire's largest farms were also held by the Earls of Ross. The Earldom of Ross was thus one of the most extensive and valuable in the Highlands and was the envy of royalty. Many of these ancient castles are now in ruins but some have been rebuilt on their original sites.

### *The Royal Castle of Dingwall*

King Alexander II in 1226 made Dingwall a royal burgh and granted the town its first charter. He also conferred the original Castle of Dingwall (held earlier by the Mormaers, who preceded the earls) upon Farquhar Mac-An-T-Sagairt after granting him the title of Earl of Ross. It passed out of the hands of the Earls of Ross for a time, but after reconciliation of King Robert the Bruce with William, third Earl of Ross, the castle was granted to this Earl, (it had previously been withheld from him by King Edward I of England). The castle thus again became the seat of the Earls of Ross and remained in their possession until the forfeiture of the earldom in 1476, when it reverted to the Crown.

This ancient castle held a dominant place in Highland history. After it came into the possession of the Crown, King James IV visited Dingwall Castle on many occasions, and renovations and improvements were made for his visits. He seemed to take a special pride in keeping the castle as up-to-date as possible, and it was there he received the clan chiefs and their retainers from the surrounding districts.

The Crown appointed governors to the castle; Sir John Munro of Foulis, as Chamberlain of Ross, was the first Governor. The castle was granted in 1584 to Sir Andrew Keith, who was then created Lord Dingwall. It was also used during the fifteenth and sixteenth centuries as a general prison for the north of Scotland because of its extensive underground dungeons. By the middle of the eighteenth century, this ancient stronghold of the once powerful Earls of Ross had become a complete ruin.

*Balnagowan Castle*

This castle has been very well preserved to the present time, having been frequently renovated by its occupants. It is situated on large grounds near the northern boundary of Ross-shire with wide, deep ravines on both sides. The castle was the seat of Clan Ross and of the Rosses of Balnagowan for more than three hundred years, until the beginning of the eighteenth century, when it was sold by David Ross in 1711, the last of the old line of Balnagowan Rosses.

The Balnagowan estates were, until recently, one of the largest single land-holdings left in the British isles, three hundred thousand acres extending across the northern Scottish Highlands, almost from coast to coast. Miles and miles of heather and gorse-covered moors stretch out in the distance, making it one of the greatest game preserves in Scotland. Grouse, partridge, pheasants, and, more especially, deer are still in abundance. There are also more than fifty miles of the finest salmon and trout streams to be found in Scotland. The Oykell River runs through the property and is one of Scotland's most celebrated salmon rivers.

A steep old bridge, known as "King's Bridge", crosses the Oykell River. It is supposed to have been named after King James IV, since he and his knights frequently crossed over this bridge on pilgrimages to St. Duthac Chapel.

Crowning this vast domain is Balnagowan Castle, a great, rambling, grey stone structure of the Scottish baronial style, with many turrets and battlemented parapets. It dates back over five hundred years and is one of the oldest continuously inhabited castles in Scotland. There are thirty-four bedrooms in the castle, and in the eighteenth and nineteenth centuries it was filled with priceless antiques and fine paintings. The west tower, the oldest part of the castle, with its high pointed roof and turrets, was probably built in the fifteenth century. David Ross, thirteenth Chief of Clan Ross, rebuilt the main part of the castle and added another wing in the later part of the seventeenth century. In 1838 the castle was again renovated and the east wing was added to conform with the older parts. Above the fireplace in the main drawing room of the portion built by Chief David Ross is the following carved inscription "Soli-Deo-Gloria" (to God above be Glory). Another inscription, which surrounds the picture of a ministerial figure wearing a Geneva hat and gown, is "Servire-Deum-Est-Reg-Nare" (To serve God is to rule). An escutcheon bearing the date

1680 and the three lions rampant, carries the motto "Nobilis-Est-Ira-Leonis" (Noble is the wrath of the lion).

Much of the life of the Highlands used to centre around Balnagowan a few centuries ago. The Ross Clan with their guests and tenants went out to the moors on hunting parties, accompanied by many beaters, loaders, stalkers, gillies, and their ponies. These would deploy in various directions to raise the game and provide the sport for which the Highlands were famous. In the days of the Balnagowan Rosses, the hunting and fishing rights on the moors and salmon rivers were jealously guarded, and poachers were severely dealt with.

Balnagowan Castle and estates passed out of the hands of Clan Ross in the year 1711. They were inherited under entail by the Lockharts and, although they took the name of Ross, the Lockharts did not have a direct connection with the Ross family and failed to establish title to the principal arms of that family. They could not properly be called Chiefs of Clan Ross. Sir Charles Ross, who was the last of the Lockhart Rosses at Balnagowan, assumed the title of Chief of Clan Ross because of his possession of Balnagowan Castle, but he was not rightly entitled. More recently, the castle was owned by the Hon. Francis de Moleyns, who married Sir Charles Ross's widow. Lady Ross died in 1957 and de Moleyns himself died at the castle at the age of 63, on May 1, 1964. The castle is now held in his estate.

*Urquhart Castle*

Urquhart Castle on Loch Ness, the Royal Castle of William the Lion, was built in the twelfth century for the purpose of suppressing the Highland clans. It was besieged and taken by Edward I in 1297. King Robert Bruce later held it as a royal castle. In 1450 it was given to the Earl of Ross but reverted to the Crown when his estates were forfeited. Finally, James IV presented it to the Grants, in the year 1509, as a reward for their services against the Lords of the Isles. The ruins are still an impressive sight on the bank of the beautiful Loch Ness with the massive stone walls towering fifty to sixty feet above the sandstone hill on the shore of the lake.

*Balconie Castle*

Balconie Castle, sometimes referred to as Ballone Castle, was situated on the Tarbat Isthmus overlooking the ocean. It was a former seat of the ancient Earls of Ross, and is now an imposing ruin. From this castle the Lady of Balconie set out on her strange adventure to the Black Rock Gorge of "Alt-Grannda", as related elsewhere. The castle was originally built by William, second Earl of Ross about the end of the thirteenth century. It was held by the Earls of Ross for many years but later came into possession of the Earls of Cromarty and finally it was held by the Mackenzie Clan. The castle became the centre of a clan feud between the proprietor Alexander Macdonald of Lochalsh and the MacKenzies, when young Kenneth MacKenzie felt himself slighted at a Christmas party which was held at the castle. Many brave highlanders lost their life over this trifling incident.

*Inverness Castle*

Alexander, Earl of Ross and Lord of the Isles, was imprisoned at Inverness Castle in 1427 by King James I. When released he soon raised a group of his kinsmen who pillaged and burned the town of Inverness but was unable to take the castle itself. Earl John, the last Earl of Ross, was more successful. In 1455, he took the castle and imprisoned the garrison as the result of a surprise manoeuvre. Later, Earl John was compelled to surrender his castles of Dingwall, Inverness, and Argyll to the Crown at which time he forfeited the earldom. All traces of the ancient castle of Inverness have now disappeared and the new buildings have been erected on the site.

*Ruthven, Loch-an-Eilean, Delny and Lochindorb Castles*

From these four ancient fortresses Lord Alexander, the "Wolf of Badenoch," held ruthless sway over all the surrounding country. The "Wolf" was the fourth son of Robert II and played a prominent part in the history of Clan Ross. He became the second husband of Euphemia, Countess of Ross, and thus took the title Earl of Ross, but the marriage was not a happy one and soon ended in a separation. The Countess made her home at Dingwall Castle while Lord Alexander resided at Ruthven Castle.

Ruthven, the grim old stronghold in Badenoch, was in existence in the days of Bruce. It was besieged, taken, and later rebuilt on a grander scale by Edward I during one of his raids into Scotland, when he was attempting to overwhelm the Scots. The present structure was built in 1718 but was burned after Culloden in 1746 and is now in ruins.

The notorious "Wolf" also held Loch-an-Eilean, a thirteenth century castle, which was built by the Comyns on an island in the picturesque Loch-an-Eilean at the base of the Cairngorme. Nothing remains now of the former stronghold.

Delny Castle, which is also in complete ruin, was the stronghold of William, third Earl of Ross. The Earl died here in 1322. In later years the "Wolf" obtained possession of the Castle and used it as a headquarters for his raids on the surrounding countryside. In more recent times the castle was held by the Mackenzies.

*Castle Avoch*

This ancient castle in Ross was held by the loyal Scots in 1297 during the Scottish War of Independence, while Dingwall, Inverness, Urquhart, and Nairn Castles were held by the English.

During the first half of the fifteenth century the castle was in possession of the Earls of Ross. The ruins are close to the village of Avoch on the northern shore of Munlochy Bay.

*Dundonald Castle*

This castle, now in ruins, was situated between Irvine and Ayr, and was the home of King Robert II and his Queen, Euphemia Ross. Here the "Wolf of Badenoch" was born.

*Castle Swin, Ardtornish Castle, and Aros Castle*

These three estates, although not in Ross-shire, have considerable significance in the struggles of the Lords of the Isles, which will be discussed in Chapter 2.

The ancient Castle Swin is said to have been named after Sweno, or Sweyn, of Denmark, by whom it was founded. It was situated on the west coast of Argyllshire on the Sound of Jura. It was a key fortress in the continual warfare between the Scots and the Scandinavians in the eleventh century. A century or so later it held a dominating position during the feuds between the Lords of the Isles and the Scottish Kings. Here Robert the Bruce beseiged and conquered Alexander of the Isles and the Castle reverted to the Crown. For a number of years it was under the charge of a "heritable keeper". Later, Castle Swin was burned and demolished by Alistair MacCholla.

The ruins of Ardtornish Castle stand on the Morven side of the Sound of Mull, opposite Duart. It was the stronghold of John, first Lord of the Isles, who built the castle in the mid-fourteenth century. In the next generation John de Yle, Earl of Ross and fourth Lord of the Isles, called a council of his chiefs at the castle and appointed two of the kinsmen as ambassadors to sign a treasonable alliance with Edward IV against the Scottish throne in 1462. The Lords of the Isles used this castle as one of their headquarters for four generations.

The fragmentary ruin of another once powerful stronghold of the Lords of the Isles, Aros Castle, stands on a high promontory on the shore of the Sound of Mull. Here, in 1608, the King summoned the Lords of the Isles and the chiefs of clans. They were all assembled in the castle and then were informed that they were being held as prisoners of King James IV. They were forthwith carried off individually to other royal castles such as Dingwall and Redcastle and held as prisoners in order to ensure a term of peace in the western Highlands.

## RELIGION IN THE HIGHLANDS

The religion of the Picts before their conversion was considered to be Druidism by a majority of writers. This cult prevailed also in most of Britain. The trees, rivers, and lakes, as well as the heavenly bodies, were objects of religious regard, and not a few of the customs and superstitions of later years in Scotland were inherited from their Pictish ancestors. The Picts of northern Scotland above the Grampians were pagan until the year 565, when St. Columba and his twelve disciples arrived.

St. Columba after emigrating from Ireland, resided in a monastery which he had built on Iona, near the Island of Mull. He gradually converted the northern Picts on the mainland to Christianity. This conversion paved the way for a reconciliation of the Picts and the Scots and contributed to their union as the kingdom of *Alban*. A few generations after the arrival of Columba, Christianity was established as the universal religion of Scotland and the celtic places of worship eventually became the clan churches.

The ancient Scottish Church of St. Columba was superseded by the Catholic religion in 1128 and popery flourished for upwards of four hundred years. Monasteries were built and abbeys established on the east and west coasts. The abbey of Applecross was one of the earliest on the west coast.

Fortrose was the seat of the mediaeval Bishops of Ross. The Cathedral of Rosemarkie a religious centre on the Black Isle was built by Robert, Bishop of Ross, about the middle of the thirteenth century. One of the later bishops was John Leslie, a relative of Sir Walter Leslie who became an Earl of Ross after his marriage to Euphemia, Countess of Ross.

A writ dated 1380 preserved in the Charter Chest of the Munros of Foulis, grants as follows: "To the blessed Virgin Mary and St. Boniface, Patron of the Church of Ross, the whole farm of Drum forever, for the sustinance of the Chaplain during Divine worship in the Chapel adjacent to the town of Rosemarkie . . .", signed Walter de Lesley, Lord of Ross, and Euphemia.

The great John Knox, an eloquent orator, took up the cause of Protestantism and did more to firmly establish this church in Scotland than any of his predecessors. In 1560 he was instrumental in introducing the Court of Elders, the Book of Common Prayer, and other innovations in the mode of worship. The Liturgy and prayerbook of John Knox were translated into Gaelic by Bishop Carswell in 1567 for use in the Scottish Reformed Church. These were used for the religious teachings in the Highland parishes for two centuries.

Protestantism was legally established in Scotland in 1563 and a commissioner was appointed by the General Assembly of the Protestant Church of Scotland to "plant kirks in Ross". Master Donald Munro was the first commissioner; he held the parochial charge of Lenclair, near Waterloocroft. His parishioners, however, lodged a complaint that he was not as proficient in the Gaelic language as might be wished.

The Catholic Abbot of Fearn in 1560 was Nicholas Ross and it is rather surprising to find that in his capacity as Peer of Parliament in 1560 he voted for the establishment of Protestantism in Ross-shire. He was, however, probably forced to make this decision by the circumstances of the time. On the memorable 17th of August 1560, the Abbot of Fearn, Nicholas Ross, and Robert Munro of Foulis, representatives of the Barons of Ross, voted with the overwhelming majority of Highlanders for the abolition of the mass and the Pope's supremacy, and for the adoption of the Protestant faith.

The Scottish Presbyterian Church established in Dingwall was called the Presbytery of Chanonry and Master Walter Ross held the office of reader, since there were not sufficient ordained ministers to fill the Presbyteries.

Later under the guidance and supervision of the Good Regent, the Reformation in Ross-shire went on apace. The town of Tain soon attained a prominence all its own, and the Regent presented the church with a finely carved pulpit, a creditable work of Scottish craftsmen. Tain, Edderton, Tarbat, and Nigg were joined in one parish under the spiritual guidance of Master Finaly Manson, who was their minister.

The ruins of one of the early Presbyterian churches near Waterloocroft was still to be found at the beginning of the twentieth century.

One of the first Protestant ministers in Ross who preached at the Kincardine Kirk was Hutcheon Ross who replaced the Catholic abbot, Nicholas Ross, about the year 1600. Amongst the Balnagowan documents was found a receipt dated 1602, which stated: "I Hutcheon Ross persone and minister at Kincardine . . . receavit fra . . . George Ross of Balnagowan one hundred punds complete payment . . . personage and vicarage . . . Witness—Alexr. Ross of Invercharron, Robert Ross minister at Alnes."

The Rev. Thomas Ross followed the Rev. Hutcheon Ross as minister at Kincardine and became the most famous of all the early ministers in the Highlands. He is described as "a singularly pious minister". He was a strong Covenanter who was finally imprisoned for his principles.

Charles I of England made an ill-fated attempt to introduce English episcopacy into Scotland in 1638. The great majority of the nation however declared their determination "by the great name of the Lord their God" to defend their religion against what they considered to be "errors and corruption." The Covenanters met at the assembly in Glasgow with representatives from every presbytery, where they passed a mandate that in spiritual matters the kirk was independent of civil power. They then assumed all the powers of legislation, and abolished episcopacy, as well as excommunicating the bishops. The Highlanders watched these proceedings with great joy, and testified their approbation by a national thanksgiving. The Earl of Sutherland, the Earl of Montrose, the Laird of Balnagowan, the Rosses, the Munroes and others were the leaders of the Covenanters north of the river Spey.

Later the Earl of Montrose, influenced by King Charles, changed over and gave his allegiance to the royalists. He and the Marquis of Huntly became the leaders of the royalist forces in the north. The spirits of the royalists were somewhat subdued by the severity of the attacks of Covenanters, who had large bodies of well-trained troops in the field, and after a number of preliminary skirmishes, the Royalists began to consider their cause a rather hopeless one. But the Earl of Montrose continued to harass the lands of the Covenanters, and defeated the Earl of Argyll's forces at Glenlevis. Montrose then proceeded to lay waste Argyll and Lorn and the warlike sound of his trumpets resounding through the glens struck terror in the towns and villages. In spite of these struggles the Scottish Presbyterian Church gained the supremacy.

Kirkton, in writing of the religious influences of the Reformation, is quoted here. "It is not to be forgotten, that from the year 1652 to the year 1665 there was great good done by the preaching of the Gospel in the West of Scotland. And, I verily believe, there were more souls converted to Christ in that short period of time, than in any since the reformation."

The Shandwick Rosses were a very religious family and supplied many of the Scottish parishes with ministers in the early days of the Reformed Church. The Rev. Robert Ross, son of Donald Ross, second of Shandwick, preached at Alness in the early seventeenth century, as did others of his descendants.

The long religious struggle came to an end in 1688 with the landing of William of Orange who was successful in restoring presbyterianism.

## ANCIENT ABBEYS AND CHAPELS IN ROSS-SHIRE

### *Edderton Abbey*

The Edderton Abbey was one of the earliest monasteries in Ross-shire. It was founded about 1227 by Farquhar, first Earl of Ross. The abbey was situated near the present town of Edderton, on the Dornoch Firth, and remained as a religious shrine for four hundred years. It crumbled and became a ruin about 1617. The pious Earl Farquhar had travelled from Applecross on the west coast of Scotland to the east coast, to establish his abbey on the Dornoch Firth.

The first religious order to take up residency at the abbey was that of the Premonstratensian Monks from Whithorn in Galloway. The abbey was apparently poorly constructed by the local guilds, because we find that Earl Farquhar about the year 1246, decided to transfer the monastery to "Nova Farina", (New Fearn). The building of Fearn Abbey was Farquhar's crowning religious achievement.

### *The Abbey of Fearn and Chapel of St. Duthac*

In the parish of Fearn, on the east coast of Ross-shire near the Moray Firth are several antiquated abbeys and castles. Fearn is said to have derived its name from the alders which grow plentifully along the rugged coastline. The cliffs in these parts of Ross-shire are wild and precipitious.

This abbey is one of the most ancient in Ross-shire, and was founded on the site of an earlier Celtic place of worship. Originally it was under the jurisdiction of the Celto-Pictish Church of Ninian, but in 1617 the abbey was united to the See of Ross and became known as the Monastery of Ross, (in Gaelic, Monochain Rois). It was rebuilt in 1321 of rough stone, and, as was the custom, it had a thatched roof. Many years later the roof fell in after a heavy snowfall and thirty-six of the congregation were killed. The abbey was rebuilt, (about 1742) and, after the Reformation, the Scotch Presbyterians held services there. One of the tombs in the floor of the church was pointed out as being that of Farquhar, first Earl of Ross.

The ancient and Royal Burgh of Tain, near Dornoch Firth, is regarded as the capital of Easter Ross. The Burgh of Tain was incorporated by charter of King James II in 1457. In the town of Tain stands the small ivy-covered ruins of *St. Duthac Chapel*, where the patron saint of the town is said to have been born. St. Duthac was the last of the Celtic saints of Ross-shire, and was killed in 1088, probably by the Vikings. He was deemed a martyr, and his shrine was visited by many pilgrims, since Tain was known far and wide as a place of sanctuary. To this place King

Robert the Bruce sent his wife and daughter and ladies of the court in the dark days of 1306, but the sanctuary was violated by William, third Earl of Ross, who captured the Royal hostages and delivered them to King Edward I of England. This despicable act does not reflect to the Earl's credit.

Near the ruins of the ancient St. Duthac Chapel, stands a building of which the town is justly proud, *St. Duthac Church*. It was erected before 1371 by William, fifth Earl of Ross, and, for over four hundred years, was used for public worship. King James IV made seven pilgrimages to this ancient church during his reign. It fell into disrepair but was restored in 1877 and stained glass windows were installed. This beautiful little church is seventy feet long by twenty feet wide and contains a full-sized duplicate of the Regent Moray's hand-carved pulpit.

## BROCHS, INSCRIBED STONES, AND VITRIFIED FORTS

In the parish of Edderton, on the south shore of Dornoch Firth, are found the remains of some remarkable stone structures or towers, called *brochs*, which were erected by the Picts between 300 *B.C.* and 400 *A.D.* These brochs were round, thick-walled, lighthouse-like structures originally over forty feet in height. The circular stone walls, ten to twenty feet thick, enclosed the well-like court, which was about thirty feet in diameter. Through the wall there was only one tunnel which formed the doorway. A guard chamber was constructed halfway along this entrance, where a single spearman could defend the passage against an enemy seeking to enter, while a guard above the entrance could thrust his spear downward through the openings between the lintels. A series of small rooms were hollowed out of the stone walls and lighted by windows overlooking the central court, where those living inside the broch could sleep in perfect safety.

Apparently these brochs were places of refuge for the peaceful inhabitants when hostile invaders swept over the Highlands. Some of the brochs have been given names. On the Island of Lewis there is a broch called *Dun Borve Broch,* near Borve. It is one of the largest and best preserved brochs in Ross-shire. Another, at Loch Cromore, is called *Dun Cromore.* At Glensheil there is a Broch called *Caisteal Gruguig.* One of these round stone brochs may still be found just east of Easter Fearn. The remains of another is seen near Ardgay.

The Picts have also left many large *Standing Stones* in various parts of the country. One such stone is found at Shader, fifteen miles from Stornoway, on the island of Lewis. This stone, called *Clach an Truiseil,* is a large unhewn gneiss monolith, six feet six inches broad and twenty feet six inches high, the tallest menheir in Scotland.

Early Christian Celtic crosses and inscribed stones can also be seen in certain districts. *Clach a Charridh* is an upright stone slab eight feet, six inches in height situated near Shandwick village in the parish of Nigg. It is a good example of one of the early Christian Pictish sculptured stones. It has a cross on its seaward face, with a panel underneath the cross filled with interlacing ornament, and on the sides are depicted two animals which are now indistinct. On the back of the stone the depressed carvings depict hunting scenes, processions, and combats. *Cloch a Mhearlich* is a symbol stone near Rosskeen. Another fine example of a Pictish Standing Stone is found in the "Moor of the Grave Plot" (*in Gaelic Blar a Charaidh*) near Edderton village. This is a rough, unhewn freestone about ten feet high and three feet wide, with the outlines of a fish incised on one side, and, on the other, the double disc and sceptre. Another Pictish carved stone is found in Kincardine churchyard.

A further purely Scottish structure dating from early Celtic times is the *vitrified fort.* In such a fort there has been a fusion of the stones, which is thought to have been produced by the great heat of the beacon fires set by the ancient Britons. One of the best examples of a vitrified fort can be seen at the top of Knockfarrel.

In the parish of Logie-Easter there is another relic of the days when clan feuds were common occurrence. At this well-marked site of the "pit and gallows" of olden days, there is the "drowning pool", or *Poll a Bhathaidh,* for women, and "hanging hill", or *Cnoc na Croich,* for the men.

## LEGENDS AND BALLADS OF ROSS-SHIRE

The Celts were a very superstitious people, and their superstitious beliefs involved their rivers and streams, their moors and mountains. There is little doubt but that they offered human sacrifices. Nature appears at its wildest and most romantic in the Highlands, with rugged mountains, dreary wastes of moor land, wide lakes, and rapid torrents, over which the tempests and thunders exhaust their rage. This aspect of the country vividly impressed the imagination of the Highlanders and gave them a tendency to ascribe to the elements supernatural powers.

One of the most dangerous and malignant creatures inhabiting the lakes and rivers was the *kelpie,* or water-horse, who had the power of luring women and children to his under-water haunts, where he devoured them. Deprived through the influence of Christianity of their due offerings, these river spirits were believed to lie in wait for the unwary, especially at fords, and thus obtain the human lives they sought. The water-horse usually appeared as a sleek well-fed animal grazing peacefully by a loch side. On being approached, he quietly remained to be caught or even mounted. Frequently three or four children mounted him at the same time, but woe betide those who did. The water-horse immediately rushed into the loch and there was no possible escape, for whoever touched him stuck immovably fast. The lungs of the water-horse, which floated ashore afterwards, remained the only evidence of the disaster. Perhaps because of this, Loch Scaven is said to take its name from *squamhain*, meaning "lungs, or lights".

"Alas for the man who would clutch the mane,
There is no spell to help and no charm to save
Who rides him will never return again,
Were he as strong, O were he as brave
As Finn-mac-Coul, of whom they'll tell,
He thrashed the devil and made him yell."
(Author unknown)

Another legend involves the *Lady of Balconie*. This legend centres around the village of Evanton, where the River Glass enters the Black Rock Gorge. This chasm, called in Gaelic *Alt-Grannda,* is a mile and a quarter long and has a depth of about 110 feet. Tradition informs us that some three centuries ago the Lady of Balconie lived near the Alt-Grannda gorge. She was of a retiring nature, and spent much time wandering in this beautiful gorge. She set out one evening for the gorge and induced a maidservant to accompany her. They arrived there about sunset, and on coming to the wildest part of the chasm, the lady desired the maid to accompany her down the rock-face. When the maid demurred, the lady said that there was quite a good path leading down to the water and that she had taken it hundreds of times; she insisted that her maid should accompany her that night. The girl again refusing, the lady seized her and attempted to drag her towards the chasm, but while they were struggling, a tall dark man suddenly appeared beside them. The Lady of Balconie immediately released the girl, whereupon the dark stranger took the lady's arm and, leading her towards the chasm, said "You may remember that your surety had to be a willing one." At the edge of the precipice the lady turned and looked despairingly behind her. She untied her household keys and threw them up the bank towards the girl. In falling, the keys struck a large granite boulder, and sank into it as if it were a mass of wax.

The girl, frantic with fear and horror, rushed home and told her strange tale to the lady's husband. He and his retainers hastened to the gorge and minutely searched it, but no trace of the ill-fated lady could they find. But the imaginative can perhaps still trace the impression in the rock, now known as the Balconie Boulder, of the keys supposedly flung there by this lady, as the devil was taking her over the precipice.

A singular practice of *Deis-iuil* existed in the Western Isles. In this ancient custom a person carrying a fire brand in his hand, makes a fiery circuit around a certain house or farm, to protect the members of the household against evil spirits. The fire-round was also believed to be especially effective for preserving a mother and her new-born infant from the power of these evil spirits. The spirits sometimes carry away the infant. If the infant was returned to the family later it would be as an emaciated skeleton and not likely to survive. On the island of Lewis some of the poorer people were in the habit of making the fiery circuit sunwise about their benefactors three times, and followed this by blessing such persons that had shown them kindness. Before setting out to sea, the sailors would row their boat in a circle sun-wise. If this precaution was neglected their voyage was likely to prove unfortunate.

Diarmaid and Fionn (Fingal) are favourite characters in the Gaelic poems and ballads written in the early days of Scotland and Ireland. Stories about them were related at great length throughout the regions wherever Gaelic was spoken. The legend of Diarmaid is mentioned in an old Irish document as being one of the favourite stories which the bards used to recite before kings and princes.

The story is localized over an area of northern Scotland from Cape Clear to the Ord of Caithness. The place known as Beinn Gulban, which is frequently mentioned, is on the island of Skye. Gleann Sith is on the island of Tiree. The well and knoll where the tragedy ended are in Kintyre, Ross-shire.

Diarmaid is described as a man gifted, like his comrades, with superhuman attributes. He is invulnerable, save for a small mole on the sole of his foot. If this mole is injured he will bleed to death. On Diarmaid's brow is a love mark, *sugh seirce*; the woman who will see it is destined to fall in love with him, which Graihdne, Fingal's wife, does, and they elope together. After many adventures, and through the cunning of Fingal (whose gift was a "Knowledge Tooth") Diarmaid is enticed into a boar hunt. He slays the boar, which no one else could overcome. His uncle bids Diarmaid measure the boar with his bare feet against the bristles; he wounds the mole on the sole of his foot with a poisoned spike, which was the boar's miraculous endowment, and unfortunately his uncle refuses to cure him with his magic cup. After Dairmaid dies, Graihdne is restored to her husband and a happy feast follows.

Three verses out of the many Gaelic ballads dealing with Diarmaid and Fingal are here reproduced in the original Gaelic.

Dyth Wylelyss Myschi Zraynnyth
Dyth wylelyss myschi zraynnyth
Hwnggis nayrri w'cowle
Wee myr it tayme sin nagyn
Is bert nach fadyr a wllryng.

Dyth zhagis clwycht is couzar
Er chompan zaw neyss tayr
Dyth zhagis mnan gin gillaa
Is dyth wilelis myschi a zraynna.

Dyth zhagis murnd is meygzegr
Curme is greygzin is garae
Dyth zhagis clwithi fylli
Is dyth willis myschi a zraynnaa.

The *Diri Moir*, or Reay Forest, is a wild and desolate region extending over much of the western side of Sutherland and Ross-shire which has always been famous for a variety of birds and beasts of prey. A prevalent superstition of early times has it that the grey-furred and green-eyed wolf which lived in these districts, here takes the form of the *were-wolf*, or witch disguised in the shape of a wolf. The following verses are from a modern version of the ballad.

THE WOLF OF EDERACHILLIS

In the gloomy Diri Moir
One aged man, 'twas said
Knew all the former life
The witch of Loch Stac had led,
And why so oft by the stony cairn
She made a sleepless bed.

At the rise of Autumn's wind
The witch was seen no more,
And raging tempests beat
On Ederachillis' shore;
And the billows leapt o'er sinking boats
With fierce sepulchral roar.

In the churchyard on the hill
Was heard a growling loud;
By the shifting, stormy moon

That panted through the cloud
The grey wolf was seen at rifled grave,
And it champed at a corpse's shroud.

Thus every grave we dug
The hungry wolf uptore,
And every morn the sod
Was strewn with bones and gore;
Our mother earth had denied us rest
On Ederachillis' shore.

Many ballads were composed to record important events in Scottish history, and more particularly to record the stirring battles and feuds between the clans and the Norse invaders.

Hardyknute is probably one of the most ancient and celebrated of the historical ballads of Scotland. Written anonymously and first published in 1719, it is attributed to Lady Wardlaw, sister-in-law of Sir John Bruce of Kinross and wife of Sir Henry Wardlaw of Balmulie. The ballad deals with the invasion of the western coast and islands of Scotland by Norsemen. John Finlay, who records this ballad in his book, *Ancient Scottish Ballads*, in 1808, states: "It is difficult which most to admire, the mind capable of producing such a ballad, or the modesty of sending it into the world anonymously. It must be remembered too that Hardyknute was composed at a period unusually dark in the literary history of Scotland, and when poetical genius in particular seems to have slumbered; at least no composition of these times exists, possessing, in a nearly equal degree, the vigour and lofty versification of 'Hardyknute'."

The following historical events are celebrated in the ballad. In 1263 Haakon King of Norway invaded the Western Isles of Scotland with a powerful fleet. He conquered and laid waste Kintyre and the islands of Bute and Arran. A storm arose and several of the ships were driven on shore near Largs. The Scottish army led by William, second Earl of Ross, attacked them in the famous battle of Largs, 1263. The Earl of Ross had an army of about five hundred foot soldiers well accoutred with bows and spears; also a number of mounted knights, their horses clad in breastplates and armour. As the Scots attacked furiously with darts, spears and stones, the Norwegians on the hill began to retire towards the sea. Showers of arrows were poured upon the Norwegians, who were routed and began to push off from shore in their boats. Many ships were sunk and the rest of the Norwegian fleet wheeled about towards the sea. The battle of Largs proved to be the decisive engagement in driving the Norwegians from the coast and islands of Scotland.

Hardyknute refers to a Scottish knight called Sir Perus Curry, of distinguished birth and fortune. He is said to have worn a helmet plated with gold and set with precious stones. Before the battle commenced he rode gallantly up to the Norwegians and galloped back and forth along their battle lines, taunting them and then riding back to his own followers. He finally fought with a Norwegian, Andrew Nicholson, who was later killed in the battle. The Norseman struck at the knight's thigh with such force that his sword severed the thigh through the armour and penetrated to the saddle. This was the signal for the start of the battle. Many fell on both sides, but the Norse invaders were finally driven from the shores of Scotland, back to their strongholds in the Western Isles.

Hardyknute's Castle was an impressive Port, standing "Hie on a hill" beside a mountain stream, near the Firth, where the Norwegian ships were anchored.

HARDYKNUTE

Stately stept he east the wa'[1]
And stately stept he west;
Full seventy ziers[2] he now had sene,
With skerss[3] seven ziers of rest.
He livit quhen[4] Britons breach of faith
Wroucht Scotland meikle wae,
And ay his sword tauld, to their cost,
He was their deidly fae.

Hie on a hill his castle stude,
With halls and touris a hecht,
And quidly[5] chambers fair to se,
Quhair he lodgit many a Knicht.
His dame sae feirless anes, and fair,
For chast and bewtie deint,
Nae marrow[6] had in all the land,
Saif Elenor the Quene.

Full thirteen sons to him scho[7] bare
All men of valour stout,
In bluidy ficht, with sword in hand
Nine lost their lives bot[8] doubt;
Four zit remain; Lang may they live
To stand by leige and land;
Hie was their fame, hie was their micht,
And hie was their command.

[1] Wa'—the castle rampart
[2] ziers—years
[3] skerss—scarcely
[4] quhen—when
[5] quidly—goodly
[6] marrow—equal
[7] scho—she
[8] bot—without

Great luve they bare to Fairly fair,
Their sister saft and deir,
Her girdle shawd her middle jimp[9]
And gowden glist[10] her hair.
Quhat waefow[11] wae her beautie bred,
Waefou, to Zung[12] and auld;
Waefou, I trou, to kyth and kin,
As story ever tauld.

The King of Norse, in summer tyde,
Puft up with powir and micht,
Landed in fair Scotland the yle[13],
With many a hardy knicht.
The tydings to our gude Scots king
Came as he sat at dyne,
With noble chiefs, in braif aray,
Drinking the blude-reid wyne.

"To horse, to horse, my ryal leige!
Zour[14] foes stand on the strand;
Full twenty thousand glittering spears
The king of Norse commands."
"Bring me my steed, Mage dapple gray,"
Our gude King raise and cryd:
A trustier beast in all the land,
A Scots King never seyd.[15]

"Go, little page, tell Hardyknute,
That lives on hill so hie,
To draw his sword, the dried[16] of foes,
Ant haste and follow me".
The little page flew swift as dart,
Flung by his master's arm;
"Cum down, cum down, Lord Hardyknute,
Ant red[17] zour King frae harm."

"Late, late zestrene, I weind[18] in peace
To end my length'ned life;
My age micht weil excuse my arm
Frae many feats of stryfe:
But now that Norse dois proudly boast
Fair Scotland to inthral,
It's neir be said of Hardyknute,
He feird to ficht or fall".

[9] jimp—slender
[10] gowden glist—shone as gold
[11] waefou—woeful
[12] Zung—young
[13] Yle—Isle
[14] Zour—your
[15] Seyd—rode
[16] dried—dread
[17] red—rid
[18] weind—wished

"Fareweil, my dame sae feirless gude,"
And tuke hir by the hand,
"Fairer to me in age zou seim
Than maids for bewtie fam'd:
My zoungest son sall here remain,
To guard these stately towirs,
Ant shut the silver bolt that keips
Sae fast zour painted bowirs."

Syne he has gane far hynd attowre[19]
Lord Chattan's land soe wyde;
That lord a worthy wicht was ay,
Quhen[20] foes his courage seyd:
Of Pictish race, by mother's syde.
Quhen Picts ruld Caledon,
Lord Chattan claim'd the princely maid
Quhen he saift Pictish crown.

Now with his ferss[21] and stalwart train
He reicht a rysing heicht,
Quhan brard[22] encompit[23] on the dale,
Norss Menzie lay in sicht;
"Zonder my valziant sons, and feris[24]
Our raging revers[25] wait.
On the unconquerit Scotish swaird[26]
To try us with thair fate."

To join his king, adown the hill
In hast his merch he made,
Quhyle play the pibrochs[27] minstralls meit[28]
Afore him stately strade.
"Thryse welcum, valziant stoup of weir;[29]
Thy nation's scheild and pride,
Thy king nae reason has to feir,
Quhen thou art be his side."

Quhen Bows went bent, and darts were thrawn,
For throng scarce could they flie,
The darts clave arrows as they met
The arrows dart the trie.
Lang did they rage, and fecht full ferss,
With little skaith to man;
But bludy, bludy was the field
Or that lang day was done!

[19] Far hynd attowre—far beyond, over the country
[20] Quhen—when
[21] ferss—fierce
[22] brard—companions
[23] encompit—encamped
[24] feris—companions
[25] revers—spoilers, robbers
[26] swaird—grassy ground
[27] pibroch—martial air on the bagpipes
[28] meit—proper
[29] weir—war

The King of Scots that sindle[30] bruik'd
The war that lukit lyke play,
Drew his braid[31] sword, and brake his bow,
Sen bows seint but delay.
Quoth noble Rossay, "Myne I'll keep,
I wate its bleid a skore."
"Hast[32] up my meny men," cry'd the king,
As he rode on before.

The king of Norse he socht to find,
With him to mense the faucht[33];
But on his forehead there did licht
A sharp unsonsie[34] shaft:
As he his hand put up to find
The wound, an arrow kene,
O waefu[35] chance! there pinned his hand
In midst between his ene.

Proud Norse with giant body tall,
Braid shoulder and arms strong;
Cryd, "Quhair is Hardyknute sae fam'd,
And fierd at Britain's throne?
Tho' Britons tremble at his name,
I sune sall make him wail,
That eir my sword was made sae sharp,
Sae salf[36] his coat of mail."

That brag, his stout heart coud na byde,
It lent him zouthfu[37] micht:
"Im Hardyknute. This day," he cryd,
"To Scotland's king I hecht[38],
To lay thee law[39] as horses' hufe,
My word I mean to keip:"
Syne with the first strike eir he strake
He garrd[40] his body bleid.

Norse ene lyke gray gosehauk, staird wyld,
He sicht[41] with shame and spyte;
"Disgrac'd is now my far fam'd arm
That left the power to stryke,"

[30] sindle—seldom
[31] braid—broad
[32] hast—hasten
[33] mense the fancht—measure, or try the battle
[34] unsonsie—unlucky
[35] waefu—woeful
[36] salf—soft
[37] zouthfu—youthful
[38] hecht—promised
[39] law—low
[40] garrd—made
[41] sicht—sickened

Then gaif his head a blaw sae fell,
It made him down to stoup,
As law as he to ladies usit,
In courtly gyse to lout[42].

In thrawis of death, with wallowit[43] cheik
All panting on the plain,
The fainting corps of warriors lay,
Neir t'aryse again:
Neir to return to native land;
Nae mair wirh blythsom sounds
To boist the glories of the day,
And schow[44] their shyning wounds.

There on a lie, quhair stands a cross
Set up for monument,
Thousands full fierce, that summer's day
Fill'd keine waris[45] black intent.
Let Scots quhyle Scots praise Hardyknute,
Let Norse the name ay dried[46];
Ay how he faucht, aft he spaird,
Sal[47] latest ages reid.

Loud and chill bleu the westlin wind,
Sair beat the heavy shower,
Mirk[48] grew the nicht eir Hardyknute
Wair[49] neir his stately towir:
His towir that us'd with torches bleise[50]
To shyne sai far at nicht
Seem'd now as black as mourning weid:
Nae marvel sair he sich'd.

"As fast I haif sped owre Scotland's faes"
There criest his brag of weir
Sair schamit[51] to mynd ocht[52] but his dame,
And maiden Fairly fair.
Black feir he felt, but quhat to feir
He wist not zit with dried:
San schuke his body, sair his limbs,
And all the warriors fled.

[42] lout—bend low
[43] wallowit—faded
[44] schow—show
[45] waris—war's
[46] dried—dread
[47] sal—shall
[48] mirk—dark
[49] wair—arrived
[50] bleise—blaze
[51] schamit—ashamed
[52] ocht—none

## THE WIFE OF USHER'S WELL

This is the story of two sons of a clerk, who fell in love, each with a daughter of the Mayor of the parish in which they were ordained. They are sentenced to death by the Mayor for the shame which they bring upon his house. The father of the two sons, on hearing that they are "bound in prison strang", hastens to try and obtain a pardon for them. The ballad opens with a picture of their mother waiting hopefully at the Castle wall for her sons' homecoming, but ends with their having to return to prison early the following morning.

His lady sat on her castle wa',
Beholding dale and doun;
And there she saw her ain gude lord,
Come walking to the toun.

Ye're welcome, ye're welcome, my ain gude lord,
Ye're welcome hame to me;
But where away are my twa sons?
Ye suld hae brought them wi' ye."

"O they are putten to a deeper lear,
And to a higher scule:
You ain twa sons will no be home
Till the hallow days o'Yule".

"O sorrow, sorrow, come mak my bed;
And, dule, come lay me down;
For I will neither eat nor drink,
Nor set a fit on groun!"

The hallow days o'Yule were come,
And the nights were lang and mirk
When in and cam her ain twa sons,
And their hats made o' the birk.

It neither grew in syke nor ditch,
Nor yet in any sheuch:
But at the gates of Paradise
That birk grew fair eneuch.

"Blow up the fire now, maidens mine,
Bring water from the well;
For a' my house shall feast this night,
Since my twa sons are well.

O eat and drink, my merry men a',
The better shall ye fare;
For my twa sons they are come hame
To me for evermair."

And she has gone and made her bed,
She's made it soft and fine;
And she's happit[1] them wi' her grey mantil,
Because they were here ain.

Up then crew the red, red cock,
And up and crew the grey
The eldest to the youngest said,
"Tis time we were away."

The cock he hadna crawed but once,
And clapped his wings at a',
When the youngest to the eldest said,
"Brother we must awa'."

"The cock doth craw, the day doth daw,
The channerin'[2] worm doth chide;
Gin we be mist out o' our place
A sair fain we maun hide.

Fare ye weel, my mother dear!
Fairwell to barn and byre!
And fare ye wel, the bonny lass
That kindles my mother's fire."

[1] happit—covered [2] channerin'—fretting

During the reigns of James III (1460-88) and James IV (1488-1513) Scotland was undergoing great internal changes in its social organization. The poet Dunbar wrote a number of poems describing the changing times and the new order of things. John M. Ross, LL.D. states: "When we consider the originality, strength and richness of Dunbar's genius, we have no scruple in assigning him the highest place after Burns in the ranks of Scottish poets." The following poem on the evils of covetousness, illustrates the Scottish dialect of the latter half of the fifteenth century;

COVETYCE

In burghis to landwart and to sie[1],
Quhair[2] was plesour and grit plentie,
Vennesoun, wyld-fowill, wyne and spice,
Ar now decayid thruch Covetyce.

[1] sie—sea [2] Quhair—there

Husbandis that grangis[3] had full grete,
Cattell and corne to sell and ete,
Hes[4] now no beist bot cattis[5] and myce;
And all thruch causs of Covetyce.

Honest yemen in every toun,
War want to weir baith reid[6] and brown,
Ar now arrayst in reggis[7] with lyce;
And all thruch causs of Covetyce.

Man, pleiss thy Makar, and be mirry
And sett nocht by this world a chirry;
Wirk for the place of Paradyce,
For thairn ringis na Covetyce.

[3] grangis—grain
[4] hes—has
[5] cattis—cats
[6] reid—red
[7] reggis—rags

The following contemporary verses were written by Dr. A. C. Gordon Ross of Glasgow, in 1963. They depict the life and times of Alexander Ross, sixth laird of Balnagowan, and his son Sir David. The account of the bitter clan feud and final pitched battle between the Rosses and the Mackays at Alt A'Charrais, resulting in the death of Alexander, Chief of Clan Ross, is described.

AN OLD OLD TALE OF ROSS-SHIRE

October 1496 in Inverness
My Lord of Balnagowan had a keep
A summer house, not far from Tarbat Ness,
Where in the gentle season he would go
To take his ease, to look on sand and sea,
And give a summer grazing for his beasts.
He had with him his mother, full of years,
The Lady Christian, a Macleod of Lewis
Daughter of Torquil, and his grown sons
David and William, and his servitors
Upwards of nine men only.

And Balnagown was sad, remembering the past.
His wife was dead, his daughter dead to him,
They called her Grizel of the golden hair:
Last year while bathing with her servant maid
They vanished into the bleak north lands,
Taken in a raid by Angus Roy Mackay;
None saw them go, or heard what was their fate.
Grizel was beautiful, and strong, and tall,
The princess of the province known as Ross.

The Lady Christian had the second sight,
But yesterday she said she thought she saw
The sun set over Tarbat Church.
And now to-day
She dreamt two strangers came to call,
It boded ill for all of Balnagown,
Or so she said to Alexander:
He humoured her, for she was very old
And full of fancies, like a Dornoch witch.
This second dream was better than the first
For over Tarbat Church would come the dawn.
But she was proud about her second sight
And prouder still when suddenly, — behold!
Simon, the pedlar man from Inverness
Appeared within the courtyard with his pack
Complete with linens, cottons and good tweed
From Harris and the islands.
Stuff to make
The hearts of women glad.
The widow Christian knew
Some of the islanders who made the cloth.

And she had news of them,
For Simon knew his trade and every girl
Had need of something from the pedlar's store.
And so they fell to bargaining, while the Laird
Sat silent in his grief for Grizel gone . . .
When suddenly
The lookout man came running from his tower
In panting haste he knelt before his Lord:
"My Lord! My Lord! Along the bridle path
I see a horseman come in grievous speed.
He rides bareback with Hell upon his heels."
"We are expecting him", Christian replies.
"He is the second stranger, let the girls
Prepare more food and keep him out my way
Till I conclude my business.

Chief Balnagowan
Meantime kept looking where the sentry said,
And then his heart leapt up for he did know
That none with in the broad fair lands of Ross
Could ride as did this rider — save Grizel!
He saw her tresses gleaming in the sun,
He saw her leap the fallen blasted oak.
He saw her take the stone dyke in a stride

And breast the burn beside the wishing well.
The many months of waiting fell away
For in a flash his lass was by his side
And all were glad to see her look so well
But she had news for them that could not wait . .
Some three days since, she heard her captors say,
The lands of Ross are fair and fat with kine,
With grain and fodder, let us make a raid
To bring back plunder to Strathnaver bare.
Now is the time when they are by the sea
And Balnagowan Castle miles away
Where dwell the Tacksmen and the armoury.

Grizel had watched the Mackay men prepare.
And followed them, a band of ninety men,
To Bonar Bridge she went, and left them there
To make her way along the northern shore
Of Dornoch Firth, where she did swim the gap
At Meigle, where the tide is not so strong.
And then she stole a horse, as daybreak came,
And rode to warn her father of his peril.
He took the fiery cross from off the wall
And told his men prepare, then called his son
William, the Fleet of Foot, "Run through the land,
Bring out our men to put Mackays to rout."

Then Grizel spoke with resolutions bold:
"Father, at most you have but forty men,
The odds are in their favour, let me go
And lead the raiders through the Quarry Den
While you lie hid among the heather banks,
I'll take the pedlar's horse." And so she went
By devious ways where long ago she played,
And so it was within the narrow den
All afternoon was heard the clash of arms.
BRATACH BHAN MHIS AOIDH. Mackay's war cry
And death was there and slaughter
Mighty grim . . .

Hugh Vass and William Ross brought Grizel home
And she was dead: between her shoulder blades
Someone had plunged a dagger to the hilt.
They laid her down beside the pedlar's stuff
Where now the cottons, torn into shreds,
By Christian and her girls were binding up,
The gaping wounds of many men of Ross.

The Lady Christian spoke: "How goes the fight?"
And William said:
"Forty Mackays are dead or wounded, what remains
Are cornered safely in the Tarbat Church
And father guards the door with his broad axe."

She plucked two brands from off the blazing fire:
"For her sake, lads, take these and fire the church.
Let none escape. Remember Grizel here,
'Tis not for nothing I have second sight,
The sun will set high in the east tonight!"
And so they took the torches and were gone
All night the old church burned. A crimson fire,
When morning came only the four walls stood.
But in the night the pedlar stole away
A frightened man, he could not suffer blood.

Five years went past
The Lady Christian died at Balnagown.
The pedlar man came for her funeral.
It was a time of famine. No rains came
To bring the harvest on, that hot July
The pedlar spread a tale —
A mighty run of salmon from the sea,
A late spring run of many splendid fish
Far up the Carron River. Thus begun
The rumour spread about the province wide . . .
With rod and net, and line, and right good cheer
The men folk gathered. Every one intent
To fill his larder empty half a year.
At Alt A'Charrais, where they made a camp
The Mackays surprised them at an evening ceidilh
And slaughtered them — the gentlemen of Ross.
Alexander the laird was slain, and William Ross,
Three brothers Vass, John, Hugh and Thomas too.
John Mitchell and the Tarrells: many more
One hundred dead, in fourteen eighty six.

Up on the Struie Brae on quiet spring nights,
A ghostly piper plays a sad lament
For all the men of Ross who died that day.
The 'Coronach of Carron' is the tune.
Some folks say
" 'Tis Balnagown's piper, Peter Ross,
Who killed three Mackays with a salmon cleek
Before he fell by Alexander's side ——"

# 2. THE EARLS OF ROSS

## 1215-1493

### THE ORIGINAL LINE OF SUCCESSION

The earliest origins of the Rosses as a family or clan date back to the thirteenth century when the Earls of Ross held jurisdiction over extensive territories in the northern and westerly part of the Highlands. The first of the ancient Celtic Earls of Ross was Farquhar a descendant of the O'Beolain family who lived in the small village of Applecross, on the west coast of Scotland, just north of the Kyle of Lochalsh. This family is said to be descended from Gilleon na-h-Airde (Colin of the Aird) who lived in the tenth century and was one of the ancestors of the lay Abbots of the Monastery of Applecross. It was to this abbacy that Farquhar belonged. These Abbots were the Lords of the western section of the County of Ross in the twelfth century.

A previous Earl of Ross is recognized with much justification by some authorities, namely Malcolm MacAedth who held the Earldom from 1157 to 1168. In 1160 this abbot was placed in charge of the Monks of Dunfermline, but very little is known of him other than this. He is said to have married a sister of King Somerled of the Isles.

In the old manuscripts the Rosses are referred to as Clann Aindreis. The name "Ross" as a family name was not in use until the fourteenth century however, when the Barons of Balnagowan adopted it to indicate their descent from the Earls of Ross and from the county of Ross where they held their lands.

Donald MacKinnon, an authority on clan history, did not entirely agree with this derivation of the name and states that the name Ross is Gaelic, and in the Gaelic literature Clan Ross is Clann Rois, not Clann Aindreis. A Ross is either Rosach or Ros.

I Earl FARQUHAR (Fearchar Mac An T-Sagairt)
descended from the Celtic O'Beolain family.
Was created Earl of Ross by Alexander II in 1234.

II **EARL WILLIAM, second Earl of Ross, "Lord of Skye and Lewis". Married Jean Comyn daughter of Earl of Buchan. Died 1274..**

MALCOLM de Ross

EUPHEMIA married Sir Walter Moray (Walter de Moravia)

**CHRISTINA married Olaf, King of Isle of Man.**

III **EARL WILLIAM, third** Earl of Ross married Euphemia who became Countess of Ross. Died 1322

IV **EARL HUGH, fourth** Earl of Ross, married (1) Lady Maud Bruce

SIR JOHN de Ross married with no issue.

**SIR WALTER de Ross killed at Bannockburn 1314**

**ISABELLA**

**DOROTHEA married Torquil McLeod of Lewis**

(2) married Margaret daughter of Sir David Grahm

JOHN De Ross died young

MARJORY married the Earl of Strathearn, Caithness and Orkney

**HUGH** of Rarichies and Balnagowan Progenitor of CLAN ROSS 1371, and of thirteen Barons of Balnagowan

EUPHEMIA married (1) Earl of Moray (2) Robert, Earl of Strathearn. He afterwards became King Robert II of Scotland. Euphemia became **QUEEN OF SCOTLAND**

**JANET**

V **EARL WILLIAM fifth Earl of Ross married Mary, daughter of Angus Og. Compelled by** King David to forfeit the Earldom of Ross in 1370

**EUPHEMIA** his daughter, created Countess of Ross by King David. Married **(1) to Sir Walter Leslie (2) to Lord Alexander "The Wolf of Badenoch", Son of Richard II**

**WILLIAM**

**JANET**

FARQUHAR, *first Earl of Ross*

Fearchar Mac-an-t-Sagairt (Farquhar MacTaggart) was the son of a Sagairt or priest as the name implies, and was hereditary Abbot of the lands of Applecross. He was given the title Earl of Ross by Alexander II in 1234 for his valiant services as a military leader in Alexander's army.

Earl Farquhar, was a man of restless activity, chivalrous, physically powerful, and of superb courage, a heroic figure in his time. He regularly attended the court of King Alexander II, who succeeded William the Lion, and was one of the Commission of Scottish noblemen who went to Rome to inform the Pope that Scotland and England had concluded a treaty of peace. It was at this time, while a guest of the English king, that Farquhar took part in one of those knightly combats which were a favourite pastime of royalty.

Challenged by a French courtier who was renowned for his prowess with sword and lance, Farquhar agreed to show what a Ross-shire highlander could do. He won handsomely in the encounter. He had vowed that if he survived the combat, he would found a religious house in Ross-shire. This was no idle boast as he later built both Edderton Abbey and Fearn Abbey.

Farquhar was one of the leaders of the military forces in northern Scotland. He led his Highland troops in the suppression of a rebellion which had broken out in Moray. The rebel leader was Donald Bane MacWilliam of the old Celtic line, who, with the assistance of an Irish Chieftain, marched with a strong force into Moray. Young King Alexander, at the age of seventeen, led his army, which was much inferior in numbers, to meet the rebels. The King's forces were in desperate straits when Farquhar with a band of rough-clad, brawny hillmen came to his aid and routed MacWilliam's forces by a circling manoeuvre. Farquhar slew MacWilliam and presented his gory head to the King. For this timely assistance Alexander honoured him with a knighthood on the field of battle in 1215, and granted him the Royal Castle of Dingwall for his personal use.

In 1232, the King again marched with his army of loyal subjects to subdue the Bretons and Norse pirates in Galloway, who were proving particularly troublesome to successive Scottish monarchs. Farquhar and his band of lightly armed, mountaineers arrived late at the appointed place to assist King Alexander, and found that the King's forces had been drawn into a trap. The Earl promptly altered his line of march and assailed the Gallowegians in the rear, converting what would have been a national disaster into an important victory. The Gallowegian leaders soon appeared before King Alexander with ropes around their necks, signifying total submission. As a politicial manoeuvre, the King allowed them to go free instead of spiking their heads on the battlements.

The Earldom of Ross was conferred on Sir Farquhar Mac-an-t-Sagairt, in 1234 in recognition of the valuable service he was able to render to King Alexander in this campaign against the Gallowegians. Earl Farquhar was hereditary Lord of all the Churchland of Applecross extending along the north-western coastline of Scotland from Glenelg to Lochbroom and far inland. The monastery of Applecross was originally founded by St. Maelrubha in 673 and was known as the "Sanctuary", (in gaelic A' Chromraich). After Farquhar was created Earl of Ross, the extensive territories of the newly created Earldom were also placed under his jurisdiction, and he was given lordship rights over lands in Ross, Skye, Lewis, and Moray*. In the gaelic *ros* signifies a peninsula, such as the major part of Easter Ross which is situated between the Dornoch and Moray Firths. With these vast lands he became the most powerful chieftain of his time in the Highlands. His steadfast support of King Alexander enabled him to rise to a postion of great influence throughout the north, at the expense of the Norse earldoms of Orkney and Caithness. Earl Farquhar was undoubtedly the most important of the northern earls in the early part of the thirteenth century, and was an important factor in enabling Alexander III to finally overthrow the powerful Norse influence in Scotland and the isles.

As became a good son of the Church, Earl Farquhar was duly affected by the religious ideas of the times, and since the erection and endowment of monasteries was considered to be a duty most acceptable to heaven, he founded in 1230 the Abbey of Edderton. This abbey was apparently poorly constructed by the local contractors of those days however, and in 1238 it was abandoned and a new abbey was erected at Fearn some miles distant. This abbey became known as Fearn Abbey or "Abbacia de Nova Farina". The relics of St. Ninian were said to have been installed in the original abbey, and when these were transferred to the new Abbey they gave it a special aura of sanctity. Earl Farquhar is also said to have built the Castle of Eilean Donain about the year 1220. It became one of the strongholds of the Earls of Ross until it came into possession of the Mackenzies in the fifteenth century. After the battle of Glenshiel in 1719 the Castle was restored and became the seat of the Macrae's.

The years 1214-86 are known as Scotland's "Golden Age". The country was experiencing a period of unusual quiet and prosperity after the suppression of the revolt in Moray, and the later conquest and subjugation of the Hebrides, which had remained so long under the control of Norway. The establishment of good relations with England and peace

*See map on front endpaper.

on the borders, the growth of towns with their prosperous middle class, the building of churches and abbeys, and the spread of culture and religion, all added to this improved standard of living. Earl Farquhar and the later Earls of Ross contributed in no small way to this age of prosperity.

Earl Farquhar died in his Castle of Delney in 1251 and was buried in the abbey at Fearn that he had built. The stone effigy of a warrior is said to have marked his grave.

For more than one hundred years, from the time when Farquhar was created first Earl of Ross, to the death of William, fifth Earl, in 1372, the maintenance of law and order in the Highlands was ably administered through most of northern Scotland by the Earls of Ross. The proud record of Farquhar led the way for the earls who succeeded him.

The name of Earl Farquhar's wife is unknown, but he left as issue two sons and two daughters, (1) William, second Earl of Ross, (2) Malcolm de Ross, mentioned in the writs of the Lovat estate as having donated the lands of Craigorm to William de Bisset, a transaction confirmed by King Alexander III, (3) Euphemia, who married Sir Walter de Moravia, (4) Christina, who became the third wife (according to tradition) of Olaf, King of Man and the Isles.

## WILLIAM, *second Earl of Ross*

William, eldest son of Farquhar, became one of the most important Scottish nobles in the reign of Alexander III.

Previous to this time there had been considerable strife between Scotland and England. Earl William was one of the nobles who gave their bond that they would not sign any separate peace treaty with England without the consent of the Prince and nobles of Wales.

William carried on his father's religious crusade in northern Scotland and continued the donations for the upkeep of Fearn Abbey in 1258. He was a staunch supporter of Alexander III and he, along with other nobles, bound himself to maintain and defend Princess Margaret's title to the Crown of Scotland in the event that Alexander III should die without male issue.

At this time, King Haakon of Norway and his island chiefs held control of the Western Isles. These included the Hebrides, Skye, Mull, Jura, Islay, and the smaller islands. King Alexander III was trying to gain possession of these islands, and, at his request Earl William undertook to subdue King Haakon and his islanders. In 1263, Haakon, with a large and powerful fleet, determined to enforce acknowledgement of his claim as ruler of the Western Isles. He anchored his flotilla in Clyde

Firth and proceeded to Largs where his men effected a landing. Here they were met by a mixed army of Scottish cavalry and foot soldiers under the able command of Earl William of Ross, who was fighting under the banner of King Alexander III. King Haakon's men were completely routed by the men of Ross. Haakon escaped and returned to the Orkney Islands, where he soon died. In 1266 his successor, King Magnus IV, negotiated with King Alexander, and in return for certain money payments, all the Western Isles, from the butt of Lewis to the Isle of Man, were annexed in perpetuity to the Scottish Crown. For this distinguished service Earl William was given the title "Lord of Skye and Lewis" by Alexander III and was further rewarded with the hand of Jean, daughter of William Comyn Earl of Buchan and niece of the King. Thus for the first time the island of Lewis became identified with the Earldom of Ross. The second Earl of Ross died at Erles-Allane in 1274.

## WILLIAM, *third Earl of Ross*

William, Earl of Ross of the O'Beolain line, succeeded his father. At this time the death of the Maid of Norway caused a dispute over the succession to the throne. Thirteen separate claimants came forward, among them Robert the Bruce and John Balliol. King Edward I of England decided in favour of Balliol, who was thereupon crowned King of Scotland. (The document pronouncing this succession still exists, signed with the seal of the Earl of Ross as witness.) At first the Scottish Highlands approved this decision, and also approved the fact that Scotland was made an English dependency. But King Edward gradually became oppressive and after many humiliating experiences, the Scottish king, the Earl of Ross and other Scottish nobles, and the people themselves broke away from the English tyranny.

In 1296 the army of Scotland, led by the third Earl of Ross, Earl Monteith, and Earl Athole, was mobilized and marched into England, devasting the country as it advanced. The army leaders succeeded in occupying and holding the Castle of Dunbar for a time, but, the Scottish army of King Balliol was ultimately routed by the English. Ten thousand men were lost, and a number of prisoners were taken. The Earls, who had taken refuge in the Castle, were quickly taken prisoner by King Edward's forces. Earl William of Ross was sent to the Tower of London, where he was condemned to live on sixpence a day. Here he was kept in close confinement for the next seven years.

After defeating the Scottish army at Dunbar, King Edward marched in triumph through Scotland and on his way northward received the surrender of King Balliol and the latter's renunciation of his throne.

After his seven years of imprisonment in the Tower, the Earl of Ross was released under the escort of Sir Francis le Vylers and a squadron of soldiers. This was largely the result of the efforts of his wife Euphemia, Countess of Ross. She was a very remarkable woman, who had ingratiated herself so thoroughly with Edward, that the King not only released her husband but appointed him Warden of Scotland beyond the River Spey. King Edward's object in treating Earl William so leniently was doubtless to attach him more firmly to the English cause, a move that later proved to be successful.

In 1306, Robert the Bruce was crowned King of Scotland at Scone, and was the reigning monarch at the time the Earl of Ross was released from the Tower.

To satisfy the English sovereign and to ensure his retention of the Earldom, Earl William violated the sanctuary of the church and seized Bruce's Queen and stepdaughter, Lady Marjory, who had taken refuge in St. Duthac's Church at Tain, as previously mentioned. After being held under guard for several years by King Edward, these distinguished prisoners were later released.

To retaliate King Robert the Bruce invaded Ross and Sutherland in 1307. The inhabitants of these regions under the leadership of the Earl of Ross petitioned the English king for assistance, but the required aid did not come. Bruce devastated the lands of the Earl of Ross and destroyed his fortifications. The Earl sued for pardon, made a truce, and swore fealty to King Robert at Auldearn. This reconciliation was cemented by the marriage of the Earl's son, Hugh, to the Princess Maud, the King's sister. Eventually the Earl of Ross became Bruce's staunch vassal and personal friend, and was granted the Castle and Estates and Ferncrosky (Croick). The great Castle of Dingwall again became the seat of the Earls of Ross and remained in their possession until 1476 when the Earldom was forfeited to the Crown. Earl William as a friendly gesture invited King Bruce to his hunting reservation on the Island of Kinellan, and there entertained him royally.

In 1309, Earl William was present at Bruce's first parliament held at St. Andrews, and later appended his seal to the agreement between the kings of Scotland and Norway. He had the honour to lead the men of Ross, Sutherland, and Caithness at the Battle of Bannockburn in 1314, where his younger son Sir Walter de Ross was killed. He was also one of those who addressed the famous letter to the Pope on the Independence of Scotland. Earl William's shield bore three heraldic lions rampant.

Earl William and Euphemia had three sons and two daughters; (1)

Hugh, fourth Earl of Ross; (2) Sir John de Ross, who married the Lady Margaret, daughter and co-heiress of John Comyn, Earl of Buchan. The lady died without issue and the lands acquired through her passed to her nephew, William, fifth Earl of Ross; (3) Sir Walter de Ross, was a scholar at Cambridge in 1306, he was also a close friend of Edward Bruce, Earl of Carrick and was one of the few Scottish nobles who fell at Bannockburn; (4) Isabella, who contracted to, but probably did not marry Edward Bruce, Earl of Carrick, self-styled King of Ireland, and brother of Robert I; and (5) Dorothea, who married Torquil McLeod, second Baron of Lewis, by whom she had issue.

The "Kalendar of Fearn" bears the record that Earl William died at his Castle of Delny on January 28, 1322.

## HUGH, *fourth Earl of Ross*

Hugh succeeded his father William in 1322. He was made Sheriff of Cromarty, and through various royal charters granted by King Robert I he received the lands of Rarichies, the isle of Skye, Strathglass, Strathconon, and other lands, thus increasing the vast territory over which the Earls of Ross ruled. Earl Hugh was a patriot and strong supporter of the King. As a young man he was placed in command of the troops loyal to the government at the siege of Urquhart Castle on Loch Ness in 1297.

Hugh was married twice, first to Lady Maud Bruce, sister of King Bruce, and second to Margaret, daughter of Sir David Graham of Old Montrose. By the first union he had two sons and a daughter: (1) William, fifth Earl of Ross; (2) John de Ross, who died in 1364, and (3) Marjory, who married Malise, Earl of Strathearn, Caithness, and Orkney.

The children of his second marriage to Margaret were (1) Hugh, who was known as "*of Rarichies*", and who afterward became the progenitor of the *Rosses of Balnagowan* and *first Chief of Clan Ross.* (2) Euphemia, who married first John Randolph, Earl of Moray, who died at the battle of Durham in 1346, and second Robert, who afterwards became King Robert II of Scotland; (3) Janet, who married first Monymush of that Ilk, and later Sir Arthur Murray of Abercairney.

Earl Hugh met an untimely death in 1333 at the battle of Halidon Hill near Berwick, where he commanded the Scottish army against the English. Many brave men of Ross were also killed in this battle. It is said that in battle the Earl wore the shirt of St. Duthac, which was supposed to render its wearer invulnerable. Perhaps it was in a spirit of irony rather than generosity that the English removed the shirt from the Earl's body and returned it to its resting place in the Sanctuary at Tain.

## WILLIAM, *fifth Earl of Ross*

William, fifth Earl of Ross, was the eldest son of Hugh, by his first wife Lady Maud Bruce. He was living in Norway when his father was killed and did not take possession of his earldom until three years later, in 1336. This nobleman has been described as a man "of great pairts, worth, and honour". He assisted Robert, the High Steward of Scotland and Governor of the Kingdom, and exerted a steadying influence in Scottish affairs. He behaved gallantly on every opportunity against the enemies of his country, and was appointed "Justiciar of Scotland benorth the Forth". Earl William of Ross also held the honour of being called "Lord of Skye." His armorial shield showed the three lions rampant.

In 1346, ten years after he succeeded to the earldom, he unfortunately committed a deed that dishonoured his good name. David II had assembled an army at Perth with a view to invading England. The muster was the greatest that had taken place for many years, with troops drawn from all parts of the Highlands and the Islands of Scotland. Unfortunately some of the Highland chiefs brought their personal jealousies with them, which terminated in bloodshed, as the following incident reveals.

In the reign of Robert Bruce certain lands belonging to Roderick of Bute had been forfeited to the Crown. King David II had restored these properties in North Argyll to Roderick's son Reginald (Ronald). Earl William apparently disputed the possession of these lands and a bitter feud ensued.

In 1346, King David II summoned the barons of Scotland to meet him at Perth, where Reginald and Earl William with others obeyed the call. Reginald and his men from the Isles took up their quarters in the monastery of Elcho, a few miles from Perth. To the Earl of Ross this seemed a favourable opportunity to revenge himself on his enemy. He surprised the keeper and entered the monastery in the middle of the night killing Reginald and seven of his followers. Then, dreading the royal vengeance, he led his men back to their homes in the Highlands instead of proceeding to join King David at Perth. Reginald, the slain chieftain, was the son of "Rory of the Isles", and the last male representative of Roderick of Bute, grandson of the great Somerled of the Isles. As a result of Reginald's death, John and later Donald of the Isles, claimed the succession to that principality, and became the first and second Lords of the Isles.

Not withstanding the desertion of the Earl of Ross, with members of his clan, as well as a large number of Reginald's Islesmen, King David pressed forward into England and on Oct. 17, 1346, fought the Battle of Durham. David himself was taken prisoner and sent to the Tower, where he was confined for eleven years.

Nine years later, the northern lords had thrown off their allegiance and refused to contribute towards the payment of King David's ransom, which amounted to 10,000 merks Scots, a fabulous sum in those days. Among those who took a leading part in this rebellion were the Earl of Ross and his brother Hugh. No doubt, like so many of the nobility of Scotland, they disapproved of the repeated attempts on the part of King Edward to make Scotland subservient to England, and they took courage from those in power.

Scotland was experiencing a difficult period at this time with the ravages of war as well as the onset of the Black Plague which had spread from England.

In 1350, Earl William with the approval of his sister Marjory, Countess of Strathearn, (her husband Malise, the eighth Earl of Strathearn, had granted the lands of Hawkhead to his kinsmen Godfrey de Ros about 1367,) and—be it noted—upon condition of obtaining the King's consent, appointed his half-brother Hugh of Rarichies as his heir to the Earldom of Ross.

After his release from the Tower of London, King David returned to Scotland and took vengeance on Earl William, who had not only failed to support him in his campaign against the English, but who had murdered one of his chieftains. He would not sanction Earl William's proposal that his half-brother Hugh of Rarichies be declared his heir, to the Earldom of Ross. Instead the King drew up a *new Charter for the Earldom of Ross and the Lordship of Skye,* and created a new line of succession.

He first compelled Earl William to forfeit all his vast lands to the Crown for reinfeftment, in the year 1370. The Earldom of Ross was then conferred upon the Earl's daughter Euphemia, and her husband, Sir Walter Leslie, with the exception of the lands of Balnagowan which were given to the rightful heir, Hugh of Rarichies. In this way Sir Walter Leslie, who was unrelated to the Earls of Ross, became the sixth Earl upon the death of William, fifth Earl in 1372, and his wife became the Countess of Ross. The earldom was diverted from male heirs exclusively to a female heir, and thus began the new line of succession of the family of Leslie. This change of succession resulted in a great deal of dissatisfaction in succeeding generations, and consequently there was a continual struggle to gain possession of the earldom by the rightful heirs, and by the Lords of the Isles.

While Earl William did merit punishment, it is generally conceded that he was too severely treated by King David, in being forced to forfeit his vast possessions. In a later section it will be shown how the true line of succession of Clan Ross came down through Hugh of Rarichies and the house of Balnagowan.

## THE SECOND OR LESLIE LINE OF SUCCESSION OF THE EARLS OF ROSS

### SIR WALTER LESLIE, *sixth Earl of Ross*

At this time the Clan Ross became closely associated with royalty. Not only did the Clan provide a queen for the Scottish throne, but one of the king's sons married a Countess of Ross.

King Robert II married, as his second wife, Euphemia, sister of Hugh of Rarichies, first chief of Clan Ross. Euphemia was then crowned Queen of Scotland in 1371. She was the daughter of Hugh, fourth Earl of Ross, and we are proud to claim her as the most notable female member of Clan Ross. She bore King Robert four children and was a gracious figure in the early Scottish Court.

Robert II is said to have arranged the marriage of Queen Euphemia's niece, the Countess of Ross, who was also called Euphemia, with Sir Walter Leslie. The Countess Euphemia was the daughter of William, fifth Earl of Ross. This marriage, however, was an unhappy one, and after Sir Walter Leslie's death in 1379, Euphemia, with King Robert's consent, married Sir Alexander Stewart, King Robert's fourth son by his first wife Elizabeth Mure.

This Alexander Stewart was a wild and lawless character and he is known in history as "The Wolf of Badenoch". Even his childhood was turbulent. When his father was fighting the nobles, Robert (who later became Robert II) and his sons, including the "Wolf", were incarcerated in various strongholds, one of them Lochleven Castle on Loch Leven. The "Wolf" was a notorious troublemaker and spent most of his time seizing the property of others, stirring up clan feuds, plundering church properties, and finally burning two towns. Alexander, the "Wolf," in this way gained possession of four great castles. Delney Castle, Ruthven Castle, Loch-an-Eilean Castle situated on the lovely loch of the same name, and Lochindorb Castle as previously mentioned.

His childless marriage to Euphemia, Countess of Ross, was an unhappy one; the "Wolf" had only married her to secure control of the Earldom of Ross. But while married to Euphemia, the Wolf's exotic

## THE EARLS OF ROSS

*The New Leslie Line of Succession Created by King David II, 1370*

VI Sir Walter Leslie,
married Euphemia Countess of Ross
and became sixth Earl of Ross, died 1379.

VII Alexander Leslie, seventh Earl of Ross
married Isobel Stewart,
no heirs male. Died 1402.
Euphemia, Countess of Ross
illegally resigned the Earldom of Ross to her uncle.

VIII Sir John Stewart, eighth Earl of Ross. Killed 1425.
King James I annexed the Earldom of Ross to the Crown.
Earldom of Ross granted to Lady Margaret, widow of
Donald, Lord of the Isles, she became Countess of Ross.

IX Alexander MacDonald, ninth Earl of Ross and third Lord of the Isles. Succeeded on death of his mother, Countess of Ross.
He married Margaret, daughter of Sir Alexander Seaton, died 1448.

X John, tenth Earl of Ross and fourth Lord of the Isles. Died 1493.
Forfeited the Earldom of Ross to the Crown in 1476.
Married Elizabeth Livingstone.
Angus Og, an illegitimate son of Earl John was not granted the earldom. Killed by his Irish harper in the castle at Inverness.
Donald Dubh, called Black Donald, also an illegitimate son
of Earl John was not granted the earldom of Ross.
He was confined to prison for sixty years.

mistress Mariota Athyn, bore him five lusty sons. The unfortunate Countess Euphemia soon applied to the Bishop of Ross for a separation. The Bishops of Ross and Moray met in the Church of the Preaching Friars at Inverness in 1389 and endeavoured to settle the matrimonial difficulties of Lady Euphemia. Separation was granted to Euphemia by the Church dignitaries. The "Wolf" was excommunicated and in revenge, he and a group of "wild, wikked heilandmen" razed the Priory of Forres, sacked and burned the Elgin Cathedral, and proceeded to establish his claim to the lands of Strathnairn by devastating the countryside and slaying the Sheriff. For these deeds he was prosecuted and obliged to make reparation. When the "Wolf" died, his effigy was duly placed in Dunkfield Cathedral.

Two of the "Wolf's" sons deserve mention. One, Duncan Stewart, led a great raid into the Braes of Angus. Another, also called Alexander proved to be as wild and lawless as his father. He took a fancy to Isabel, Countess of Mar, sister of the second Earl of Douglas. This lady was well endowed but was already married to Sir Malcolm Drummond, brother of the late Queen. In no time at all Drummond was murdered, and at Kildrummie Castle, young Alexander forced the widow to marry him at sword point. Then he got the Bishop of Ross to deed over all the Countess' property to him. After this he went to sea as a pirate and captured one of Dick Whittington's ships—he of the Nursery Rhyme—before becoming a great success in Paris as a courtesan. He returned to Scotland in time to lead the Burgess of Aberdeen against his cousin, Donald, second Lord of the Isles, at the Battle of Harlaw, where he gained a pyrrhic victory over the men of Ross and the Isles. He finally became Warden of Marches under James I, full of years and honour, justice notwithstanding.

After the "Wolf's" death, Euphemia ruled the vast estates for a time as Countess of Ross in her own right, meanwhile seeking a husband after her own heart. It appears that the Countess had set her heart upon Alexander of Kintail, and that she took the initiative in proposing marriage. The Chief of Kintail, however, refused her offer. Still pressing her suit, she invited him to the Castle of Dingwall, where he still refused her advances. She promptly made him a prisoner in one of the strong rooms of the castle. The unfortunate clansman's escape was finally effected by Macaulay, Governor of Eilean-Donan Castle. This led to the desperate battle between the clans of Macrae, MacKenzie, and Ross on one side, and a mounted troop of King's men under Lord Lovat and the Munros of Foulis on the other. The battle took place at the Glen of Peffery, with much bloodshed.

The unhappy and disillusioned Countess Euphemia entered the convent of Elcho, near Perth, and after her death was buried at Fortrose.

## ALEXANDER LESLIE, *seventh Earl of Ross*

Alexander Leslie, seventh Earl of Ross, was Countess Euphemia's eldest son. He became Earl of Ross on the death of Sir Walter Leslie in 1372. He married Isabel Stewart, daughter of Robert Stewart, Earl of Fife and Duke of Albany, who was Regent of Scotland at that time.

Earl Alexander led a rather uneventful life and died at Dingwall in 1402, leaving only one daughter, Euphemia.

## SIR JOHN STEWART, *eighth Earl of Ross*

Countess Euphemia illegally resigned the Earldom of Ross to her maternal uncle, Sir John Stewart who thereafter called himself Earl of Buchan and Ross, and settled with his family and retainers in the Castle of Dingwall.

Since there were no male heirs, the rightful heir on the female side was the daughter of the late Sir Walter Leslie, Lady Margaret Leslie, who had married Donald, Lord of the Isles. Donald a fighting Scot was not prepared to be deprived of the extensive possessions and lands which the earldom of Ross comprised, and laid claim to these estates through his wife. When his claim was refused, he quickly gathered a large force of islanders, marched to Harlow where the great battle of the Clans was fought in 1416.

James I annexed the earldom of Ross to the crown after the death of Sir John Stewart at Verneuil in 1424.

For three years King James I retained the earldom in his own hands, but in 1424 he revoked his previous decision and granted the earldom to Margaret, wife of Donald, Lord of the Isles, who had fought so hard to recover it. Margaret's son Alexander then succeeded to both titles, Lord of the Isles and Earl of Ross, on her death, his succession was confirmed by King James.

From this point the history of the Earls of Ross and of the Lords of the Isles run concurrently for two generations. Alexander, the ninth Earl of Ross, and John, tenth and last Earl of Ross, will be considered in the next section.

# THE LORDS OF THE ISLES, 1354-1493

Skye and Lewis were under Norse jurisdiction before they were incorporated into the territories of Ross. Somerled, King of the Isles was the progenitor of the once powerful Lords of the Isles. The population of the Hebrides and the adjacent coast of Scotland at that time was a mixture of Celtic and Scandinavian blood, but the Celtic race and language predominated as we have seen.

In 1135 when King David I expelled the Norwegians (Fingalls) from the islands of Man, Arran, and Bute, Somerled appears to have obtained a grant of these islands from the King. Somerled gained further power and island territory by his marriage to Ragnhildis, daughter of Olaf the Red, who ruled as the Norwegian king of the northern islands. Reginald, one of Somerled's three sons held hereditary possession of the Island of Islay, and this island later became the headquarters of the Lords of the Isles. In 1164 Somerled collected a large force of islanders and men from Ireland and landed with his fleet of war galleys near Renfrew. Here he was met by King Malcolm's troops and was defeated in a decisive battle in which he and his son Gillecolum were slain.

The Earl of Ross had raided the island of Skye where he ravaged the country and put to death a number of the Norse inhabitants in order to bring them under subjection. The Norsemen however, drove him back to the mainland.

In the year 1263 the Norwegian forces under King Haakon invaded the mainland but were completely routed by the Scots at the battle of Largs. Following this decisive battle, the Isles were finally ceded to the kings of Scotland.

It is of interest to follow the history of the Lords of the Isles, descended from Somerled the Gaelic hero, especially since they are closely associated with the Earls of Ross, the last two of whom retained the double title.

The first Lord of the Isles was *John (Eoin) of Islay.* In 1354 John, who held hereditary possession of extensive territories in the Western Highlands and the islands near the coast, assumed the title "Lord of the Isles" and lived in the Castle of Ardtornish, which he built for himself and his knights. John had married the daughter of the Steward of Scotland. King David II began to suspect that the northern barons were becoming too powerful, so he applied to the Steward to assist him in suppressing them and bringing them under subjection to his rule. King David had to contend not only with the various clan feuds which occurred at frequent intervals, but also with a formidable insurrection against royal authority at this time. In a parliament held at Scone in 1366 a resolution was passed to seize the rebels in Argyll, Ross, Athole, and Badenoch; and among the persons mentioned in the parliamentary records who were to be apprehended were the Earl of Ross, Hugh de Ross, John of the Isles, John of Lorne, and John de Haye. These men were summoned to the parliament to give their submission, but, in a most decided manner, they all refused to do so. Since the government was at this time too weak to compel them to submit to the king's authority, they were allowed to remain independent for three more years. John of the Isles, with a numerous train of wild Highland chieftains who followed his banner, now undertook to assert his authority as an independent ruler and throw off his allegiance to King David II. The king however, with an unprecendented burst of courage, assembled the Steward and barons of the realm as well as a formidable group of vassals and retainers, and proceeded against the rebels. The expedition was completely successful; John with other Highland chieftains met the King at Inverness, where, after swearing his allegiance, he signed a treaty to this effect in 1369.

The Lord of the Isles not only gave his own oath of allegiance, under penalty of forfeiting his entire island domain if it were broken, but he also offered to deliver as hostages his lawful son Donald, his natural son also called Donald, his grandson Angus, and his father-in-law, if the terms of treaty were not carried out. In this way John, was again received into the favour of the King. Later John of the Isles was murdered under unknown circumstances.

## DONALD, *second Lord of the Isles*

Donald, second Lord of the Isles was a son of John's second marriage to Lady Margaret, daughter of Sir Walter Leslie and Euphemia, Countess of Ross. He laid claim to the earldom of Ross when Euphemia, the rightful heiress, entered a nunnery.

Donald, who was the first chief of Clan Donald called his clan together to defend his claim against the Duke of Albany, great-uncle of Euphemia, who disputed his rights to the lands and possessions of the earldom of Ross. He was supported by six thousand Highlanders and Islanders from Kintail, Islay, Eigg, and Rum, and from the hills of Ardnamurchan, Ardgower, and Mowan. In 1411 this large army, armed after the fashion of the islands with bows and arrows, pole axes, knives, and claymores, marched through Wester Ross in their kilts and sporrans, over the hills and glens to Dingwall. Here Donald defeated an army of the MacKays, Dingwalls, MacKenzies, and Munros under the leadership of "Black Angus" Dubh Mackay.

This historic march of Donald of the Isles and his Islesmen is commemorated to this day by a stone called the "Eagle Stone", an old Celtic-carved slab which was erected by the Munros at Strathpeffer. This stone (so called from the figure of an eagle which it bears) is known in the Gaelic as *Clach'n Tuindain* or the "Stone of Turning". It marks the spot where the forces of Donald of the Isles were "turned" in a desperate encounter which took place in the valley near Strathpeffer. Donald then proceeded eastward toward Dingwall which was quickly taken. He went on to Inverness, which he sacked and burned, and then to Aberdeenshire where he was stopped short by the Earl of Mar an illigitimate son of the Wolf of Badenoch. The Earl had rallied an army of many brave knights from his own districts of Gairloch and Strathbogie, together with volunteers from Angus and Mearns. This army of Saxon lowlanders was said to be only one-tenth as large as the rebel forces under command of Donald of the Isles, but they were clad in armour and had superior weapons. Donald was supported by Macintosh and MacLean and other Highland chiefs. The two armies met on the field of Harlaw, and on signal the Highlanders and Islesmen, setting up the terrific shouts and yells which they were accustomed to raise on entering battle, rushed forward upon their hated Saxon opponents. They were met with great firmness and bravery by a party of knights led by Sir James Scrymeogur, the hereditary standard bearer of Scotland and constable of Dundee. The mounted knights, with their spears levelled and battle axes raised, cut through the ranks of poorly armed Islesmen, but hundreds more poured in to fill the gaps. Sir James was finally surrounded, and since no alternative was left for him and his knights but victory or death, they chose death.

Meanwhile the Earl of Mar led the main strength of his army which consisted of the Murrays, the Leslies, the Irvings, the Lovels, the Stirlings, and other clans in the second wave of battle, and penetrated to the centre of the Islemen's ranks, keeping up the unequal contest with great bravery. Although the Earl of Mar lost almost the whole of his army during the battle, he continued the fatal struggle with a handful of men till nightfall.

The bloody battle of Harlaw made a lasting impression of horror on the minds of the many Highland and Lowland Clans which participated, and many ballads, songs, and marches were written to commemorate it. It is stated that five hundred knights and nobles from the Lowlands were slain, and nine hundred Highlanders. The Earl of Mar and a few of his followers who survived the battle remained on the field over night. When morning dawned they found to their surprise that the Lord of the Isles and the remainder of his troops had retreated.

As soon as the news of this disastrous battle reached the ears of the regent of Scotland, he collected an army, and then marched to the north, determined to bring the Lord of the Isles to obedience. He advanced into Ross-shire and took possession of the Castle of Dingwall. Donald of the Isles retreated before him and returned to his winter quarters in the islands. Donald was then forced to give up all claims to the Earldom of Ross, to become a vassal of the Scottish crown, and to deliver hostages to guarantee his future good behaviour. Donald of the Isles died in 1423.

### THE BATTLE OF HARLAW
*(A portion of the ballad)*

Grit[1] Donald of the Yles[2] did claim
Unto the lands of Ross sum richt.
Ant to the Governour he came,
Them for to haif fig that he micht;
Quha[3] saw his interest was but slicht,
And thairfore answerit with disdain;
He hastit[4] hame baith day and nicht
And sent nae bodword[5] back again.

But Donald, richt impatient
Of that answer Duke Robert gaif,
He vowd to God Omnipotent
All the hale[6] lands of Ross to haif;
Or ells, be graithed[7] in his graif
He wold not quat[8] his richt for nocht
Nor be abusit lyk a slaif[9],
That bargain sould be deirly bocht.

The armies met, the trumpet sounds,
The dandring[10] drums alboud did tank,
Baith armies byding on the bounds,
Till ane of them feild should bruik;
Nae help was thair, for nane wad jouk,[11]
Fers[12] was the fecht[13] an ilka[14] syde,
And on the ground lay many a bouk[15]
Of them that thair did battill byd.

But Donald's men at last gaif back
For they war all out of array;
The Erle of Moris men throw them brak,
Pursewing shairply in thair way.
Thair enemys to take or slay,

[1] Grit—Great
[2] Yles—Isles
[3] Quha—Who
[4] hastit—hastened
[5] bodword—message
[6] hale—whole
[7] graithed—buried
[8] quat—give up
[9] slaif—slave
[10] dandring—rattling
[11] jouk—escape by jumping aside
[12] fers—fierce
[13] fecht—fight
[14] ilka—either
[15] bouk—body

Be dynt of forss[1] to gar them yield;
Quhar[2] war[3] richt blyth to win[4] away,
And sae for feirdness[5] tint[6] the field.

Then Donald fled, and that full fost,
To maintains hich[7] for all his micht;
For he and his war[8] all agast,
And ran till they war out of sicht:
And sae[9] of Ross he lost his richt,
Thoch[10] many men with him he brocht;
Towards the Yles fled day and nicht,
And all he won was deirlie bocht.

[1] forss—force
[2] quhar—who
[3] war—were
[4] win—get
[5] feirdness—fright
[6] tint—lost
[7] hich—high
[8] war—were
[9] sae—so
[10] thoch—though

## ALEXANDER *(Alasdair), third Lord of the Isles and ninth Earl of Ross*

The third Lord of the Isles was Alexander, son of Donald the second Lord. He succeeded without opposition to the Earldom of Ross through the claim of his mother even though his father had not gained possession of this dignity, and he thus held the double title. In the early years of his Lordship of the Isles, Alexander was well liked by King James and he was made justiciar for the Crown north of the Forth. He placed his seal on all legal documents in the northern domains.

As a result of the constant feuding of the Islesmen with the clansmen in the Highlands, James I, on his return to Scotland in 1424, decided to destroy Alexander. He invited the Lord of the Isles and his mother the Countess of Ross, and other Highland chiefs, to the castle of Inverness in 1427. When they were all assembled King James promptly arrested them and threw them into prison. After summary trials a number of the chiefs were taken to the block and beheaded.

Alexander of the Isles, after a short confinement, was pardoned. However, this royal clemency met with an ungrateful return. Shortly after the king had returned to his lowland dominions, Alexander collected a force of ten thousand men in Ross and the Isles, and with his formidable army laid waste the country, plundered and devastated the crown lands, and burned a large section of the royal burgh of Inverness to the ground. On hearing of these distressing events, James collected a force, (the extent of which has not been ascertained,) and marched with great speed into Lochaber, where he surprised the rebels. Alexander prepared for battle, but, before its commencement, he had the misfortune to witness the desertion of the Clan Chattan and the Clan Cameron who, to a man, went over to the royal standard. The king then attacked Alexander and completely defeated him on July 23, 1429. Alexander sought safety in flight.

Reduced to the utmost distress, and seeing the impossibility of evading the active vigilance of his pursuers, this haughty lord resolved to throw himself entirely on the mercy of the king by an act of the most abject submission. Arriving in Edinburgh, the humbled chief suddenly presented himself before the King on Easter Sunday in the church of Holyrood, where he and the Queen, surrounded by the nobles of the court, were seated before the high altar. The extraordinary appearance of the fallen prince denoted a very penitent attitude. Without bonnet, arms or ornament of any knd, his legs and arms quite bare, his body covered only with a plaid, and holding a naked sword in his hand by the point, he fell down on his knees before the king, imploring mercy and forgiveness, and, in token of his unreserved submission, offered the hilt of his sword to his majesty. At the solicitation of the Queen and nobles, James spared his life, but committed him immediately to Tantallon Castle, under the charge of William Earl of Angus, his nephew.

The Countess of Ross meanwhile was kept in close confinement in the ancient monastery of Inchcolm, on the small island of that name, in the Firth of Forth. Later, however, the king relented, and released the Lord of the Isles and his mother after about a year's imprisonment. The Countess of Ross died in the same year and Alexander then became Earl of Ross. Alexander died in 1448.

## JOHN, *Earl of Ross and fourth Lord of the Isles*

Earl John was the last who bore the double title. He was but sixteen years of age when his father died and in consequence, he became a ward of James II. He was rather a wild and uncontrollable youth and had become the father of at least one illegitimate child, the notorious Angus Og, before he was eighteen years of age. He was a weak man but had boundless ambitions, and he soon became involved in disputes between the English King and the King and Court of Scotland.

Earl John, Lord of the Isles, became as determined an opponent of the Scottish King as his father had been, and later his son, Angus Og, offered him the same rebellious opposition that he had offered to King James.

John, tenth Earl of Ross, assembled his clansmen at Ardtornish Castle and entered into an alliance with his 'trusty and beloved cousins' Ronald of the Isles, and Duncan, Arch-Deacon of the Isles, instructing them to proceed to London to confer with King Edward IV. As a result of this conference, the most extraordinary treaty of Ardtornish was brought to parchment in 1462. Its distinct purpose was the complete dismemberment of the Scottish monarchy. Earl John, Donald Balloch and his son John de Isles, as well as the Earls of Douglas and Crawford, had entered into this treasonable alliance with King Edward for the conquest and subjugation of the entire territories of northern Scotland. These conspirators were to become the sworn vassals of Edward IV and were to assist him in all future wars both in England and Scotland. This singular treaty stipulated further that Scotland north of the Firth of Forth was to be divided equally between the Earl of Ross, the Earl of Douglas, and Donald Balloch.

Earl John and his son Angus collected a force of Highlanders and seized the royal castle of Inverness. He then marched southward capturing Urquhart Castle at the head of Loch Ness, and stormed and demolished the fortalice of Ruthven in Badenoch. King James' position was so weak at this time that he resorted to condoning rather than suppressing the rebellion. Earl John was accordingly allowed to retain possession of both Urquhart and Glenmorriston Castles, on condition that he pay into the royal exchequer an annual rent of 100 pounds. These payments are shown in the books as a column of arrears.

The Earl of Ross continued his raids, and stormed the Castle of Blair where he dragged the Earl and Countess of Athole from the chapel of St. Bridget and carried them off as prisoners to the island of Islay. The Earl however, lost many of his war-galleys in a storm off the coast as well as the rich plunder he had taken in the raids.

The Scottish Crown supported by a number of Highland clans and Scottish barons instigated proceedings against Earl John as a convicted traitor and rebel. He was summoned in 1476 at his castle of Dingwall, to appear before a parliament in Edinburgh and answer these charges. The Earl sued for pardon and threw himself on the royal clemency as his father had done. James III agreed to pardon his relative, and also his son Angus, and the parliament formally restored to him all his forfeited estates.

King James IV succeeded to the throne in 1488. He had established in his Lowland dominions a system of law and order, and was resolved to establish the same administration of civil and criminal justice throughout the Highlands and Islands. For this purpose, in 1490, he rode from Perth with his court, across the Grampians to visit the Highland chiefs, in a spirit of goodwill and friendliness. In 1493 and 1494 he again visited the Highlands on three occasions and extended his trips to the Isles. Many sailing vessels were fitted out to accommodate the king and his retinue, and the grandeur which surrounded the King impressed the islanders with his importance and wealth. One ship of 26 oars and two ships of 16 oars were supplied for the King's use by Alexander "Crottach" the Humpback (Alexander Macleod). In return for this kindness, King James, in a charter under the great seal, granted him all the Macleod of Harris lands on the islands. James IV increased his prestige among the islanders by his friendly attitude, and particularly by his ability to speak to them freely in their Gaelic tongue. The only opposition which the young King James experienced on these trips was from the Lord of the Isles himself, who resented his visits to the islands. His Majesty was not to be trifled with, however, for he summoned the island prince to stand trial "for treason in Kintyre". In a parliament held in Edinburgh shortly after the King's return from the north "Sir John of the Isles" as he is named in the treasurer's report, was again stripped of his power, and his possessions were forfeited to the crown forever.

Earl John made a "voluntary" surrender to the Scottish Crown in 1475 of the Earldom of Ross, the lands of Kintyre, Knapdale, Urquhart, Glenmorriston and others, with all the castles belonging thereto. The Earldom of Ross was now subdivided. South Ross was placed under the control of Alexander "The Upright", Chief of the Mackenzies, and North Ross, together with the administrative offices, were placed under the command of John, Baron of Fowlis. Earl John himself, stripped of all his possessions, retired in disgrace to the Abbey of Paisley. He died a pauper, in a common lodging house at Dundee in 1498. He was not altogether neglected however, as he received an honourable burial in the tomb of his ancestor King Robert II.

Since John of the Isles had no legitimate son, succession was granted to his illegitimate son Angus Og. Angus Og, as noted previously, turned against his father and they came to blows at Mull not far from Tobermoray, in an event which was later called the "Battle of Bloody Bay", (1480). Earl John and his followers were completely defeated and the unsavoury Angus Og turned next against Alexander Mackenzie the Upright. This brave highlander was taken by surprise but during the skirmish Angus himself was assassinated by one of his own men, an Irish harper who held a grudge against him.

The union of the Earldom of Ross and the Lordship of the Isles under one authority had long been considered by the Crown to be a potential menace to peace in the Kingdom of Scotland. James IV therefore, decided to prevent such a union in future generations.

Thus after nearly three centuries, the authority of the Earls of Ross, the great rulers of the Highlands, came to an end. Their Castle of Dingwall and the estates were taken over by the Crown. The advice which

King Robert the Bruce had left for the guidance of his successors, in regard to the Lordship of the Isles, was certainly dictated by sound political wisdom. He foresaw the danger which would result to the crown if the extensive territories and consequent influence of the island chiefs and of the Earldom of Ross were to be concentrated in one individual.

During the tenure of the Lords of the Isles, from 1354 to 1493, and in spite of the numerous clan uprisings, the Gaelic culture flourished in the Western Highlands. Law and justice were for the first time established on the islands and on the mainland. There was a judge on every island and in the territorial districts. Governing councils composed of sixteen heads of important families were established.

In the reign of James IV the castles and territories of Ross-shire were placed in the hands of Chamberlains and Custodians (*Custodiers*). In 1507, King James appointed Andro, Bishop of Caithness, as his Chamberlain and Captain of the lands of Ross and Ardmannach, and keeper of the Royal Castles of Dingwall in Ross, and Redcastle in Ardmannach. The same bishop had also a grant for three years of "the Conane River and all other fishings in the Lordship of Ross and Ardmannach, for the yearly payment of four last salmon, to be delivered free on the shore from Dingwall to Leith".

Queen Mary appointed George Munro of Davoch-carte her Bailie and Chamberlain over her lands in Ross and Ardmannach in 1561. This appointment was later confirmed by James VI.

In 1584 the Castle of Dingwall became divested of its royal character, and the lands of Ross settled into more law-abiding habits. Sir Andrew Keith was later granted the Castle and lands of Dingwall as his Barony, and he was given the title Lord Dingwall.

*Claimants for the earldom of Ross and lordship of the Isles*

Following the death of John, last Lord of the Isles and Earl of Ross, the titles were forfeited, but succeeding generations made strong efforts to regain them. The right of inheritance to the lordship of the Isles was held by Alexander of Lochalsh, son of Celestine, an illegitimate son of Alexander, ninth Earl of Ross. Alexander of Lochalsh for many years called himself Earl of Ross and fifth Lord of the Isles without any authority whatever. He was murdered on Oransay in 1498 by one of the Macdonalds of Ardnamurchan, and was buried in the tomb of his royal ancestor, King Robert II, in the abbey of Paisley.

Alexander of Lochalsh had a son, Sir Donald Galda (Donald the Stranger), who was knighted at Flodden. He in turn laid claim to the title, calling himself Sixth Lord of the Isles, again without justification.

After Earl John was deprived of the earldom, a *Dukedom of Ross* was created in 1492 by King James IV in favour of his brother James. The ducal estates were later relinquished by James and there were no successors to this title.

In 1503, Donald Dubh, a fiery son of Angus Og, who as we have seen was the illegitimate son of John of the Isles, also set up claims to the earldom of Ross and the lordship of the Isles. To cool his ardour he was taken prisoner, and confined for forty years in Tantallon Castle. He escaped in 1544 and rose again in rebellion. He assumed the titles of Earl of Ross and Lord of the Isles and entered into a treaty with King Edward to uphold his claim, but he died at Drogheda the following year.

Donald Corm was another claimant for the earldom of Ross. He was the representative of the kindred illegitimate house of Sleat, and set up his claim after the failure of male descendants of Celestine. In 1562 Donald followed Mary Queen of Scots everywhere, begging her to confer the earldom upon him, but she refused to do so.

The Earldom of Ross was again revived in 1565 when Lord Darnley was created Earl of Ross in May of that year. In July of the same year the banns of marriage were proclaimed between "Harie Earl of Ross" and Queen Mary, which accounts for the conferring of the title upon the weak and cowardly Lord Darnley. The unfortunate Darnley did not merit the title, and was the last to enjoy the earldom.

Aeneas Macdonell of Glengarry also became a late claimant of the dignity. The grounds for his pretensions were that his great-great-grandfather had married the granddaughter of the illegitimate Celestine of Lochalsh. Macdonell did everything in his power to assist King Charles I in the hope of being rewarded with the earldom of Ross. In 1646 he wrote to King Charles from Castle Leod professing loyalty and obedience: "being only desyrus that your Majesty may kno of a particulare faithful servand to receive and act your commands."

At the Restoration, King Charles II had apparently created him Earl of Ross but this did not take effect. He was given the title Lord Macdonell, however, for his services to the King.

In the reign of James III the office of King's Advocate was established to help the Royal authority settle disputes of succession and other legal matters. The first Advocate on record was Sir John Ross of Montgrenan, who held office in 1488.

# 3. CLAN ROSS OF BALNAGOWAN

**1371-1903**

Having dealt with the Earls of Ross who were leading members of the highland aristocracy in the later half of the thirteenth century, we now proceed to the Rosses of Balnagowan who succeeded the Earls. They became chiefs of the Clan Ross and as such they were largely responsible for maintaining law and order throughout the County of Ross for over three hundred years.

The Rosses of Balnagowan were the oldest and original branch of the Clan Ross, the true descendants of the Celtic O'Beolain Earls of Ross. The succession of the Rosses of Balnagowan (frequently spelled Balnagown), the first of whom was Hugh of Rarichies, remained an unbroken line from father to son for over three centuries.

The succeeding generations of Rosses of Balnagowan, who were in direct line of male descent through Hugh of Rarichies, continued to dispute the arbitrary decision of King David in conferring the Earldom of Ross on Sir Walter Leslie, and much bitterness was expressed from time to time at the loss of the title "Earl of Ross" by the true heirs.

HUGH OF RARICHIES, *first Chief of Clan Ross, Laird of Balnagowan*

Hugh of Rarichies was the third son of Hugh, fourth Earl of Ross, and, after the death of his brother, he became the direct heir male to the Earldom of Ross, but he was deprived of his rightful title, as we have seen.

On the death of William, fifth Earl of Ross, the earldom passed to the Leslie line, while the chiefship of the clan passed to his brother Hugh of Rarichies, to whom was given the lands of Easter Allan and Balnagowan. The gift of these lands was confirmed in a charter by King David II in 1371 and Hugh took the name of the county — Ross — as his surname. Nesbet, in his *System of Heraldry* writes: "Hugh Ross of Rarichies, son of Hugh, Earl of Ross, who was killed in the battle of Halidon Hill, got from his father the lands of Rarichies, as also the lands Westray and of Easter Allan from his brother William Earl of Ross in 1357, and these lands were confirmed by a charter of King David II".

In 1333 Hugh Ross of Rarichies had also received from his father the greater part of the family lands of Buchan, but on his death his heirs were apparently deprived of these lands, along with the earldom. In 1365 Hugh is styled *Lord of Philroth,* and these lands he later exchanged for the lands of Wester Ross, Strathglass, and Eilandonan.

Hugh was the eldest son of Earl Hugh and Margaret Graham, daughter of Sir David Graham of old Montrose. He himself married Margaret Barclay of Ury and had as issue William, who became second Baron of Balnagowan, and Jean, who married Robert Munro, eighth Baron of Foulis.

WILLIAM ROSS, *second Baron of Balnagowan*

He succeeded his father and became the second Laird of the estates, and second chief of the Clan Ross. He married Christina, daughter of Lord Livingstone. In Reid's *Earls of Ross,* this lady is credited with having built the Kirk of Alness. According to an old charter which had been preserved at Balnagowan Castle, William, Laird of the estates of Balnagowan, Wester Ross, Strathglass, Eilandonan, Westray and Easter Allan, was confirmed as having possession of these lands in 1374 by King Robert II who was his uncle by marriage. He therefore had undisputed possession of this vast territory in the Scottish Highlands. William was succeeded by his son Walter when he died in 1398.

# CLAN ROSS OF BALNAGOWAN AND CADET BRANCHES 1371-1711

I. Hugh of Rarichies and Balnagowan, 1st Chief
marr. Margaret Barclay, and died 1374.

II. William of Balnagowan, 2nd Chief
marr. Christine, dau. of Lord Livingstone, and died before 1398

III. Walter of Balnagowan, 3rd Chief
marr. Catherine, dau. and heiress of Paul McTyre,
and died 1412.

IV. Hugh of Balnagowan, 4th Chief
said to have married Janet, dau. of Earl of Sutherland.

V John of Balnagowan,
said to have marr. Christian, dau. of
Torquil MacLeod of Lewis

Hugh

1st Cadet Branch
William of Little Allan
Killed 1486

Rosses of Shandwick

Rosses of Balblair

Rev. Thomas

VI. Alexander of Balnagowan
marr. Dorothy, dau. of Alexander
Sutherland of Duffus and killed
at Alt a'Charrais, 1486

2nd Cadet Branch
Donald

Rosses of Priesthill

VII. Sir David of Balnagowan
marr. (1) Helen Keith, with issue,
(2) dau. of Duke of Albany,
without issue

VIII. Walter of Balnagowan,
marr. dau. of Sir John Grant
of Grant, and slain at Tain
in 1528

3rd Cadet Branch

William of Ardgay

Rossess of Invercharron

Rosses of Braelangwell

Rosses of Easter Fearn

4th Cadet Branch

Hugh

Rosses of
Achnaclioch

IX. Alexander of Balnagowan,
marr. (1) Janet, dau. of John,
3rd Earl of Caithness,
(2) Katherine, dau. of Kenneth,
MacKenzie of Kintail
Died 1592

5th Cadet Branch
Alexander (legitimated)
Rosses of Little Tarrell
Rosses of Pitkerrie
Rosses of Cromarty

Hector | Catherine | Agnes | Malcolm | Robert

6th Cadet Branch
Nicholas
Rosses of Pitcalnie
Rosses of Kindeace
Rosses of Invercastley
Rosses of Calrossie

X. George of Balnagowan,
marr. (1) Marion, dau. of Sir
John Campbell of Cawder
and (2) Isobel, dau. of Angus
MacKintosh, without issue
Died 1615

Colin Earl of Seaforth | John of Lockslin | Kenneth

XI. David of Balnagowan,
marr. (1) Lady Mary Gordon, dau. of
Alexander, Earl of Sutherland
and (2) Lady Annabella Murray, dau. of
John Earl of Tullibardine, without
issue, Died 20th Nov. 1632

XII. David of Balnagowan,
marr. Mary, dau. of Hugh,
Lord Lovat, and died 1667
Buried in Windsor

XIII. David of Balnagowan, 13th Chief
Last of the Barons of Balnagowan
of the original line,
marr. Lady Anne Stewart, dau.
of James, Earl of Moray, without issue
Died 17th April 1711
Lady Ross schemed to transfer
estates to her brother Francis Stewart.

WALTER ROSS, *third Baron of Balnagowan and Chief of Clan*

Beside the lands of Balnagowan which he inherited, he was granted the lands of Cullisse (Cullys) in the Parish of Nigg, by Alexander Leslie, Earl of Ross of the extraneous line. He married Katherine, daughter of Paul McTyre the freebooter of Strathcarron. This Paul was the grandson of Olaf the Red, King of Man, a Norwegian raider of royal rank, whose name caused as much terror in the land as Rob Roy had done in the Southern Highlands. In the *Chronicles of the Earls of Ross* he is described as "a very takand man", which implied taking by force men's goods, cattle and lands. In this way he made himself owner of a large part of Sutherland and the Parish of Kincardine in the County of Ross. Another old chronicle states that Paul McTyre "was a valiant man who forced Caithness to pay him blackmail–nyne scoir of cows yearly so long as he was able to travel." McTyre's stronghold was Dun of Creich, and isolated rock standing out in the upper Dornoch Firth, on which is located one of the vitrified forts that Paul is said to have constructed to repel his enemies.

In Taylor's *History of Tain* it is stated that "this 'gentleman' became so powerful that the family of Balnagowan appear to have been reluctant to give him a daughter of their house in marriage, and along with her a legal grant of the lands of Kincardine, which he had already seized".

Walter Ross of Balnagowan and his wife Katherine McTyre had received in dowry the lands of Strathcarron, Strathoykel, and Westray. Their son Hugh succeeded his father in 1412.

HUGH ROSS, *fourth Baron of Balnagowan and Chief of Clan*

On the authority of the *Chronicles of the Earls of Ross,* this laird is said to have married Lady Janet, daughter of the Earl of Sutherland, but there is no confirmation of this union to be found in the pedigrees of the house of Sutherland. Hugh had as issue: (1) John Ross, who became fifth Laird of Balnagowan; (2) Hugh Ross, of whom nothing is known; (3) William Ross of Meikle Allan, who became first laird of Shandwick (it is with this William Ross that the direct line of descent of the Shandwick Rosses originates and from whom the late Chief Designate of Clan Ross, Sheriff Charles Campbell Ross, traced his descent[1]), and (4) Rev. Thomas Ross, who became Sub-dean of Ross and Rector of the Collegiate Church of Tain.

[1] See the Shandwick Rosses, page 96.

JOHN ROSS, *fifth Laird of Balnagowan*

John was married to Christina, a daughter of Torquil Macleod of Lewis. They had as issue (1) Alexander, who became sixth of Balnagowan; and (2) Donald, who became first of Priesthill and Dean of Caithness; and three other sons. After the forfeiture of the Earldom of Ross (by Earl John in 1476) there was much fighting in the Highlands and part of the Earldom was wasted and seized by other clans. Repeated attempts were made at this time in the name of 'Lord John of the Isles' (John of Balnagowan) to recover the Earldom of Ross, but these were unsuccessful.

ALEXANDER ROSS, *sixth Laird of Balnagowan and Chief of Clan*

Alexander Ross suffered one of the greatest disasters in the history of the Clan Ross. Gordon, in his *Earldom of Sutherland* describes a bloody encounter which took place between the MacKays and the Rosses at Alt'a Charrais. The Kalendar of Fearn gives the date of this battle as June 1486.

The Rosses and MacKays had been bitter enemies for some years previously. The feud began when Angus MacKay, son of Angus Dubh and his band of wild highlanders began raiding the territories of Ross, killing and plundering as they went, and returning with goods and cattle which they had seized. At last however, the Rosses surprised him at Tarbat, shut him up with his men in the church and set the church afire. This brutal act could not go unavenged and Angus MacKay's son, John Raibhaich MacKay, was bound by the clan code of honour to take up the feud and avenge him. John MacKay, as soon as he was old enough, applied for help to the Earl of Sutherland and obtained a select company of soldiers under Robert Sutherland, the Earl's uncle. The combined bands made a raid into Strathoykell and there "wasted many lands appertaining to the Rosses". Alexander of Balnagowan gathered his clansmen at once and met the raiders at Alt'a Charrais, on a small northern tributary of the Oykell River, the spot which has since been called Doir a Chatha, or Grove of the Flight. The fight was obstinate and bloody but at last Chief Alexander Ross was killed, and the loss of their chief decided the day against the Rosses. They had to flee, no quarter was given, and the slaughter was terrible. Among the other leaders who fell were William Ross first of Little Allan and of Shandwick, Alexander Terrell, Angus McCulloch, William Ross, Thomas Vass, John Vass, Hucheon Vass, and John Mitchell. The victors, had secured great booty, but the avarice of Clan MacKay got the better of them. They persuaded John Raibhaich MacKay to take Sutherland and his company unawares, cut them off, appropriate their share of the booty, and give out that they had been killed in the fight. The Sutherlands were warned of the plot and were on their guard. Young John MacKay saw that the scheme was frustrated and went home to Strathnaver.

Alexander of Balgowan who thus fell, had married Dorothy, daughter of Alexander of Sutherland and had as issue—(1) David who became seventh Baron of Balnagowan (2) Isabella who married George Munro, tenth Baron of Foulis. George of Foulis was killed in a fight as disastrous to his family as Alt'a Charrais had been to his father-in-law.

The custom of *manrent* was in vogue at this time in Scotland and is illustrated by the bond of *manrent* which is said to have been given by Angus McCulloch to Laird Alexander as follows: "I, Angus McCulloch, to be bound and strictly obliged, and by the faith of my body leally and truly, bind and oblige myself, in the straitest style of obligation, to a noble and mighty lord, Alexander, in true manrent, homage and service, for all the days of my life; that I shall be ready to ride and pass with my Lord at his warning, in all his lawful and honest quarrels, and give leal and true counsel . . . and abide and remain with his lordship against whosoever, my allegiance to our sovereign and my service of law only accepted, because my said Lord is bound to defend me, and give me a fee at his pleasure. . . . In witness of which I have affixed my seal to this the 8th of December, 1482",

These baronial alliances or bonds of manrent had been suppressed by James I on his return to Scotland, after his imprisonment in the Tower; he endeavoured also to reduce the Isles to obedience and respect for royal authority, before his tragic murder at Perth in 1437. The curious custom of manrent or vassilage still persisted to the end of the century.

## SIR DAVID ROSS, *Chief of Clan Ross*

On the death of his father Sir David became the seventh Laird of Balnagowan. He was twice married, first to Helen Keith, daughter of the Laird of Inverguie, and second to a daughter of the Duke of Albany. For some reason unknown this laird was made a knight, probably through the patronage of his second wife or for unrecorded valour. Very little is known of this highlander but he seems to have been an honest and upright laird, and two of his sons became progenitors of the houses of Invercharron and Achnacloich.

By his first wife he had four sons: (1) Walter, who became the eighth of Balnagowan; (2) William, who became first Laird of Invercharron; (3) Hugh, who became first of the Rosses of Achnacloich; and (4) Angus, who married the daughter of William MacCulloch of Plaids.

WALTER, *eighth Laird of Balnagowan*

Walter was married to Marion, daughter of Sir John James Grant of Grant and had as issue: (1) Alexander, (2) Katherine, who married John Denoon of Cadboll, one of the magistrates of Tain, and (3) Janet, who married the fifth Lord Lovat. According to the Kalendar of Fearn, Walter Ross of Balnagowan was slain at Tain in 1528. He was probably involved in a clan feud.

ALEXANDER ROSS, *ninth Chief of Clan Ross*

Alexander, who succeeded in 1528, was one of the most powerful and also one of the most unscrupulous men in Ross. This colourful Scot and his clansmen took advantage of all the modern military equipment of the day, not only to defend their property, but also to make raids on neighbouring clans. In 1553 he invested in a culverin, the eighteen-pounder cannon of those days, and also in coats of mail for himself and his band of raiders, to prepare himself for any emergency. Just at this time the troubles between the Queen Regent, mother of Mary Queen of Scots, supported by the Catholics on one side, and the Lords of the Congregation of Reformers on the other side, were coming to a head. Laird Alexander was fined £80 for refusing to join the royal standard.

Between 1553 and the calling of the Great Parliament of 1560, which enacted the Reformation, there were many transactions between Alexander lord of Ross, and Nicholas Ross Abbot of Fearn. The Abbot granted several of the abbey lands to the laird, for which the laird signed a *band* or bond of alliance and protection with the Abbot. This bond is still preserved on one of Balnagowan parchments, dated 1559, and written at the time of the reformation. It reads as follows: "Me. Alexr. Ross of Balnagowan forasmeikle (forasmuch) as I am infeft . . . lands of Myd Garry, Petkare (Pitkerry), Balmawquby (Balmuchy), Wester Ferne . . . fischings of Bonoch[1] . . . part of Maurs (Moors) of Ferne . . . by Nicholas Ross, commendator of Ferne and Provost of Tayne (Tain) . . . and for many years . . . Quid deids . . . I obleiss me and my airs and assignais faytfillie (faithfully) in ye stratest form . . . yt (that) can be devisit . . . to manten and defend ye said Nicholas . . . contrar all mortals, ye authorite beard (King) except . . . nevu (never) to heir, sie, nor wit . . . dampnage (damage) nor skayt (hurt) . . . to his bady (body) land or quids (goods) bot I sall advertyse him yrof (thereof) and keep him skaytless at the utmost of my power . . . I shal use ye counsell of ye said Nicholas in all effars perteyning to my hous, kin and freynds induring my lyftyme . . . Notwithstanding ye said commendator hes astrickit in . . . charter made to

[1] Fishing the waters of the River Bonach in the Abbey lands of Ferne.

me . . . in case I falazie (fail) in . . . delyvering merts, mutons, Reik hens . . . to pay for everie mert fourty shillings . . . muton four shillings . . . capoun eight-pence . . . hen four-pence be it not deliverit . . . in due tyme . . . to serve ye said Nicholas wt. my kin and freynds (clan) wtin., ye bounds of Ross . . . att Ferne ye auchtein day of November 1559 . . . Alxr. Ross of Balnagowan." (His seal also is affixed.)

Nicholas Ross, Catholic Abbot of Fearn and Provost of the Collegiate Church at Tain, was fighting for the old privileges of the Catholic Order, but against him were the Laird of Balnagowan, (in spite of the above bond of friendship), the hereditary baillie, and the town of Tain. It was a losing battle for Nicholas, for in 1567 he resigned both the Abbacy and the provestry, and the Presbyterian Church of Scotland became established in that area. The members of Clan Ross wholeheartedly accepted this new form of religion. The Church of Scotland evangelist readers and ministers were already present in the highlands and ready to take over the ministery. Hutcheon Ross was the first minister at the Kirk of Kincardin, and Farchar Reid, "exhortar at Kincardin", was a Gaelic reader of the scriptures for those who could not read.

In the Collegiate Church at Tain were kept the relics of the patron St. Duthac, cased in gold and silver. Relics of saints had a great vogue in the Scotland of the late fifteenth and early sixteenth centuries, attracting many pilgrims. By 1560 the day of relics and pilgrimages was over, for the doctrines of the Reformed Church of Scotland were spreading. Clearly Nicholas Ross, the Catholic priest, dared not leave the relics of his monastery at Fearn behind him when he went up to attend the Parliament of 1560 in his last official appearance as an Abbot. He therefore consigned them to the strong custody of Alexander Ross at Balnagowan Castle and took a receipt for them. It bound the laird either to return them on demand or pay 2000 marks—equivalent to 1,333 pounds Scots or 111 pounds sterling. This receipt was found amongst the documents at Balnagowan.

Another document shows that the Laird of Balnagowan, like many other landed proprietors of the time, was intent upon grasping as much as he could of the church lands and property. In the absence of Nicholas he compelled three monks of the Monastery of Fearn to sign a deed conveying to him part of the Abbey lands, on the ground that they had been granted to him by Nicholas' predecessor. When Nicholas returned, these monks signed in his presence another deed revoking their signatures to the former one, as having been given under duress.

Laird Alexander, some years after, had a feud with Innes of Plaids, proprietor of Castle Cadboll and of lands near Moray Firth; he raided these lands, driving off cattle, sheep and horses, and seized corn and other stores. Then as a condition of getting these back, Innes had to agree to give over part of his lands to Laird Alexander Ross of Balnagowan. But since Innes had to have a place to keep his movables, he was allowed to retain his tower at the castle. Next we find Alexander has "cassin down the fortalice and barrailed Tower of Cadboll." This led the powerful Regent Morton to summon chief Alexander before Parliament in Edinburgh and, finding him guilty, he shut him up in Tantallon Castle for his misdeeds. Only on signing an agreement to rebuild Castle Cadboll and pay compensation for the destruction he had caused, was Alexander released and allowed to return to Balnagowan. He continued his wild raids on neighbouring properties, and within a year Alexander revoked his signature to the agreement, on the ground that it was given under duress.

Amid the plots and intrigues that began to shake the Regent's power, this fiery Scot Alexander seems to have travelled north and defied the Government, till, in 1583 letters of "fire and sword" were issued against him. His own son George Ross was actually one of those charged to "Convocat the lieges" and pursue him. George was at this time in possession of Balnagowan Castle but the old man was by no means suppressed. He levied rents on land belonging to his son and relatives.

He also seized the Chapter House belonging to the Church at Tain and was putting it to the "prophane use as a girnell (granerie) and larder" till in 1588 an order of the King in council charged him to "redd himselfe quids and geir therefrae" and give up the Chapter House to the Presbytery Church of Scotland, which had just been established. This demand is found in an old Balnagowan document, dated 1588, in which the Commissionaire of the Kirks of Ross and "Mr. Johne Ross moderator of the presbiterie of Tayn", declared that "whereas the chapter-house of the colledge Kirk of Tayne being a place dedicated to the commisionare and brethren of the said presbiterie becaus Alexander Ros of Balnagowan hes witholden and reteinit the said Chapter this lang tyme begane lykas he yit with-holdis the same and maks his girnell (granerie) and ladner (larder) hous yrof wit (with) uyr (their) prophain usis and keipis to that effect and will nocht deliver the same to the saidis complenaris (complainers) is proper and convenient place. . . . And sichlyke their being foundat besyde the said colledge Kirk and Chapter an hous of auld dedicat for sculhous (school house) callit the boith (little cottage) is alsua occupat pritilie (presently) be Johne Ros of Littill Allane . . . the sme be maist necessar for upbringing of the youth in edification of verteu and gude letteris, he aluterlie (utterly) refussis to deliver . . . bot . . . deteines (detains) the same to his prophane (profane) usus . . . to yr (their) grite (great) hinder and skaith qif sua be as alledget (if it be as it is alleged) therefor ye charge the saidis Alexander Ros and Johne Ros . . . ceis (cease) from furder occuper . . . of the said Chapter (chapter-house) and scuilhous (schoolhouse) and red (clear out) thame-selfis (themselves), quids (goods) and geir yrfa (therefrom). . . ."

The ruins of the old chapter house still stand a few yards away from the old Kirk—roofless, but some of the thick stone walls are still fairly sound.

Strangely enough, in spite of his misdeeds, Alexander was later accepted, not elected, as Provost of the borough of Tain in a letter of appointment from the previous Provost.

Alexander was married twice, first to Janet, daughter of John, third Earl of Caithness, and second to Catherine, daughter of Kenneth MacKenzie of Kintail. By his first marriage he had as issue: (1) Robert, (2) Hector, (3) George, who became tenth of Balnagowan, (4) Catherine, (5) Agnes, who married Duncan Campbell of Boath, and (6) Christian, who married Kenneth MacKenzie, third of Dochmaluak. By his second wife he had an issue: (1) Nicholas, who became the first laird of Pitcalnie (2) Malcolm, who died without issue.

Superstitions and witchcraft were flourishing at this time and it is related that one of Alexander's daughters, Catherine, second wife of Robert Munro of Foulis, was tried for witchcraft. Two accomplices Christina Ross and Thomas McKean who assisted her in a plot to poison chief Alexander's wife were brought to trial, convicted and burned at the stake in 1577.

Chief Alexander Ross the ninth of Balnagowan died at Ardmore in 1592 and was buried with his kith and kin at Fearn.

## GEORGE ROSS, *tenth laird of Balnagowan*

At this time Clan Ross was numerically the largest of the highland clans and wielded great influence and power throughout northern Scotland.

George was educated at St. Andrew's and was the first of the Chiefs of Clan Ross to receive a university education. In spite of his higher education, young George apparently inherited many of the lawless characteristics of his father. In June 1592, George Ross and his son were charged with high treason for having sheltered and assisted the Earl of Bothwell, arch enemy of the King. They were charged with having knowingly "resetted the said Francis, Earl of Bothwell, within their houses and boundis, and in conveying him to and fro fra Caithness over the ferries of Ardersier, Cromarty and Dornoch, speciallie at the tyme when the said sumtyme Erl, returning South fra Caithness, interprised that most treasonable and wicked deid agains his Hienes (Highness) own personne, and personne of the Queen, his darest bedfellow. The Lords of the Secreit Counsall accordingly ordain letters to denounce these rebels. . . ."

Another document, dated 1592, records the complaint of John Ross of Edinburgh as follows: "Upon twenty-four of April last, while he was in the Channonrie of Ros, doing his lesum affairis, George Ros of Balnagowan, Nicholas Ros, Gillicallum Ros, brothers of the laird of Balnagowan, Alexander Ros of Invercharron, William Ros of Preisthill, Hircheon Ros, apparent of Tolbie, Johne Ros of Mulday, Johne Ros of Little Tarrel, Walter Ros apparent of Balmuchie, Donald Ros of Mudgarry, William Innes of Candieruffe, James Innes apparent of Inverbreakie, with their accomplices to the number of threescore persons, put violent hands on the dias complainer, John Ross, and tuke him as captive and prisoner to the place of Balnagowan, quhair they detainit him in sure firnance and captivitie quhill the twenty-ninth day of May next thereinafter." The parties concerned were charged to answer, and, not appearing were denounced as rebels.

In 1589 an act of parliament, commonly called "The General Bond" for maintaining order, both on the borders and in the Highlands and Isles, was passed. The main purpose of this act was to suppress the clan feuds, and it was made imperative for all chiefs of clans and bailies to find sureties for the peaceful behaviour of those under them. Heavy fines were exacted by the King in 1591 from Donald Gorme of Sleat, Macdonald of Islay, and Maclean of Dowait, for their participation in clan feuds. Fortunately the Rosses of Balnagowan were not involved and did not incur the King's displeasure at this time.

Chief George Ross and his tenants seem to have lived in open feuds with most of his neighbours in that district however. "The men and tennantis" were charged with personal lawlessness along with the laird. The following document accuses them of organising a raiding party dressed in full armour with steel helmets, swords, bows and arrows and all the modern equipment of the day, and raiding the house and property of "the complainer, Maister Johnne Ros, person of Logg" (Logie). It further relates that they destroyed his salmon storage bins and stole eight stone of cheese, four stone of butter and two mares with foal. They also killed four cows and four sheep. The text of this ancient document is as follows:

"Here George Ross, Macean MacLomash, in Strathcarron; John Dow Macdonald, in Ardgay; Finla Macrawis, in Soyall; John MacLucheoun Mor, these with convocation of the lieges to the number of four score persons, all armed with havershorns, jacks, steill bonnetis, hagbuttis, culverings, bowis, swordes and utheris wapponis, cam at night to the complainer's heus, in Strathcarron in Ros, belonging heriditably to him the complainer, Maister Johnne Ros, parson of Logg, where he and his men were taking their night's rest, and thair maist unhonestly brak up the hail duris of the said complaners heus, hurt and dang his servantis, sornit and destroyit his hail salmond fishes quilkes (which) were saltit in fattis, fert, spulyst and awaytuke aucht stone of cheis, foure stone of butter, two mareis with foal, and slew four key (kine) and four scheip." The accused parties failing to appear were denounced as rebels.

The hunting and fishing rights of the lairds were jealously guarded on their own estates. In a report of the inquiry by the "Lordis of Secreit Console" in 1577 regarding the complaint by Walter Urquhart, Sheriff of Cromartie that Johnnie Dingwall contravened the "Actis of Parliament, forbidand to schute at wyld beist daar (deer) and uther vennersoun, in sa far as he with his complices, to the nowmer of XVI personis, in the month of September last bifast, and at dwers (divers) utheris tymes preceding, come to the forest of Bray witgin the Earldom of Ros, pertaining heritable to the said Sheriff, and there slew with hagbuttis, bowis and pistolettis, XV or XVI greit daar, to his hurt and skayth, and manifest contempt of our laws."

A certain John Ross apparently had cause to borrow money at this time from the laird of Clan Ross and the following receipt describes the transaction: "1608—I, George Ros of Balnagowan be yir prts confess me reallie and wt (with) effect to haiff recavit (recovered) in friendlie borrowing frae my belovit kinsman Mr. Jon Ros, persoun of Logie . . . sex hundreth merks usuall money of Northe Britaine. . . . Witness Walter Ross speirand of Invercharron, Alexr. Denune portioner of East Drum of Fearn. (John Ross was the son of Alexander Ross, first of Little Tarrel, legitimized son of Walter Ross, eighth of Balnagowan, thus George's kinsman.)

George Ross, Chief of Clan Ross was twice married, first to Marion, daughter of Sir John Campbell of Calder (Cawdor). By this marriage George had as issue a son, David, who became eleventh of Balnagowan, and four daughters. The eldest Jean married Kenneth, first Lord of Kintail. Of George Ross's second marriage there were born: (1) Colin, who afterwards became the first Earl of Seaforth, (2) John of Lochalin, and (3) Kenneth, who died unmarried. George died in 1615 and left his estate heavily encumbered with debts, the result of lawless behaviour and poor management.

### DAVID ROSS, *eleventh of Balnagowan and Chief of Clan*

This chief was much more law-abiding than either his father or grandfather had been. He was married to Lady Mary Gordon, second daughter of Alexander, Earl of Sutherland, who is described in Gordon's

*Earldom of Sutherland* as "a virtuous and comley woman, a lady of an excellent and quick wit." She died without issue at Overskibo and was buried at Dornoch.

David later married Lady Annabella Murray, daughter of John, Earl of Tullibardine and had issue of an only son David, who succeeded his father as twelfth laird of Balnagowan.

In the Highlands at this time there were a number of clan uprisings which were organized to settle petty differences and avenge ancient wrongs. One of these was the insurrection of Clan Chattan against the Earl of Murray and his clan, who had previously been faithful friends. The marauding party of Clan Chattan to the number of 200 gentlemen and 300 servants spoiled and laid waste certain territories in Moray, Ross, Sutherland, Strathawick, Urquhart and others, as is vividly described in an old document: "They keeped the feilds in their Highland weid, upon foot with swords, bowes, arrowes, targets, hagbuttis, pistollis, and other Highland armour, and first began to rob and spoulizie the earlie's tennents, who laboured their possessions of their haill goods, geir, insight, plenishing, horse, nolt, sheep, corns and cattell, and left them nothing that they could gett withing their bounds; syne fell in sorning throwout Murray, Strathawick, Urquhart, Ross, Sutherland, and diverse other parts, takeing their meat and food per force wher they could not get it willingly, frae friends aseweill as frae their faes; yet still keeped themselves from shedeing of innocent blood. Thus they lived as outlawes, oppressing the countrie, besydes the casting of the earle's lands waist, and openly avowed they had tane this course to gett thir own possessions again, or then hold the country walking."

The Earl of Murray and his men met the marauders at Inverness, but were unsuccessful in defeating them. James VI supported the Earl and appointed him as his lieutenant in the Highlands to proceed against the offenders. The Earl then issued "letters of intercommuning", against the Clan Chattan prohibiting all persons from harbouring, supplying or entertaining them in any way under severe penalties of losing their estates. These measures quelled this formidable uprising without bloodshed. Some idea of the unequal administration of the laws at this time may be formed when it is realized that the heavy fines exacted in the present instance, went into the pockets of the chief judge, the Earl of Murray, himself.

Chief David died on 20th November 1632 and was buried in the family vault in the Abbey of Fearn.

DAVID ROSS, *twelfth of Balnagowan*

He succeeded to the ancestral estates of his father while yet a young man. In later life David became a brave warrior and led his clansmen

in battle in support of Charles II. A Balnagowan document relating to the suppression of crime in Ross-shire at this time reads as follows:
"1638 Forasmeikle as the crimes of theft, cutting of green wood, killing of blackfish, deer and roe and sorning upon our good subjects is become verie frequent within the bounds pertaining to David Ross of Balnagowne . . . we understanding . . . disposition to retane his owne tennents under our peace . . . constitute him and his baillies our justices in that part. ourfull auctoritie (authority) . . . all persones . . . being teenants or servants . . . delate guiltie of the said crimes . . . fines . . . half to our use, half to our said justices . . . commission for one yeare . . . given at Stirline 15th Febil 1638, Charles M. Ross."

At his own expense David raised a regiment of 800 men of Clan Ross, joined with the Scottish army and marched to the fatal battle of Worcester, which was fought in 1651. On that occasion, it will be recalled, the Scottish army marched to England in order to try to reinstate Charles II, but they were defeated by Cromwell, who called the battle his "crowning mercy". David and the surviving members of his clan were taken prisoner. King Charles with difficulty escaped to France. More than 2,000 of the Royalists were slain, and of 8,000 prisoners, the greater part were sold as slaves to the American colonists or "bound out" to serve English taskmasters. The hardships and privations of these early colonists to America will be dealt with in a later section.[1] The considerable expense involved in fitting out the men of Clan Ross in uniforms which on this occasion consisted of trews of the red Ross tartan rather than the kilt, and supplying them with the necessary fighting equipment, involved the House of Balnagowan in considerable debt, from which it has never completely recovered.

The Laird of Balnagowan was taken and committed to the Tower, where, after two years imprisonment, he died. He was buried at Westminster on December 29, 1653.

After the defeat and capture of Chief David Ross, fines and exactions were levied against the Balnagowan estates and as a result they became more deeply involved in debts. To hold the Rosses under subjection, a number of Cromwell's troops were quartered in Balnagowan castle and in the homes of the tenants.

This sacrifice of David Ross was not forgotten by Charles II when his opportunity came, for it is recorded that the King settled a pension of £200 on his eldest son David. He had married Marie, the eldest daughter of Lord Fraser of Lovat. Marie died at Ardmore on December

[1] Among the prisoners taken in this engagement was James Ross, who settled in Sudbury, Mass., and was the ancestor of Hon. Leonard Warren Ross, second President of Clan Ross in America in 1914.

22, 1646, leaving as issue: (1) David, who became thirteenth and last laird of Balnagowan of the old family, (2) Alexander, who died at the age of twenty, (3) Isobell, who was married to James Innes of Lightness, brother to Sir Robert Innes of that Ilk, and (4) Catherine, who married John Mackenzie, fourth of Inveraul.

David's bravery and leadership were admired by all his clan. He left a will which has been preserved among the archives at the Castle. It was written in 1651 before he marched away at the head of his clan to the fatal battle of Worcester: "Forasmeikle as I am, God willing, to goe presentlie southward to His Majesties services in his expeditions which is to the glory of God for religione, Covenant, King and Kingdom, and not being certain when it shall please the Lord in his mercy to send me ane happie returning." "If I come not hame" . . . (here follow the nomination of his executors and the disposition of his estates). As it is seen, David came not "hame" again.

## DAVID ROSS, *thirteenth Chief of Balnagowan*

As chief of Clan Ross he succeeded to the estates after his father's death. He was nine years of age when his father died, and David Ross of Pitcalnie was appointed his legal guardian until he came of age. This David was the last Ross of Balnagowan of the old lineage, as the male representative of the O'Beolain Earls of Ross. The Balnagowan estates at this time comprised over thirty different properties in the county of Ross, and the laird of Balnagowan was the central administrator as chief of the clan.

David was looked upon with great favour by King William of Orange. He was appointed sheriff of Ross and governor of Inverness, and was instructed to form a garrison to uphold Presbyterianism in the north, and to protect Inverness from a possible threat by Claverhouse, in 1688.

As we have seen, the lands of Balnagowan had become very much encumbered with debts, a state of affairs which gave much anxiety to friends and tenants of the family, since it afforded excellent opportunity for covetous parties to resort to questionable means in endeavouring to gain possession of the property.

Chief David built a new wing and refurnished the older sections of Balnagowan during his residence in the Castle, and most of the present day improvements are attributed to him. His clansmen considered him a wise and just laird and rallied to his support on all occasions.

The fatal battle of Worcester and the capture and imprisonment of David, twelfth of Balnagowan, had increased the debts of the family so greatly that his son David thirteenth was obliged to "wadset" (mortgage) the lands he owned to the value of 5,000 pounds sterling. David had further increased his debts by extensive renovations to Balnagowan Castle, repairs to the churches in Ross-shire, and generous assistance to his clansmen, all of which were badly needed. In spite of his weakness of character he was well liked because of his interest in community affairs.

David was married to Lady Anne Stewart, daughter of the Earl of Moray, but unfortunately there were no children of this marriage. He died in 1711 and the succession then passed out of the hands of the Ross family and into the possession of strangers.

## Disputes for the Succession

The lands and Castle of Balnagowan, which had been in the possession of the Rosses for nearly four hundred years, were now usurped by an unrelated family of Rosses of Hawkhead. But first it fell into the hands of a family of Stewarts, who took the surname of Ross. Neither the Stewarts nor the Rosses of Hawkhead were in any way connected with the original Balnagowan line of succession, from the O'Beolain Earls of Ross.

The account of the diverse manipulations and negotiations of unrelated families to obtain possession of the Balnagowan estates in the late seventeenth century and in the hundred years following the death of laird David thirteenth in 1711, were primarily financial, rather than for family and blood relationships.

### *Lady Ross, the Earl of Moray, and Francis Stewart*

The case of Alexander Stewart, Earl of Moray, is a complicated affair. He and his son, Francis Stewart, with the help of his sister Laird David's wife Ann Stewart (Lady Ross of Balnagowan), began scheming to gain possession of the estates for members of the Stewart family.

Since there was now no hope of David thirteenth of Balnagowan, having male issue, a transaction was made in 1685 between Balnagowan and Alexander Stewart for conveying the estate to Francis Stewart, Alexander's son, by which the Earl advanced £10,000 Scots to laird David Ross to relieve the debts of the estate. David then resigned the estate to himself in lifetime and to the said Mr. Francis Stewart in fee, and to other heirs therein named. It is noted also that Lady Ross took a prominent part in inducing her husband David to relinquish his estate to

## FOLLOWING THE ROSSES OF BALNAGOWAN A NEW LINE OF SUCCESSION OF CLAN ROSS OF UNRELATED LINEAGE WAS ESTABLISHED 1711-1903

I. Frances Stewart
Chiefship and Estates gained by purchase. Nominal posession only

II. Twelfth Lord Ross of Hawkhead
Chiefship obtained by purchase. Nominal possession only

III. Lt.-General Charles Ross
Infefted in 1713 by purchase

IV. Col. Charles Ross

V. Lady Grizel Lockhart and Sir James Lockhart (Ross)

VI. Sir William Lockhart

VII. Sir James Lockhart

VIII. Sir George Lockhart

IX. Admiral Sir John Lockhart-Ross

X. Sir Charles William Augustus Lockhart-Ross

XI. Sir Charles Henry Augustus Fredrick Lockhart-Ross

## THE ORIGINAL LINE OF SUCCESSION RE-ESTABLISHED

### *A. The Rosses of Pitcalnie*

I. Miss Ethel Frances Sara Williamson Ross, 1903—1957

II. Miss Rosa R. Williamson Ross
Chief of the Clan Ross 1957—1968

### *B. The Rosses of Shandwick*

I. The Late Charles Campbell Ross Q.C.
Chief Designate of Clan Ross, died 1966

II. David Campbell Ross
Chief of Clan Ross 1968—

Alexander Stewart, even though there was a rightful heir at this time in the person of Malcolm Ross, fifth of Pitcalnie. She has received considerable censure for this, in spite of the fact that she was said to be a person "endowed no less with the gifts of nature than those of grace" and had bequeathed the sum of 3,000 merks Scots "for behoof of some indigent persons fearing the Lord in the County of Ross."

Francis Stewart was then to assume the surname and the arms of the Clan Ross after David's death.

It was only natural that the next heirs of the blood should try to regain Balnagowan from the possession of strangers. The nearest male heir, was Malcolm Ross, fifth of Pitcalnie, one of the Cadet branches of Clan Ross. Malcolm had descended from Alexander Ross, ninth of Balnagowan, through Nicholas Ross, Alexander's second son, who became first of Pitcalnie. He rested his claim on two grounds; first, that David Ross, thirteenth, the last of the old Balnagowan family, had been in possession under letters of entail, and second, that David was so weak-minded as to have been susceptible to undue influence from his wife, Lady Ann Stewart. Malcolm Ross, however, lost his claim.

The litigation to gain their rightful possession of the Balnagowan estates was continued unsuccessfully by Alexander, sixth laird of Pitcalnie and also by his third wife, Naomi Ross, daughter of John Dunbar of Burgie, on behalf of her son, Munro Ross, who became seventh of Pitcalnie. This strong willed lady, Naomi Ross is to come into these pages again.

Lord Ross of Hawkhead now started his campaign to gain possession of the Balnagowan properties from Frances Stewart. The accounts of his endeavours to secure Balnagowan and the chiefship of Clan Ross are very involved. In a letter to Hugh Ross of Kilvarock (who was on friendly terms with the Balnagowan family), Lady Ann Stewart (Lady Ross) was promised a countess' coronet by Lord Ross of Hawkhead if she would help him to accomplish his object. Since Lord Ross[1] was not a descendant of the Earls of Ross, or related in any way to the Rosses of Balnagowan, a rather scathing dismissal of his claim was contained in a letter written at that time by Lord Tarbat. He stated that: "Lord Ross had no more relation to the Earls of Ross, directly or indirectly than the Miller of Carstares had to the Prince of Parma." He went on further to state that "there are very considerable families now owning parts of the Earldom of Ross . . . such as the Earls of Seaforth and several other considerable hereditors . . . the Earls of Cromartie, Rosehaugh, Scotwell, Gairloch,

[1] See Appendix 3 for genealogy of Lord Ross of Hawkhead.

Coul, Redcastle, Culcoy, Fowlis, Cubrain, Kilvarock, Cadboll, Fairburn, Tulloch, Macleod of Lewes, Macdonald of Applecross, Mackenzie of Davochmaluach and Mackenzie of Suddie, many of whom do not think my Lord Ross fit to be their superior."

It is apparent that the extensive territories of the old Earldom of Ross had now been divided into many different estates, each under its own proprietor. These chiefs declared that they would not submit to being governed by Lord Ross of Hawkhead, since he was not of the true line of descent from the Earls of Ross.

It was also pointed out that Lady Ann Stewart was much under the influence of a certain clergyman, also named Stewart. In order to advance his ambition to gain possession of Balnagowan, Lord Ross of Hawkhead wrote to the Reverend Mr. Stewart: "I am informed ye have a considerable interest with Lady Balnagowan. If you would be so kind as to use your interest with the lady to get my affair to succeed, I do assure you, I will never fail in any occasion wherein I can serve you, and if thereby you bring me to an interest in that country, ye will thereby put me in a condition to serve you more effectually."

In the Rev. Mr. Stewart's answer, dated Kiltearn, 6th of February 1700, he writes: "After mature thoughts thereinat, I am fully persuaded and inclined to judge it my duty to obtemper your lordship's desire. . . . It is true I see some difficulties in the undertaking, not with respect to duty but success, which your Lordship may easily conjecture, but on the grounds above mentioned, and because success and events belong to the Lord, I shall use such means, leaving it to the Lord—whose sovereign providence has the determining hand in all the actions and transactions here below—to dispose of the event."

To summarize the many complicated claims to the Balnagowan estates at this time, we find that Mr. Francis Stewart, son of Alexander, Earl of Moray, came into ownership but not into possession of the Balnagowan estates after his father purchased them for him. He was to assume the surname of Ross and take the heraldic arms of Clan Ross after the death of David thirteenth. Francis Stewart still found himself and the estates under heavy appraisings for debt, and he was finally induced to sell them to Lord Ross of Hawkhead, who had been planning for some time to gain possession of the Balnagowan Castle, the valuable lands, and especially the title and arms as Chief of Clan Ross.

In spite of the strong criticism of Lord Ross, the Rosses of Hawkhead proved to be a noble and worthy family who, after they took possession, ably administered the estates, and gained the respect of the members of the Clan.

## THE HAWKHEAD LINE OF SUCCESSION OF BALNAGOWAN

Lord Ross, twelfth of Hawkhead[1] advanced the sum of 6,300 merks to Francis Stewart and agreed to relieve him of all debts against himself and the Balnagowan estates. Fraser Mackintosh in his *Letters of Two Centuries,* states that "In the annals of Scotland there is, perhaps, no greater case of fraud and wrong than the unscrupulous, but ultimately successful attempts of Lord Ross and his brother General Charles Ross, strangers to the Family, to possess themselves of the estate of Balnagowan." In spite of all opposition Lord Ross was infefted in the Balnagowan estate in 1707. His crest was a Hawkshead on the Ross arms.

Since David thirteenth was still alive and in residence at the Castle at this time, Lord Ross of Hawkhead's ownership of the properties was merely nominal for four years. At the end of this period he sold the estates to his brother Lieutenant-General Charles Ross.

### *Lt.-General Charles Ross of Balnagowan*

This worthy Highland gentleman was infefted in 1713 by charter under the Great Seal on payment of £3,500 sterling to redeem the wadsets against the properties. The General came into full possession of all the properties, and of Balnagowan Castle after the deaths of David Ross thirteenth, who died in the year 1711, and of Lady Ross, who died in 1719. He also became Chief of Clan Ross.

Lt.-General Charles Ross, when a Colonel of the Dragoons, had distinguished himself under the colours of William of Orange in the wars against Louis XIV. In civilian life he was elected Provost of Tain and during his tenure of office he was able to lift this town out of debt, and put it under better management. In 1715, the year of the first Jacobite rising, the Town Council of Tain, under the leadership of General Ross, considering the confusion likely to occur throughout Scotland in consequence of the efforts of the Pretender, ordered all male inhabitants to take up arms, and appointed a nightly guard of ten men and a captain, to watch for prowlers in the town. All men between sixteen and sixty were called to rendezvous on the Links, and volunteer for duty. They received orders from the Magistrates to prepare the town for defence against any who might attempt to enter it to proclaim the Pretender. At the same time they despatched fifty fencible men under command of Hugh Ross of Achnacloich, with the best clothes and arms and four days provisions, to march at once to Alness in order to join Captain Robert Munro of Foulis, in defence of the present government.

[1] For geneology of the twelfth Lord Ross of Hawkhead see Appendix IV.

Balnagowan Castle
The Ancient home of the Clan Ross

The late Chief Rosa R. Williamson Ross

The late Sheriff Charles Campbell Ross Q.C., right
with son, David Campbell Ross Chief of Clan and grandson.

Clan Ross Association of Canada
First Annual Meeting, Ontario Branch
Granite Club, Toronto, December 1961.
Left to right: Dr. Colin Ross, Toronto, Hon. Secretary; Dr. James W. Ross, Toronto, Member Exec. Council; Dr. John R. Ross, Toronto, Vice President; Major James J. Ross, Montreal, President; Mr. Jack Ross, Montreal, Vice President; not shown – Prof. H. U. Ross, Toronto, Member Exec. Council.

As a member of Parliament for Ross-shire General Ross served in five parliaments, and was appointed one of the commissioners to investigate the affairs of the South Sea Company.

Lt. General Ross, a very wise and just laird, retained possession of Balnagowan for eighteen years. He greatly improved the properties and renovated the estates. He was unmarried, however, and on his death the Balnagowan estates passed to his grand-nephew, Colonel Charles Ross, the "Hero of Fontenoy".

*Colonel Charles Ross* came into full possession and took up residence at the castle in 1732. After being in possession of Balnagowan for only a short time, this great soldier was killed at the battle of Fontenoy.* A lengthy ode was written by the poet Collins to commemorate his prowess, the first four stanzas of which are here given:

ON THE DEATH OF COLONEL CHARLES ROSS
IN THE ACTION AT FONTENOY

While lost to all her former mirth
Britannia's genius bends to earth
And mourns the fatal day.
While stained with blood she strives to tear
Unseemly from her sea-green hair
The wreaths of cheerful May.

The thought which musing pity pays,
And fond remembrance loves to raise,
Your faithful hours attend;
Still Fancy to herself unkind
Awakes to grief the softened Mind
And points the bleeding friend.

By rapid Scheldt's descending wave
His country's vows shall bless the grave
Wher'ere the youth is laid.
That sacred spot the village hind
With every sweetest turf shall bind
And Peace protect the shade.

O'er him whose doom thy virtues grieve
Aerial forms shall sit at eve
And bend the pensive head;
And fallen to save his injured land
Imperial honour's awful hand
Shall point his lonely bed.

* Col. Ross fought gallantly with his regiment of the Black Watch in this engagement.

Balnagowan now reverted to his father George, thirteenth Lord Ross in 1745, after Col. Charles Ross had died at twenty-four years of age. On the death of Lord Ross the estates were again transferred to his brother William, fourteenth Lord Ross who died unmarried. Lacking male heirs in the Hawkhead line the succession reverted to heirs female in the person of Lady Grizel Lockhart Ross who was the sister of the thirteenth Lord Ross.

## THE LOCKHART ROSSES OF BALNAGOWAN, 1754-1942

The important and influential family of Lockharts followed the Rosses of Hawkhead as owners of Balnagowan. Although not of the same line of descent and not in any way related to the Earls of Ross, the Lockharts adopted the surname Ross. They failed to make up title to the principal arms of the Ross family however, and could not rightly be called chiefs of the Clan. On many occasions, however, the Lockhart Rosses assumed the title.

As nominal Chiefs of Clan Ross they were noted for their integrity and sincerity in dealing with their crofters and tenants, and they did many things to improve their lot, especially when a year of famine struck the Highlands and left many of the people destitute. Two of these Lockhart Rosses had gallant and distinguished careers as naval and army officers, and the last member of this family, Sir Charles Ross, was the inventor of the famous Ross rifle.

### *Lady Grizel Lockhart and her husband Sir James*

After the death of William fourteenth Lord Ross in 1754 the Balnagowan estates passed to Grizel and her husband Sir James Lockhart of Lockhart Hall, Carstairs.

Sir James succeeded his father as second Baronet of Nova Scotia and received his knighthood from King James VI. Sir James and Lady Grizel had five sons, four of whom in turn inherited Balnagowan, and became Baronets.

### *Sir William Lockhart-Ross, laird of Balnagowan*

The eldest son of Sir James and Grizel inherited the Balnagowan estates when Sir James died in 1755. Sir William was married twice, first to Miss Agnew, and secondly to Catherine, daughter of John Porterfield of Fullwood, by whom he had two daughters. When Sir William died in June 1758 the title and estate devolved on his brother James.

*Sir James Lockhart*

Sir James Lockhart of Lanark, the second son, then inherited Balnagowan. Sir James married a daughter of Major Croslie, but dying in September 1760 without issue, was succeeded by his brother George.

*Sir George Lockhart*

Sir George was unmarried, and after possessing the estate for eighteen years, he died in 1778 without issue, and was succeeded by his younger brother John.

*Admiral Sir John Lockhart-Ross, fifth Baronet, and laird of Balnagowan*

He was one of the most important and influential of the Lockharts to inherit the castle and estates of Balnagowan. The fifth son of Sir James Lockhart and Lady Grizel, he was born at Lockhart Hall in Lanarkshire in 1721. He joined the navy at fourteen years of age. In 1756 he was placed in command of the *Forfar,* a frigate of 24 guns, in which he rendered gallant service for his sovereign and his country. In the course of his naval command he captured nine enemy ships of war in the British Channel. For this distinguished service he was promoted to Vice Admiral of the Blue.

On the death of his brother, Sir George, in 1788, he also succeeded to the Baronetcy of Nova Scotia which the family had inherited.

As a commentary on events taking place in the Highlands and the administration of justice in Ross-shire when the Lockhart Rosses were in possession of the Balnagowan properties, the following excerpt from a document dated 1762, in the archives at Tain is of interest.

"I received yours just now with the letters to our magistrates concerning the use of the Executioner, which I delivered to them, and they very frankly agreed to the request as an neighbouring burgh, for which they have great regard. A person of the Executioner business is not very easy to deal with, as they are not easily got, and the magistrates and I thot it best for your town to settle as to his demand (for money). He said he wd. take not less than five pounds Stl. but . . . we got him to agree to take fifty shillings and his expenses back and fore. . . ."

Some of the accounts relating to the executioner are then given: "For erecting a new gibbet, and to Executioner from Inverness, and execution of Katherine Ross for Witchcraft £7 6s. 6d.

To cash given the Hangman when he engaged 1s. 1d.

To cash given Hangman 3s. 6d.

Hangman's Croft 9."

Smuggling was very prevalent in Ross-shire at this time to the detriment of legitimate business enterprise. A Strathconan free-booter named Farquhar (unrelated to the first Earl of Ross) became a notorious smuggler and arsonist, and his name as a gunman, a distiller and smuggler of whisky soon became a legend in the country.

Sir John and his family settled at Balnagowan Castle and proceeded to make extensive renovations. He greatly improved the estate lands by agricultural plantings.

In the year 1782 the Highlands of Scotland were visited by a famine, and the crofters were hard pressed to make a living for their families in this "black year". Sir John Lockhart-Ross distributed bountiful supplies of vegetables and flour to his tenants, saving them from starvation conditions; as well, he supplied the Highland crofters in Kincardine with seed grain for next year's planting.

The Rev. Hector Allan writing in the *Statistical Account* makes the following reference to the event: "Sir John, with a liberality which does him the highest credit, understanding the lamentable situation of the poor people, sent to be distributed to the sufferers on his own estates a seasonable and bountiful supply of pease, barley, flour and potatoes; to which noble beneficence many hundreds owed their lives. He also ordered his factor to give to his highland crofters in Kincardine, who did not save as much as would sow their crofts, seed from his farms in the low country, where the failure was not nearly so great as in the high ground and straths, and upon his return home at the conclusion of the war, he discounted one third of the arrears of rent over the whole of his estates."

Sir John Lockhart-Ross was the first laird to introduce Cheviot sheep into Ross-Shire. As a result, many crofters were forcibly evicted from their lands and homes to make way for the sheep pastures. Many of the evicted tenants suffered severe hardships and privations following these "clearances".

At Beauley on the Black Isle the men of Ross made a determined but futile stand in an attempt to drive the sheep from their lands. These protest marches took place in 1792, the "Year of the Sheep". Many crofters were taken prisoner by army troops who were called out to quell the riots, but their prison sentences were never carried out, as the men of Ross broke out of Dingwall prison by night with the aid of clansmen on the outside.

Sir John and other proprietors received considerable criticism for the cruel and uncompromising eviction of the tenants on many of the Ross-shire estates where they and their families had lived for centuries. These evictions are vividly described by Donald Ross in his book "The Massacre of the Rosses". The crofters realizing however that further resistance was useless, submitted to the "Clearances" with as good grace as possible.

Sir John was married to Elizabeth Dundas of Arneston and had five sons (1) Charles his heir, (2) James who became a captain in the Royal Navy, (3) George a Judge of the Court of Scotland, (4) John, a Colonel in the Coldstream Guards and was killed at Talvera in 1809, (5) Robert, a Colonel in the Dragoon Guards.

*Lt. General Sir Charles Ross of Balnagowan, and Chief of Clan*

Sir Charles Ross made a name for himself, both as a military officer and as the Parliamentary representative for the County of Ross. Sir Charles was twice married: (1) to Matilda Theresa, a Countess of the Roman Empire, and (2) to Lady Mary Fitzgerald, eldest daughter of William Robert, second Duke of Leinster. By his first marriage he had as issue: (1) John, who died young, and (2) Matilda who married Admiral Sir Thomas Cochrane. Matilda succeeded to the estate of her ancestor, Sir George Wishart of Oldiston, and took the surname of Wishart. By the second marriage there were born (3) John Lockhart, who died unmarried; (4) Charles William Augustus, who became the eighth Baronet; (5) Elizabeth who died young; (6) Emilia Oliva, who married in 1819 Sir C. M. Lockhart, second baronet of Lee; (7) Mary, who in 1824 married Sir William Foulis eighth Baronet of Ingleby; (8) and (9) Louisa and Geraldine, who remained unmarried.

Sir Charles died in 1814, and the following entry was made in the Kirk Session records of the Parish of Kincardine: "General Sir Charles Ross of Balnagowan, Baronet, principal heritor of this parish, died on Tuesday, the 8th day of February 1814, suddenly, and at Balnagowan Castle—a loss irreparable to the country at large and this parish in particular. His many virtues as a husband, a parent, a master, a landlord, a patriot, and a friend endeared him to all who had the honour of his acquaintance. May the Almighty grant consolation to his afflicted lady, and spare his amiable daughters, and his infant son, to emulate his virtues."

*Sir Charles William Augustus Lockhart-Ross of Balnagowan*

Sir Charles was born in 1812 and succeeded his father as eighth Baronet of Nova Scotia, when he was only two years of age. He lived an uneventful life, taking comparatively little interest in public affairs. Eccentric in his habits, his chief pleasure lay in hunting. He was twice married; first to his cousin, Elizabeth Ross, eldest daughter of Colonel Robert Ross, 4th Dragoon Guards, fifth son of Sir John Lockhart Ross,

Bart. Sir Charles married secondly, in March 1865, Rebecca Sophia, third surviving daughter of Henry Barnes Esq., of Tufel Park, and had as issue a son, Charles Henry Augustus Frederick Lockhart Ross who succeeded him.

The estates were very valuable and extensive at this time, being situated in the counties of Ross, Sutherland and Lanark. The family possessions were located in no less than seven parishes: Fearn, Nigg, Logie, Kilmuir-Easter, Tain, Edderton and Kincardine; the gross yearly revenue from these was over £15000. Since the annual revenue of the estates in Sutherlandshire exceeded £1,800, and that of the estate of Bonnington, in Lanarkshire, exceeded £1,700, the total revenue of these two estates was £3,500.

Sir Charles was a Deputy-Lieutenant of Ross-shire and a Justice of the Peace for that county, as well as for Cromarty and Lanarkshire.

*Sir Charles Henry Augustus Frederick Lockhart Ross, Bart.*

Sir Charles, born in 1872, succeeded his father in 1893 as the seventh of the Lockhart Rosses to inherit the Balnagowan Castle and estates. He was ninth Baronet of Nova Scotia, the hereditary title having been granted to his ancestor, William Lockhart of Lockhart Hall in 1672. However, Sir Charles was not the hereditary Chief of Clan Ross, although he assumed this title on many occasions. The Lord Lyon overlooked his assumption of the title while Sir Charles was in residence at Balnagowan Castle, and he also overlooked the fact that Sir Charles made use of the undifferenced arms of the Chief of Clan Ross on his standard.

Sir Charles Ross was educated at Eton and Cambridge; after graduating he joined the Third Battalion Seaforth Highlanders. He served in the South African war as a battery commander on General Hutton's staff. After the war he took part in the establishment of the South African constabulary. On his return to Balnagowan he took an active interest in public affairs, and held the offices of Justice of the Peace and Deputy Lieutenant for Ross and Cromarty.

Sir Charles was also a fine sportsman and had spent a good deal of his time deer hunting on the moors in his younger years. He took great pride in his rifles and frequently made modifications in the firing mechanism. He finally patented the "Ross rifle" which proved to be superior to many other rifles at that time.

The famous Ross rifle was selected as the national weapon of Canada in the first World War. The first patent for the rifle was issued in 1893, and many subsequent patents on improvements were later issued.

At this time the Canadian Government was anxious to place orders in Britain for sufficient small arms to equip the Canadian Militia. Sir Frederick Borden, the Canadian Minister of Militia, according to his own statement on the floor of the House of Commons, went to the Birmingham Small Arms Company and endeavoured to persuade them to manufacture in Canada. But neither this company nor any other manufacturer of small arms could be induced to make the venture.

The project stood in abeyance for a while. Then Sir Charles Ross volunteered to establish a factory in Canada, provided the Government would enter into a contract for the purchase of enough rifles to justify the undertaking. A commission was appointed by the government to examine and test the rifle. After a series of tests under extremely rigorous conditions, the merits and demerits of the rifle were minutely set forth, in a lengthy report published by the committee. Sir Charles later submitted another model of the rifle, in which the defects had been eliminated and this the Canadian government adopted as the standard weapon to equip the Canadian militia. The Ross Rifle Company was established at Quebec in 1908 and received an order from the British Government for 100,000 rifles which called for delivery within one year. This order meant that the factory had to be greatly enlarged as it was already running at capacity to supply the Canadian government with the same weapon.

Sir Charles also developed a sporting rifle which proved to be a very effective weapon. It was lighter than the military rifle and its chief features were its pentrating power, accuracy, absence of recoil, and its rapid fire mechanism.

In his later years, Sir Charles was not often in residence at his Scottish seats of Balnagowan and Bonnington, as his business interests in Canada and the United States occupied a good deal of his time. When he returned to Balnagowan Castle after the war, he was appointed Deputy-Lieutenant of the County of Ross and lived in the traditional chieftain style, wearing the Highland dress, which his handsome figure carried well. He was devoted to sport, particularly deer hunting on his three hundred thousand acre estate.

Sir Charles was married twice, first to Winifred Berens, sister of Olivia, Countess Cairns, a descendant of the Earl of Galloway. This marriage was dissolved in 1897. He then married Patricia Burnley, daughter of Andrew Ellison of Louisville, Kentucky, U.S.A. He died at Balnagowan in 1942 and was mourned by his many Ross-shire clansmen as well as friends and admirers in Canada and the United States.

Sir Charles died without heirs, and was survived by his wife Lady Ross. With his death, the succession of the house of Lockhart Ross came to an end, as did the Baronetcy of Nova Scotia. The Rosses of Pitcalnie being true descendants of the Earls of Ross had living descendants at this time, and during the lifetime of Sir Charles, the actual Chief of Clan Ross was Miss Ethel Frances Sara Williamson Ross. Miss Williamson Ross presented her claim to the principal arms as Chief of Clan Ross, and her claim was upheld by the Lord Lyon in 1903. There was thus an interregnum in the Chiefship from the death of David of Balnagowan in 1711 until 1903, when Miss Williamson Ross of the original line of descent became Chief of Clan.

## The Balnagowan and Tain Historical Documents

Sir Charles Ross, who was resident at Balnagowan Castle in the early years of the twentieth century, allowed access to the old documents of the sixteenth, seventeenth, and eighteenth centuries which were stored in a chest at the Castle. These documents along with the early Tain documents relating to Clan Ross were reviewed by W. Macgill and published in 1909. These are of special interest in giving us a picture of the courts of justice and the punishments meted out for even minor crimes in the seventeenth and eighteenth centuries. Some of these early documents are here reproduced.

Under the date of 1648 a case appearing before "Walter Ross provost, and bailies of Tain . . . vagabond Donald McCurrichie . . . for breaking Wm. Ross his kiln, and thereby entering his merchant buith (cottage) under claud of night, and stealing one silver dish weighing sex unce of money, four pair single soled showes (shoes) and stene (stone) and quarter weight of butter . . . ane roll of tobacco weighing twell pund, ten pieces of beefe, ane stene wt of woll and yarne." He was sentenced to "nyne months or thereby in the prison of Inverness, but upon a certaine night, wild Highland men came and brak up the dore" (door), allowing him to escape.

In 1675 two cases tried before Sir John Urquhart, Sheriff of Cromertie (Cromarty) "Andrew Kaird (tinker) accused for dailly stealing of corner stocks in 3 or 4 places, stealing the communion cup of the Kirk at Tarbet . . . stealing timber from the bulwark of Cromertie . . . false cunzieing of money, and making of it half crowns by laying on ym (them) of quicksilver."

". . . committing adulterie with Marjorie Dunune in Inverness, and poysoning his own wiffe, and for perjurie yrament (thereat) . . . for which crymes he was secured in the pit of the castell of Cromartie, and on the 28th day of May being Sunday made ane passage throw the prison wall being elleven feet thick and made his escap, and stealed and away took ane pewter stoup and ane pair of blankets he had in the prison . . . brocht (brought) to the gallows at the Ness of Cromartie and hanget yuon be the neck to the death and his bodie cut down and intered at the gallows foott. . . ."

At this time there was a preference for executions and gibbeting to be held on hills and headlands so that they would be widely seen and strike terror in the onlookers.

At Tain in the year 1695 appearing before Walter Ross provost, "Wm. McColl in Invereathis did approach to the said Margaret McKay her house, and entering her most secure room having one staff in his hand . . . did beat . . . the persons of . . . at the side of her ordinar resting bed till the sd. staff braik . . . rendering her . . . not able to travel her own length from the said bed qr. (where) she now is bedfast sorely tormented."

A case of robbery at Knockbain in 1741 was tried at Tain. (Accused) "took 4 horses out of the stable and a musket. . . . The sheriff ordains that for the Musket . . . he be taken from the prison to the bridge at Tain and there by the hands of the common hangman to receive seven lashes of the common whipping cord upon his naked body, thereafter seven (lashes) . . . opposite to the house of Bailie Monson . . . seven at the Cross, lastly seven at the bridge in the upper end of the burgh, and then to be dismissed. . . . For the horses . . . to be carried to the common place of execution . . . hanged till he be dead dead. . . ."

After the Royal edict prohibiting the wearing of Highland dress was issued many of the Highlanders were imprisoned for this offence.

A Sheriff's warrant issued in 1751 states . . . "that whereupon information Wm. Ross Son of Alexr. Ross in Dalnachleragh, now prisoner in the Tolbooth of Tain, has been taken up and incarcerate for wearing and using the Highland dress and arms . . . contrar to and in defiance of the Act of Parliament . . . summoned Hugh Rose, teacher of the grammar school at Kilmuir Easter, and Donald Ross, Roderich Ross and Alexr. Mackenzie, students at the said school . . . to bear leal and soothfast witness . . . as they shall be spured at. . . ."

# 4. CADET BRANCHES OF CLAN ROSS

The cadet branches are descended from the second or subsequent sons of the original Balnagowan families. The majority of these cadet branches, through lack of male heirs, have ceased to exist; in others the line of descent is not known at the present time.

The principal cadet branches of the Clan Ross who traced their descent from the Earls of Ross and the Rosses of Balnagowan are given in the genealogical tables in Appendix I. These are as follows: The Rosses of Invercharron, the Rosses of Braelangwell, including the Rosses of Eastern Fearn and Ankerville, the Rosses of Achnacloich, the Rosses of Kindeace, the Rosses of Invercastley (Inverchasley), the Rosses of Calrossie, the Rosses of Aldie, the Rosses of Pitkerrie and Cromarty.

These Ross families are named after the towns and villages in which they lived and owned estates, and the heritable jurisdictions passed from father to eldest son. None of these families have traceable descendants at the present time with the possible exception of the Kindeace and Cromarty Rosses.

After the death of Sir Charles Ross the original line of succession was reestablished through the Pitcalnie and Shandwick branches of Clan Ross.

The genealogy of these branches are given in the following section.

## THE ROSSES OF PITCALNIE

This branch of Clan Ross is the second oldest, the Shandwicks being the oldest. It will be recalled that the male line of the Balnagowan family terminated in David Ross, thirteenth of Balnagowan. On his death Malcolm Ross fifth of Pitcalnie, became the true male representative of the O'Beolain Earls of Ross, and was entitled to become Chief of Clan.

*Nicholas Ross, first of Pitcalnie*

Nicholas, was the eldest son by his second wife of Alexander Ross, ninth laird of Balnagowan. According to an ancient manuscript the lands of Pitcalnie were conveyed by Alexander Ross to his son Nicholas in 1587, as well as other lands in Easter Ross. Along with his father and half-brother, George, Nicholas took an active part in assisting the Earl of Bothwell in his unwise contention with the reigning monarch. He was married in 1587 to Margaret, daughter of Hector Munro of Assynt. Three years before her marriage to the laird of Pitcalnie, this lady received a charter of the western third of Arkboll from James VI, thus proving that she was a lady of the court. A son and daughter were born of the marriage. The son, David, succeeded to his father's estate of Pitcalnie and to his mother's property in Aykboll. The daughter, Catherine, married Donald Macleod, seventh of Assint.

*David Ross, second of Pitcalnie*

David succeeded his father in July, 1611. He was served heir to his uncle, his father's youngest brother, Malcolm of Cambuscurry, in October 1618. He married Jean, daughter of Alexander Dunbar of Inverness, and left three sons: (1) David, third of Pitcalnie, (2) Nicholas, and (3) Malcolm, who founded the family of Rosses of Kindeace. David died on October 14, 1646, and was buried in the family burying-ground of Fearn.

*David Ross, third of Pitcalnie*

He succeeded his father in the property. On 31st July 1655, he became tutor to his kinsman, David, twelfth of Balnagowan, whose father died while he was a youth. He appears to have taken a prominent part in public life as he was made a Commissioner of War for Ross-shire in the years 1648-9, and a Commissioner of Excise in 1661. He was fined £720 in 1662 for nonconformity to Scottish episcopacy. On the same occasion his father-in-law, Mr. MacKenzie of Kilcoy, was fined £6000; Sir Robert Munro of Foulis, Bart., £3600; and Mr. Hector Douglas, £2400. David was twice married: first to Margaret, second daughter of Alexander Mackenzie of Kilcoy and later to Catherine, daughter of Colonel John Munro of Obsdale, widow of Captain James MacCulloch of Kindeace.

By the first marriage he had issue: (1) Margaret, who married Hector Douglas of Mulderg, of a family which settled in Ross-shire about the time of the Reformation, and was located near the Abbey of Fearn in the latter part of the sixteenth century; and (2) Catherine, who married Robert Munro of Achnagart.

By the second marriage he had issue: (3) Alexander, who succeeded his father as fourth of Pitcalnie; and (4) Isobel, who married James MacCulloch of Pitnallies.

*Alexander Ross, fourth of Pitcalnie*

Alexander married Agnes, daughter of Hugh Ross of Balmuchy and had as issue: (1) Malcolm, latter known as "Callum Og", who became fifth of Pitcalnie; (2) George; (3) William, a captain in the army, who died at Antrim in 1763; (4) James, who became eighth of Pitcalnie; (5) Munro, who died unmarried in 1810; and (6) Margaret, who married the Rev. David Ross, Minister of Tarbat. Alexander died in 1763.

*Malcolm Ross, fifth of Pitcalnie*

When Malcolm's cousin David Ross, thirteenth chief of Balnagowan, died, Malcolm, who was the male representative of the House of Pitcalnie became the true chief of Clan Ross and heir to the Balnagowan estates. Malcolm Ross was deprived of the chiefship and the estates of Balnagowan however. They came into the possession of Lady Anne Stewart and her husband, who subsequently transferred these extensive properties to Mr. Francis Stewart. Shortly after this Lord Ross of Hawkhead gained possession of the estates by purchase as we have seen. *From the time of Malcolm Ross who became heir in 1763 to the present day, the Balnagowan Castle and estates have not been owned or controlled by the Rosses of Pitcalnie as the Chiefs of the blood of Clan Ross, even though they were the rightful heirs.*

Malcolm lived at the time of the Jacobite risings, and took an active part in them as a Jacobite leader. The men of Ross were mostly pro-Hanoverian. Colonel Malcolm Ross in 1715 at the head of five hundred highlanders of the clan, marched to Alness, where he was joined by the Munros and the men of Sutherland in the surrender of Inverness. The Rosses afterwards suffered for their loyalty when the Seaforths ravished their lands. About thirty years later, we find the Rosses rallying to the cause of Prince Charlie, under the banner of Malcolm's grandson, also called Malcolm Ross.

Malcolm was twice married, first to Jean, eldest daughter of James MacCulloch of Piltoun, and second to Agnes, daughter of Hugh Wallace of Igliston, and widow of George Munro, first of Culcairn.

By his first marriage Malcolm Ross had as issue: (1) Alexander, who became sixth laird of Pitcalnie; (2) James; (3) Charles; (4) Angus; (5) Ann; (6) Christian; (7) Isabel; and (8) Catherine. His second marriage was childless.

### *Alexander, sixth of Pitcalnie*

On the death of his father, Alexander succeeded to his property. He was thrice married: first to Jean, daughter of George Munro of Newmore; then to Isobel, daughter of David McCulloch of Piltoun, and finally to Naomi, daughter of John Dunbar of Burgie.

By the first marriage he had a son, Malcolm, who married and left an only daughter, who was wedded to Alexander MacPherson, solicitor of Inverness. Malcolm, who was pursuing his studies at Aberdeen when the Rebellion broke out, joined the ranks of Prince Charles Edward Stuart. His right to the property was thereby attainted and his inheritance was given to his half-brother.

There does not appear to have been any issue of Alexander's second marriage, but his third resulted in a son Munro, who became the seventh laird of Pitcalnie. His mother Naomi, was destined to play a prominent part as a litigant. As previously referred to, on the death of David Ross, thirteenth of Balnagowan, the laird of Pitcalnie claimed the estates of Balnagowan. Some time after the action was raised, Alexander of Pitcalnie died, but the litigation was continued by his wife on behalf of her son Munro. Naomi Ross seems to have been a woman of unusual ability, and of great force of character. She was very proud of her family, as can be inferred from the following letter written to one of her relatives. It is taken from *Dunbar's Social Life in Former Days*:

"To Alexander Dunbar, Esq.
Edinburgh, 20th July 1761

Sir, — In answer to yours of the 13th threatening me with caption, I can only repeat what I wrote when you acquainted me in yours of the 4th that you were obliged to raise horning on my bill. Therefore I refer to what I then wrote, and shall only add that your father may put his caption in execution against me. I can go to prison, the affront won't be mine, and before I come out the fifteen Lords shall know the merits of the cause that laid Burgie's daughter, and Pitcalnie's widow in such quarters. Not in the least finding fault with your conduct, which I verily believe is much against your inclination—I am, Dear Sir, your affectionate cousin and very humble servant,

NAOMI ROSS"

*Munro Ross, seventh of Pitcalnie*

Upon coming of age Munro Ross succeeded to his father's properties. He will be best remembered as one of the claimants to the Earldom of Ross in 1778. He based his claim on the ground that he was the lineal male descendant of Hugh Ross of Rarichies, first laird of Balnagowan, who was brother to William, the last Earl of Ross. His claim was sustained by the Court of Session and by the House of Lords who stated that the title was wrongfully assumed by Euphemia, the Countess of Ross, it being limited to heirs male, but it would appear that no decision was reached on the matter. Munro entailed his property first in favour of himself and his heirs male, whom failing, to Captain James Ross of the Royal Regiment in Dublin, fourth son of Alexander, fourth of Pitcalnie and his heirs male. He died unmarried in March, 1820, and, according to the terms of the settlement, was succeeded by his cousin, James Ross.

*Capt. James Ross, eighth of Pitcalnie*

James was served heir to his cousin on July 12, 1819. He married Sarah, a daughter of G. Johnstone of Skerries, Dublin, and by her had a family of four sons and one daughter: (1) James, who became ninth of Pitcalnie, (2) George, (3) Henry, (4) William Munro, (5) Sarah, who married Donald Williamson, for many years factor to Balnagowan and later a lawyer in Tain, from whom descended the late Chief of Clan Ross.

PITCALNIE ROSSES AFTER 1819

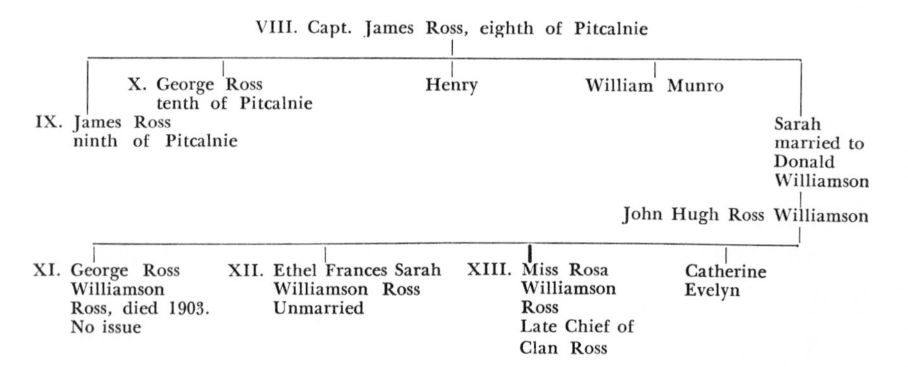


*James Ross, ninth of Pitcalnie*

James succeeded his father as ninth laird of Pitcalnie on August 23, 1821. He died unmarried in April, 1829.

*George, tenth of Pitcalnie*

On his brother's death, George succeeded to the property. He was married on June 1, 1837, to Catherine, daughter of Dugald Gilchrist of Ospisdale, Sutherland, but left no issue. His sister, Sarah, who had married Donald Williamson in 1834, bore a son, John Hugh Ross Williamson. He lived on Balnagore Farm, Fearn, which he occupied until the time of his death. He married, in October, 1865, Fanny Georgina, daughter of the Rev. Theophilus Clarke, Vicar of Tadcaster, and had issue: (1) George Ross Williamson Ross; (2) Ethel Frances Sarah Williamson Ross; (3) Rosa Ross Williamson Ross; and (4) Catherine Evelyn.

*George Ross Williamson Ross, eleventh of Pitcalnie*

George succeeded his grand-uncle, George Ross of Pitcalnie. He died on September 3, 1903. By his death there passed away the heirs male of the Pitcalnie branch of the Ross family. The two surviving sisters followed as female heirs and became Chiefs of Clan Ross.

*Ethel Frances Sarah Williamson Ross*

Miss Sarah Williamson Ross was born in 1867 at Balnagore, Fearn, in Ross-shire and was a well-educated clever woman with many artistic interests, although in poor health for the last thirty years of her life.

Sarah Williamson Ross, became heir to the title as Chief of Clan Ross in 1903, on the death of her brother, George R. Williamson Ross. She took the name of Ross as well as her family name of Williamson. Miss Ross registered arms under the Lord Lyon as "Ross of Pitcalnie", and succeeded under entail to her brother's lands and honours. She did not inherit the Balnagowan Castle or estates however. In her years of illness, her sister, Miss Rosa Ross Williamson Ross, was appointed Judicial Factor over her property and held that position until Ethel's death in 1957.

*Rosa Ross Williamson Ross, twenty-eighth Chief of Clan Ross*

Miss Rosa Ross of Pitcalnie succeeded as Chief of Clan Ross on the death of her elder sister, in 1957. She was also born at Balnagore in Fearn, and was the second daughter of Sarah and Donald Williamson.

Miss Rosa R. Williamson Ross of Ross was the granddaughter of the sister of George Ross, tenth of Pitcalnie, on whose death the male line became extinct. Her grandmother was heiress of the line of both Pitcalnie and Ross, and she therefore took the name of Ross along with her family name of Williamson. This is a legal procedure according to Scots Law.

The members of Clan Ross were recently saddened by the death of Miss Rosa Ross at her home in Tain at the age of 99 years. She had enjoyed good health, and was bright and active until her death on March 24, 1968.

Miss Rosa Ross retained the old documents, and ancient souvenirs and letters of the Rosses of Pitcalnie, and attended personally to clan correspondence from all parts of the world. Everyone who knew her admired her fine spirit and good humour, and she will be greatly missed by all her clansmen.

The chiefship and the armorial dignities are now transferred to the house of Shandwick, in the person of David Campbell Ross, eldest son of the late Sheriff Charles Campbell Ross, Q.C.

The Balnagowan Castle and estates have remained with the family of Lockhart-Rosses, the last of whom was Sir Charles Ross, and these are not inherited with Chiefship of the Clan.

Her Majesty the Queen and the Duke of Edinburgh recently (June 26, 1964) paid a visit to Ross-shire, and on this festive occasion, while at the Royal and Ancient Burgh of Tain, the Chief of Clan Ross Miss Rosa Williamson Ross, along with other notables, was presented to Her Majesty by the Lord Lieutenant of Ross and Cromarty, General Sir Richard O'Connor.

## THE ROSSES OF SHANDWICK, 1486-1968

As we trace the history of this cadet branch of the Clan Ross from Walter Ross first of Shandwich who died in 1531, to the present Chief-of the Clan, David Ross, more detailed biographies of the members of this important family will be given. All future Chiefs of Clan Ross will be chosen from the Rosses of Shandwick, as this family is the only one with proven living male descendants who can trace their origin to the ancient Earls of Ross of the twelfth century. The genealogy of this distinguished family was contributed by Sheriff Charles Campbell Ross Q.C.

A number of these Shandwick Rosses followed military careers. Two members of this family became high ranking officers in the British Army serving in India. Another, Sir Ronald Ross, had a distinguished career as a medical doctor and research scientist. While practising in India, he discovered the causative factors of malaria, and was thus instrumental in saving the lives of many people in the tropics who were affected with this disease. The world-renowned Ross Institute of Tropical Diseases in London was named after him for his outstanding contributions to medical science.

Among the few towns and parishes shown on the twelfth century map of Ross is the ancient village of Shandwick which indicates that it had attained some importance even in the very early days of Ross-shire.

The Shandwick Rosses are a very old and distinguished family, who trace their descent in direct line from the Earls of Ross, Hugh of Rarichies, and William Ross of Little Allan, who was the third son of Hugh, fourth Baron of Balnagowan.

The second son of William Ross of Meikle Allan was Walter Ross, who became first laird of Shandwick when his father was slain, along with many other members of Clan Ross at the disastrous battle of Alt a' Charrais in 1486.

*Walter Ross, first of Shandwick*

Walter Ross had a wadset from the King of the lands of Meikle Allan and also of the town and chaplainry of Dunskaith. He married six times: Janet Tulloch, Agnes McCulloch, Elizabeth Hay, Christian Chisholm, Janet Munro, and finally, Agnes Forbes. Janet Tulloch is said to have been the mother of the following four sons: (1) Donald Ross, second of Shandwick; (2) William Ross, first of Culnahall, from whom the Rosses of Marangie were probably descended; (his wife Margaret Morrison died in 1555). (3) Hugh Ross, first of Balmuchy; and (4) Nicholas Ross, first of Balon. Walter Ross died on June 10, 1531 and was buried in an aisle at Ferne Abbey which was built at his own expense.

*Donald Ross, second of Shandwick*

Donald married first Janet, daughter of Simpson, and secondly, the daughter of Clunes of Mulderg, by whom he had two sons: (1) Andrew Ross, third of Shandwick; and (2) Robert Ross, first of Keandloch.

*Andrew Ross, third of Shandwick*

Andrew Ross died on August 6, 1641, having married first the daughter of Vass of Lochlivn and secondly, Beatrice, widow of John Munro of Meikle Davoch. By his first wife he had a son, Donald, and another son, William, of whom nothing is known. On July 11, 1624, a charter was granted by Patrick, Bishop of Ross, to Andrew Ross of Shandwick and Donald, his elder son, of the lands of Shandwick. Donald, fourth of Shandwick, sold the lands of Shandwick to his cousin William Ross of Keandloch (see Chart). Donald Ross was thereafter styled "of Meikle Raynes", and his grandson John Ross, third of Meikle Raynes, was living in 1714, but no descendant of Andrew Ross, third of Shandwick, can now be traced.

# THE ROSSES OF SHANDWICK

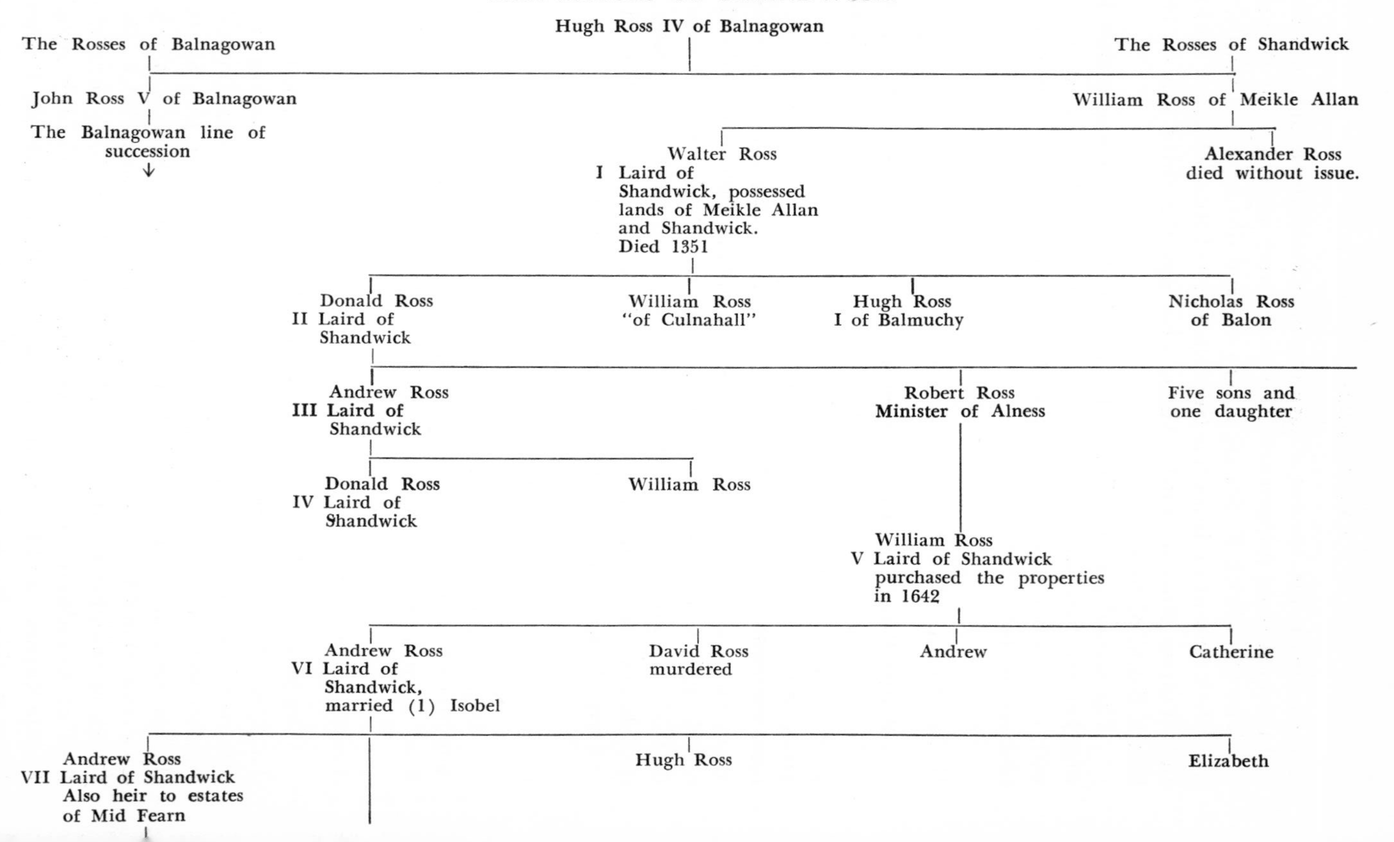

Gained possession of Shandwick
by marriage contract

Mary Ross married
David Ross of
Invercastley

No issue

William Ross
(Fer Drumgelly)
died in 1693

William Ross
purchased estates of
Kerse, Skeldon and Balblair,
unmarried,
died by drowning 1739

Bailie Hugh Ross, Magistrate of Tain.
II of Kerse. Killed Hugh Ross of
Achnacloich in a duel.
Escaped to Sweden but returned.
Succeeded to properties of Kerse
and Skeldon. Acquired Meikle Dann
by marriage

Lt. Col. Hugh Ross
**of the E.I.C.S.**

Major General Campbell
Claye Grant Ross created
a K.C.B. in 1880 married
Matilda Elderton in 1856

son
William
Ross

son

son

daughter
Wilhelmina
Ross
Married Rev.
the Hon. R. F. King

daughter

daughter

Sir Ronald Ross
Director in chief of Ross
Institute of Tropical Medicine.
Married Rosa Bloxam

Capt. Clay Ross

Maj. Gen. Charles Ross

Sheriff Charles Campbell Ross
of that ilk, younger,
Chief Designate Clan Ross
Married Beatrice R.M. Saner

Mrs. Langstaffe,
wife of Lt. Col. J.W. Langstaffe

David Campbell Ross
married Eileen Cassidy

Anne Campbell Ross

Andrew Malcolm Ross
(adopted)

Hugh Andrew Campbell Ross
born 1961

daughter
born 1964

*Robert Ross, first of Keandloch*

Robert Ross was minister of Alness in 1588, and built the manse and the west end of the church. His wife is unknown, but he appears to have had five sons and a daughter: (1) William Ross, second of Keandloch and fifth of Shandwick; (2) John Ross, who witnessed a document in 1649; (3) Thomas Ross, minister of Kincardine, described as "a singularly pious man"; (4) Andrew Ross, minister at Corton; (5) David Ross, first of Logie Easter, where he was minister and also a member of the General Assembly. He married, first, Margaret, daughter of Morrison, and secondly Janet, widow of Alexander Ross of Pitkerie. By his first wife he had two sons and two daughters. (6) Esther, who married Hugh, fourth son of Hector Munro. The eldest son succeeded.

*Rev. William Ross, second of Keandloch and fifth of Shandwick*

The second estate he purchased in 1696 from his cousin, Donald Ross of Shandwick. In 1655 he also purchased the lands of Balon from another cousin, Donald Ross of Balon. Having imprudently become cautioner for his relative, Thomas Ross of Priesthill, he became involved in numerous law suits which eventually ruined his family. He was minister at Kincardine, at Nigg, and for a time at Fearn. Born in 1593, he died at Shandwick on 20th April, 1663, having married, first, Elizabeth, daughter of William Campbell of Delnies, by whom he had a son, David Ross, described as "a most promising young man". David was murdered in 1651 in the wood of Invershie near Stirling while on his way to join the army of King Charles II. All the heritors of Scotland had been summoned to attend that monarch in his contemplated invasion of England which ended disastrously at the battle of Worchester. It is interesting to note that young Shandwick's cousin, David Ross, twelfth Baron of Balnagowan, was taken captive in that battle and died a prisoner in the Tower in 1653. William Ross had three other children: Andrew Ross, who became sixth of Shandwick; Alexander Ross; and Katherine, who married James Fraser of Pitkellyen.

William Ross married secondly, Isobel, daughter of Hector Douglas of Mulderg. She had three daughters by him who each received 3000 merks. Soon after her husband's death, Isobel Ross married Andrew Fearn, portioner of Pitkellyen. Her issue by her first marriage was: (1) Janet, who married David Ross, Dean of Guild and merchant in Tain (contract dated 7th November, 1666); (2) Isobel, who married Alexander Munro, fifth of Tennaird in 1680; and (3) Elizabeth, who married William Ross "in Shandwick" (contract dated 8th December, 1680).

*Andrew Ross, sixth of Shandwick*

Andrew Ross married, first, Isobel, daughter of William Ross of Invercharron (contract dated 13th April, 1660), by whom he had: (1) Andrew Ross, seventh of Shandwick; (2) Hugh Ross, who died before 1680; and (3) Elizabeth, who married Patrick Aitman. By his second wife Lillian, daughter of John Dallas, Dean of Ross, and widow of Alexander Urquhart of Craighall (contract dated, 1671, by virtue of which she gained possession of Shandwick), he had as issue: (1) William Ross, "fiar of Drumgell," who died in October, 1693 having disposed of Drumgelly to his other son, Urquhart of Craigton; and (2) Mary, who married first Lachlan McIntosh of Balnespick, and later became the second wife of David Ross, first of Inverchasley. Andrew Ross, sixth of Shandwick, died in October, 1675.

*Andrew Ross, seventh of Shandwick*

His property having passed to his stepmother, he was able to retain only the small estate of Midfearn. David Ross first of Invercastley, bought up the claims against Drumgelly and those of the heirs of the second marriage of William Ross, against Shandwick, and these properties terminated with him in 1708. He died in October 1733. He had married Christina, daughter of William Ross of Gladfield, and by her had a very numerous family: (1) William Ross, first of Kerse and Skeldon, who still styled himself "of Shandwick", was a Writer to the Signet in Edinburgh, where he was trying to retrieve the fallen fortunes of his family. Between 1728 and 1737, he purchased the lands of Kerse and Skeldon in Ayrshire, and he also acquired by purchase half of the lands of Drumgelly and also the town and lands of Balblair. Born in 1694, he was drowned in April 1739 between Peterhead and Orkney. He was unmarried. (2) Hugh Ross became the second of Kerse and Skeldon; (3) Andrew Ross, Bailie of Tain and Dean of Guild, 1726, was drowned while crossing a stream in India in 1739. He was married on November 6, 1724, to Margaret, daughter of Colin Campbell of Delnies. She married, secondly, in 1742, Hugh Ross, merchant in Tain, and died about 1775. Margaret bore three sons and three daughters, but none of the sons left issue. The eldest daughter Mary, married in 1748, John Reid, Bailie of Tain, whose descendants afterwards came into possession of Shandwick after much litigation. (4) Alexander Ross, sometime merchant in Gorrenburg, born at Midfearn in 1704, died at Sheldon House, Ayrshire in April 1775, unmarried. (5) David Ross, Ensign in the Master of Ross's Independent Company, raised to suppress the rising in 1745. He became tenant of the estate of Midfearn which belonged to his elder brother Hugh. Born in 1705, he died on the 21st

May, 1768 and was buried at Kincardine. He married first in 1727 Esther, daughter of George Munro of Culrain. She died in Orkney in 1740, leaving no issue. He married, secondly, on 29th July, 1745, Jean, daughter of George Law of Duddingstone, and widow of David Byres of Elie, by whom he had one son and two daughters. She died on August 19, 1776. The son, William Ross, was born on January 21, 1753, and fell in a duel with his cousin David Reid at Blackheath on May 11, 1790. He was unmarried. When a young man he was sent to India by his uncle, Hugh Ross of Kerse. Returning with a fortune he was able to *re-purchase in 1786 for his family, from his relative, David Ross, Lord Ankerville, for £17,600 the lands of Shandwick, Culliss, and Ankerville.* He gave these lands to his nieces and their heirs. The last descendant of those nieces, Christina Cockburn-Ross, died on the 16th May, 1872, unmarried and the property of Shandwick passed to the Reids. (6) George Ross, merchant in Gottenburg, died there in June 1783. He married Dorothea Schweitzer, by whom he had (in addition to four other children who died young) two sons: Andrew Ross (unmarried), East India Company's Marine, who was lost in the ship *Louisa,* which he commanded, in May, 1789; and Benjamin Ross, East India Company's Military Service, who died unmarried at Dinapore in January, 1790. Some of the claimants to the Shandwick property pretended a descent from these gentlemen. (7) Isabella married Robert M'Culloch, merchant in Tain. (8) Margaret, married Bailie Donald Ross of Tain. She died on March 4, 1753, (9) Katherine, married on September 29, 1743, George, eldest son of Bailie William Ross of Tain. (10) Christina, married in 1730, John, eldest son of Duncan Ross of Tain. She died in March, 1746.

Andrew Ross, seventh of Shandwick, had also four sons who died in infancy and three daughters who died unmarried. The second son Hugh inherited the properties of Kerse and Skeldon, and Balblair.

*Hugh Ross, second of Kerse, Skeldon and Balblair.*

Hugh Ross was a merchant in Gottenburg and London, also a director of the East India Company. He was, in addition, Bailie of Tain. It seems that on June 13, 1721, he killed, in a duel, his relative, Hugh Ross, sixth of Achnacloich, and in consequence had to take refuge in Sweden. Here he built up a considerable fortune. He inherited Kerse and Skeldon, with other properties, from his brother William and he claimed these on his return to Scotland. He married on August 24, 1749, Elizabeth, only daughter of Alexander Ross of Little Daan, and granddaughter of Alexander Ross, fifth of Easter Fearn. This lady's father was Writer to the Signet in Edinburgh and Solicitor of Appeals in London. He became offended with his son David, then a boy at Westminster (who afterwards became the famous tragic actor, second only to the tragedian Garrick), and disinherited him. Thus his lands passed to his daughter Elizabeth on his death in March, 1753. Hugh Ross was born in 1695 and died on April 13, 1775. His wife had died in July, 1739, and was buried under the altar of St. Andrew Undershaft, London. They had, with two daughters who died unmarried, three sons: (1) Hugh Ross, third of Kerse and Skeldon; (2) Alexander Ross, who died an infant in 1757; and (3) Andrew William Ross, a merchant, who died unmarried.

*Hugh Ross, third of Kerse and Skeldon*

He died on the 20th January, 1818, aged 66 years, and was buried in the Greyfriars, Edinburgh. His wife was Janet, daughter of Campbell of Delnies by whom they had three sons and three daughters who died unmarried. The sons were: (1) William Ross, described as of "Skeldon, Berbice, British Guiana", who was born about 1788 and died at Berbice on February 19, 1840, having had as issue three sons and two daughters; (his grandson William Munro Ross, who died in 1926, was the last in the male line of this family, his only son having been killed in World War I.) (2) Hugh Ross; and (3) George Ross, Writer to the Signet in Edinburgh, who died unmarried at Dresden.

*Hugh Ross*

Lieutenant-Colonel in the East India Company's Military Service, commanded the 31st and 42nd Regiments and was Town Major at Calcutta, 1833. On February 28, 1819, he married Eliza, daughter of Lieutenant-Colonel William Watson, 47th Regiment, of Farnsfield, Nottinghamshire. He died at Cawnpore in 1838, leaving four sons and two daughters: (1) Hugh Ross, who was born on August 30, 1820, and died at the age of 17, (he was drowned in a boating accident in the Firth of Forth); (2) Sir Campbell Claye Grant Ross K.C.B.; (3) William Alexander Ross. Lieutenant-Colonel, Bengal Artillery, born on September 14, 1829, who married the daughter of Lieutenant-Colonel James Sleeman, Indian Army, by whom he had, with daughters, two sons, Sleeman Ross and Hugh Ross, who were both killed in the South African War, 1899-1902, unmarried; and (4) Charles Edward Ross, a surgeon, born on July 28, 1832, who died unmarried; (5) Eliza Janet who married Major Malcolm Barwell, 90th Regiment; and (6) Adelaide, who married Brigadier-General John Tytler, Indian Army.

*General Sir Campbell Ross, K.C.B.*

Campbell Claye Grant Ross was born on the 18th May, 1824, and was educated at Edinburgh High School. He received his commission as an ensign in the H.E.I.C.S. on April 4, 1841, and, arriving in Calcutta, was posted to the 66th native infantry.

In 1850, his military life began to be more lively. The 66th was ordered from Lucknow to Umritsar in the Punjab, and was the first battalion to cross the River Sutlej to relieve the regiments that had fought the Sikh campaigns.

Campbell Ross was promoted Captain in 1852, and on April 8, 1856, he married Matilda, daughter of Edward Marrick Elderton, of Norton Hall, Dartmouth, barrister-at-law. There was issue of the marriage seven sons and three daughters. Matilda Elderton was a woman of considerable character and ability and, like her husband, took great pleasure in painting and sketching. She died in 1906.

In 1857 the 66th Ghurkha Regiment left the Punjab, and marched to Almorah in the Kamaon Hills, where they had hardly settled in their quarters when the great Sepoy Mutiny broke out. With the 66th at Almorah there was a native comany of the Bengal-Artillery (Sepoys, in fact, in artillery uniform). As reports came up daily of mutinies at the several stations in the plains, the Ghurkhas, sharper than their British officers, watched the artillerymen most narrowly. One morning they brought Captain Ross information and proof that they nightly held seditious meetings in a house in the town, and had been overheard plotting to have the British officers of the 66th cut down that very evening on the Mall, by the gunners, who calculated that the Ghurkhas would then passively join the mutiny.

The entire company was thereupon arrested, and confined in small parties of ten or fifteen in separate forts or police stations over the province.

At the foot of the Kamaon Hills lay the district of Rohilcund, at that time held by a strong force of the mutineers, cavalry and infantry. Its population was principally composed of Rohillas (a warlike and bigoted tribe of Mohammedans), who had murdered many Europeans, robbed the Government treasuries, and finally set up at Bareilly a rebel governor as the representative of the emperor of Delhi.

The suppression of the mutinous company of artillery at Amnorah undoubtedly preserved the district of Kamaon and the lives of many English officers, ladies, and children and to Major Ross who was in command of the 66th Ghurkhas goes most of the credit.

Major Ross later took command of the Ferozepore Regiment at

Peshawar. The regiment had been made the 14th Sikhs in the newly organized Bengal army. It remained at Peshawar for three years, and in November, 1863, took part in the Umbeyla campaign—a campaign against the Bonnair mountaineers, noted for severe fighting and great loss of life, especially among the British officers. Fortunately Major Ross was not wounded, although in the engagement at Craig Picket his helmet was pierced by one bullet and his field-glasses simultaneously smashed by another. For his services on this campaign he was promoted Lieutenant-Colonel in 1864.

In 1870 Colonel Ross went to England on leave, and on rejoining the 14th in 1875, was made a Brigadier-General, and appointed to the command of the Peshawar district, where the 14th joined him again. He had been promoted Brevet-Colonet just before going on leave, and in 1876 he was made a *Companion of the Bath.*

In 1877 General Ross was ordered by the Government of India to punish the very troublesome Jowaki tribe of Afridis, in conjunction with Brigadier-General Keyes, commanding the Punjab Frontier Force, who operated from Kohat. On the 6th of December, 1877, the Peshawar column attacked and utterly destroyed the seven robber villages of Bori, of which the twenty-eight strong towers were levelled to the ground. The entire country of the Jowaki Afridis was occupied by General Keyes, and Ross, and for the first time thoroughly surveyed and mapped; the tribe finally made their submission to the Lieutenant-Governor of the Punjab at Peshawar. For his successful conduct of this expedition General Ross was made *Knight Commander of the Bath.*

In 1880 Sir Campbell Ross returned to England where he resided until his death. He did not actually retire from the Army and continued to receive promotion, finally being gazetted General in 1890.

He died on the 20th June, 1892, at Eastbourne, and was buried at Oakleyne Cemetery.

*Sir Ronald Ross, LL.D., K.C.B., K.C.M.G., F.R.S., 1857-1932*

This great doctor and scientist was one of the seven sons of General Sir Campbell Claye Grant Ross and was the most important and outstanding of the Rosses of Shandwick. He was born in 1857 at Almora in the Kumaon Hills of India, where his father was serving with the 66th Ghurkhas. The other two surviving sons of Sir Campbell had distinguished military careers in India and the middle east. These were Capt. Clay Ross and Major General Charles Ross.

Dr. Ronald Ross was educated at St. Bartholomew's Hospital, and after taking his medical degrees, he entered the Madras Medical Service as a surgeon in 1881. At this time he turned to literary work and wrote several novels and plays, but later did scientific research.

In 1892 he took up the study of malaria, in search of the causes of that disease, which worked such havoc in India and throughout the East. In 1895 he undertook the verification of the mosquito theory of malarial transmission, which had been suggested to him by Dr. Sir Patrick Manson. In 1897-8 Dr. Ronald Ross successfully traced the life history of the malaria parasite in the mosquito; an outstanding accomplishment in the early days of the microscope. In 1895 he won the Parkes Memorial gold medal and prize for an essay on malaria. In 1896-9 he was on special duty to report on the tropical disease Kala-azar. After his important discoveries his health had suffered from long residence and close application to study in a tropical climate, and he found it advisable to retire from the Service, as a major, on July 31st, 1899.

He began to lecture on tropical diseases at the Liverpool School of Tropical Medicine in 1899, and became a professor in 1902. Ten years later he moved to London, where he was appointed physician for tropical diseases at King's College Hospital.

In 1908 he had taken a commission as major in the Territorial Force of the R.A.M.C., and in November, 1913, became Lieutenant-Colonel therein, on the staff of the 1st Western General Hospital, Liverpool.

Soon after the beginning of World War I, on December 21, 1914, he was appointed consulting physician for tropical diseases to the base hospitals for Indian troops in England, and in July, 1915, was sent to Alexandria to conduct an inquiry into the prevalence of dysentery in the Army at the Dardanelles. He was appointed consultant for malaria to the War Office, and in 1917 was sent out to Salonika on a malaria inquiry.

Many honours, both from the State and from scientific bodies, were conferred on Dr. Ross, beginning with his great discovery, and continuing through the next twenty years. He had gained the Parkes Memorial gold medal, the scientific prize of the State Medical Services, in 1895. In 1901 he received the silver medal of the London Society of Arts, the honorary Fellowship of the Royal College of Surgeons of England, and the Fellowship of the Royal Society. In 1902 he was given the C.B., the Cameron prize of Edinburgh University, and, in December, the Nobel prize in medicine. In 1903 he received the Barclay bronze medal of the Asiatic Society of Bengal, in 1904 the degree of D. Sc. from Trinity College, Dublin, in 1906 the grade of officer of the Order of Leopold II of Belgium, and the LL.D of Aberdeen University; in 1909 he was knighted, received the D.Sc. of Leeds, and was given the royal gold medal of the Royal Society. In 1910 the degree of M.D. Stockholm was conferred on him, in 1910 he received the K.C.B., and in 1912 the M.D. of Athens. In

1913, he was made Officier de l'Instruction Publique, France, in 1914 he received the Bisset-Hawkins gold medal of the Royal College of Physicians, London, in 1915 he was made a Freeman of the Society of Apothecaries, and in 1918 was gazetted K.C.M.G. for his services in the war. In 1922 he was elected a member of the Athenaeum Club, in 1923 he received the Albert medal of the Society of Arts, in 1928 the gold medal of the Royal Institute of Public Health, and in 1929 the Manson memorial gold medal and the gold medal of the West London Medico-Chirurgical Society.

At the annual meeting of the British Medical Association at Ipswich in 1900 Sir Ronald Ross was vice-president of the Section of Tropical Diseases and served as its president in the following year at Cheltenham. He had accepted the office of vice-president of that Section for the Centenary meeting in London.

Dr. G. Carmichael Low, President of the Royal Society of Tropical Medicine and Hygiene, writes:

"The death of Sir Ronald Ross removes another of the great pioneers of tropical medicine, and one not easily to be replaced. His name, however, will live for all time as the discoverer of the transmission of malaria by the mosquito, and the results rendered possible by this discovery are a gift to posterity. As all know, Ross joined the Indian Medical Services in 1881, and was appointed to its Madras branch in the same year. For the first years of his service he did little of note, but after Laveran's discovery of the malarial parasite his interest in that subject was aroused, an interest which was strengthened after the meeting with Manson in 1894, which led to such great results. On his return to India in 1895 Ross tackled the subject in earnest and with such energy and resolution that eventually he solved the problem, thus adding another illustrious achievement to British medicine.

"There is no question that Ross was a genius. No one but a genius could, without any practical laboratory training, have accomplished such a piece of work. A wonderful versatility is also shown by his contributions to mathematics, literature, and philosophy.

"Of an ardent temperament, it was difficult for Sir Ronald to cope with inanition and incompetence; and his desire to overcome these sometimes made him appear pugnacious. His energy and enthusiasm for his work were boundless, and he never spared himself in carrying out his schemes for the prevention and stamping out of malaria. For this purpose he visited many parts of the world, such as the West Coast of Africa, Ismalia, and Mauritius. He was appreciative of the work of others, and was always pleased to help young men beginning their careers.

"Many honours came to Ross, including the Nobel Prize in 1902. He was especially gratified by the foundation of the Ross Institute at Putney which bears his name; and also by the testimony of appreciation the nation made to him in his closing years. The world will never forget him; the names of Manson and Ross will go down to posterity together with those of Pasteur, Lister, and other benefactors of our race. The British nation should indeed be proud of the part its sons have borne in the elucidation of the problems of tropical medicine."

Sir Ronald married Rosa Bessie, daughter of Alfred Bloxam, of London, in 1889. They had two sons and two daughters: (1) Ronald Campbell Ross, born on February 11, 1895, Second Lieutenant in the Royal Scots, killed in action in France on August 27, 1914; (2) Charles Campbell Ross, Q.C., M.A. (Oxon); (3) Dorothy, who married, in February of 1916, Colonel James William Langstaff, D.S.O., Army Medical Service, and died October, 1947; and (4) Sylvia, who married, in September 1917, James Blumer, J.P., Mayor of Darlington, and died in October, 1925. Rosa Bessie Ross died on September 30, 1931. Sir Ronald, her husband died on September 16, a year later, and is buried at Wandsworth Cemetery.

*Charles Campbell Ross of that Ilk, Younger*

Sheriff Charles Campbell Ross, Q.C., M.A. (Oxon), Barrister at Law and member of the Faculty of Advocates of Scotland, was Chief-Designate of Clan Ross and direct descendant of the Shandwick Rosses. He matriculated arms at the Lyon's Court, by the Lord Lyon of Scotland on 6th June 1961. He was to have become Chief of Clan Ross on the death of Miss Rosa R. Williamson Ross, but, unfortunately, he died in February, 1967. His death was a great loss to all his clansmen.

Charles Campbell Ross was the second and only surviving son of Sir Ronald Ross of the Ross Institute for Tropical Diseases, London. He was born in Liverpool, where his father was Professor of Tropical Medicine, on October 13, 1901. He intended to pursue a military career and was a cadet at the Royal Military Academy Woolwich, but, owing to defective eyesight, was not commissioned. He then proceeded to Magdalen College, Oxford, where he graduated with a B.A. in 1924 and an M.A. in 1927. Thereafter he was called to the Bar by Lincoln's Inn and became also a member of the Faculty of Advocates in Scotland.

He was married to Miss Beatrice Rosamund Morton Saner at St. Columba's Church of Scotland, London, in the year 1930 by the late Dr. Archibald Fleming. There are two children and an adopted son. His eldest son David Ross was born February 11, 1934. His daughter, Anne Campbell Ross, was born April 15, 1943, in Nyasaland, and an adopted son, Andrew Malcolm Ross, was born February 19, 1943. David Ross succeeds his father as Chief of Clan Ross.

David completed his national service with the Royal Scots Fusiliers in Malaya, later taking the rank of Lieutenant in the Territorial Army. In 1957, he married Eileen Cassidy, granddaughter of Andrew Young of Edinburgh. They have one son, Hugh Andrew Campbell Ross, born September 8, 1961, and a daughter born May 30, 1964.

David Campbell Ross is the twenty-ninth Chief of Clan. However when the five Earls of Ross are included, David is recognized as being the thirty-fourth Chief.

The succession of clan chief from father to son is not necessarily automatic but may be changed by a possible change of entail. It is also not considered necessary to "make up title" more than once every four generations, if succession proceeds from father to son. It must be remembered, however, that no one can succeed to the chiefship unless he or she is a member of the family or clan. The Chief can, however, nominate any member of the family as his successor, even if the nominee is not in the line of direct descent.

In making application to Sir Thomas Innes The Lord Lyon, King of Arms for his Matriculation Certificate, Sheriff Charles Ross presented his credentials, and included a comprehensive history of Clan Ross as it related to his family of Shandwick. He traced the Clan history from the ancient Earls of Ross through the Rosses of Balnagowan and finally through William Ross of Little Allan and the Shandwick Rosses, to his own immediate ancestors in direct line of descent.

The Matriculation Certificate (facing p. 113) was granted to Sheriff Charles Campbell Ross by the Lord Lyon. The Arms are shown on the left and the Standard is shown on the right. The following is the text of the Certificate:—

> "Charles Campbell Ross, Sheriff Substitute; of Dunross, Stornoway, Isle of Lewis having by Petition unto the Lord Lyon King of Arms of date 2nd March, 1961 shown; that the Petitioner on 26th day of March 1936 recorded his arms in the Public Register of All Arms and Bearings in Scotland (Vol.2, fol.9) his descent being herein set forth, videlicit—that he is the only surviving son of Sir Ronald Ross, K.C.B., K.C.M.G., F.R.S., Director in Chief of the Ross Institute of Tropical Medicine, which Sir Ronald was eldest son of General Sir Campbell Claye Grant Ross, K.C.B., who was eldest surviving son of Lt. Colonel Hugh Ross who was eldest son of whom male issue survives of Hugh Ross, 3rd of Kerse[1]; Which Hugh was eldest son of Bailie Hugh Ross 2nd of Kerse who was eldest surviving son of Andrew Ross 7th of Shandwick; Which 7th Laird of Shandwick was descended from Walter Ross 1st of

[1] The estates of Kerse no longer belong to the Shandwick Rosses. Charles Campbell Ross's great-great-grandfather broke the entail and the estates were sold.

Shandwick who was eldest surviving son of William, 3rd son of Hugh Ross 4th of Balnagowan, whose great grandfather Hugh, 1st of Balnagowan was a younger son of Hugh 5th Earl of Ross who succeeded 28th January 1322-23. That the Ensigns Armorial of Ross of that Ilk[2], undifferenced by brisur[3] or mark of cadency and thus pertaining to (and demonstrative of) the Chief of the name, and Head of the Clan Ross were matriculated of date 18th October 1904 in the said Public Register in name of the late Miss Wilhelmina Ross of Pitcalnie, heir of line of the said Family of Balnagowan (elder sister of Miss Rosa Ross Williamson Ross of that Ilk, the present Chief) but that no motion was then made for inclusion in the matriculation of the Crest and supporters of old, born by the hereditary Heads of the Clan Ross. That by writ of Nomination re Chiefship of the Clan Ross by the said Miss Rosa Ross Williamson Ross of that Ilk and Pitcalnie, hereditary Chief of the Name and head of the Clan Ross of date 3rd April 1957 (recorded in Lyon Court Books 8th July 1957) the Petitioner was nominated to succeed as Chief of the Clan Ross and to the relative Armorial Bearings after the said Miss Rosa and her sisters and so constituted Tanister to the Hereditary Chiefship and Arms demonstrative thereof, in the name or title of Ross of that Ilk (as distinct from the representation or chieftaincy of the House of Ross of Pitcalnie as a House within and under the stem of the race, Name and Clan of Ross; And the Petitioner having prayed that the aforesaid Ensigns Armorial might be matriculated of new in his own name without difference and with the addition of such Supporters and crest as of old pertained to the chiefs of Clan Ross but with Brisur appropriate to him as Tanister[4] until his succession to the Chiefship the Lord Lyon King of Arms by Interlocutor of date 5th March 1961. Found in that the Petitioner had been lawfully and effectually nominated by the Deed duly recorded in the Books of the Court of the Lord Lyon of date 8th July 1957 by Miss Rosa Ross Williamson Ross of that Ilk and Pitcalnie, present Hereditary Chief of the Clan Ross to be successor to her in the undifferenced arms and appropriate Crest and Supporters of Ross of that Ilk (as distinct from the arms pertaining to the representationship of the arms of Pitcalnie) so that the Petitioner is now Tanister of the Clan Ross; (2) That the Petitioner is accordingly entitled to bear the shield without brisur or mark of cadency and external additaments of and appropriate to Ross of that Ilk and to the name and style Ross of that Ilk on being so, defeasibly matriculated in the said arms with the difference due to a Tanister or heir presumptive[5] aye, or quhill[6] any recall by the said Miss Rosa Ross William-

[2] "Of that same" that is, of the estate of the same name as the family.

[3] A mark of cadency or difference for a person other than the Chief.

[4] The Tanister is the person entitled, on the death of the Chief, to succeed him.

[5] The person named "heir" in the absence of a newer nominee.

[6] Without

son Ross of that Ilk and Pitcalnie of the said nominating; (3) That Ensigns Armorial including crest and supporters, are given at Balnagowan Castle and in the memorial to the Barons of Balnagowan, Chiefs of the Clan Ross, of a date of which parts of the same would appear to be about or anterior to the year 1672; and granted Warrant to the Lyon Clerk to matriculate in the Public Register of all Arms and Bearings in Scotland in name of the Petitioner as Charles Campbell Ross of that Ilk, Tanister of the Clan Ross, following Ensigns Armorial, videlicet;—Gules[7] three lions rampant Argent, armed and langued[8] Azure, a label of three points or for difference: Above the shield is placed an Helm befitting his degree with a Mantling Fules doubles Argent, and on a Wreath of the Liveries is set for Crest a hand holding a garland of Juniper proper and in an Escrol over the same his motto "SPEM SUCCESSUS ALIT"; on a compartment below the shield, embellished of juniper plants fructed proper, being the proper plant of the Clan Ross, are set for Supportors two savages, wreathed about the head with oak and loins with juniper, that in the dexter holding in his exterior hand a club Gules resting on the shoulder proper, that on the sinister holding a branch of juniper fructed proper in his exterior hand and also resting on his shoulder; the said Crest and Supporters being also debruised[9] by a label of three points, or as in the shield all which labels are to be borne by the Petitioner during his Tanistership; he bears for Badge a spring of juniper fructed proper which is depicted in 2nd and 4th compartments along with Crest in the first and third compartments of a standard four yards in length with end split, the arms of Ross of that Ilk in the hoist[10] of these Liveries Argent and Fules along with his Motto "SPEM SUCCESSUS ALIT" in letters Argent upon three transverse bands Azure, which standard during his Tanistership is to be raised for Miss Rosa R. Williamson Ross of that Ilk and Pitcalnie present Hereditory Chief of the Clan Ross. Matriculated the 6th day of June 1961.

Extracted fourth of the twenty-first and twenty-second page in Vol. 46 of the Publication of the Register of All Arms and Bearings in Scotland, codie. xxxx

H. A. B. LAWSON,
*Lyon Clerk Keeper of the Records*"

As shown by this document Miss Rosa R. Williamson Ross became Chief of Clan Ross in 1957 following the death of Miss Wilhelmina Ross. Both of these ladies were descended from the Rosses of Pitcalnie.

[7] The heraldic name for red.

[8] A term derived from the French word "langue", tongue.

[9] Debruised by a label of three points. This label is the mark of cadency of an eldest son during his father's lifetime.

[10] The part of a heraldic flag next to the staff.

Their ancestor Nicholas Ross of Pitcalnie was descended from the ninth Laird of Balnagowan. On the death of Miss Rosa Ross the chiefship passed to David the eldest son of Sheriff Charles Campbell Ross of the Shandwick Rosses.

Another branch of the Rosses of Shandwick is represented through the female side by Mr. James M. B. Wright of Auchinellan, Argyll. Mr. Wright's great-great-grandmother, Williamina Ross (or King), married Rev. the Honourable R. F. King, in 1800. The matriculation certificate was approved by the Lord Lyon in 1954.

Sir Ronald Ross of Shandewick, LL.D., K.C.B., K.C.M.G., F.R.S., 1857-1932. Ross Institute of the Tropical Medicines, London

Captain John Ross was the first white man to discover the Greenland Eskimos, 1819.

Captain Ross and his crew are seen sawing a passage through the Arctic ice for their ship, in the search for the North West passage.

Sir John Ross and Commander James Clark Ross on the voyage of discovery to the Arctic regions, 1829.

EXTRACT of MATRICULATION of the ARMS of SHERIFF CHARLES CAMPBELL ROSS of that ILK, younger

CHARLES CAMPBELL ROSS, Sheriff Substitute; of Dunross, Stornoway, Isle of Lewis having by Petition unto the Lord Lyon King of Arms of date 2nd March 1961 SHEWN; THAT the Petitioner on 26th day of March 1936 recorded his Arms in the Public Register of All Arms and Bearings in Scotland (Vol. 32, fol 9) his descent being therein set forth, videlicet: That he is the only surviving son of Sir Ronald Ross, K.C.B., K.C.M.G., F.R.S. Director in Chief of the Ross Institute of Tropical Medicine; WHICH Sir Ronald was eldest son of General Sir Campbell Claye Grant Ross K.C.B., who was eldest surviving son of Lt. Colonel Hugh Ross who was eldest son of whom male issue survive of Hugh Ross, 3rd of Kerse; WHICH Hugh was eldest son of Bailie Hugh Ross 2nd of Kerse who was eldest surviving son of Andrew Ross, 7th of Shandwick; WHICH 7th Laird of Shandwick was descended from Walter Ross 1st of Shandwick who was eldest surviving son of William, 3rd son of Hugh Ross 9th of Balnagowan, whose great grandfather Hugh 1st of Balnagowan was a younger son of Hugh 5th Earl of Ross who succeeded 28th January 1322-23 THAT the Ensigns Armorial of Ross of that Ilk undifferenced by brisure or mark of cadency and thus pertaining to (and demonstrative of) the Chief of the Name and Head of the Clan Ross were matriculated of date 18th October 1904 in the said Public Register in name of the late Miss Wilhelmina Ross of Pitcalnie heir of line of the said Family of Balnagowan (elder sister of Miss Rosa Ross Williamson Ross of that Ilk, the present Chief) but that no motion was then made for inclusion in the matriculation of the Crest and Supporters of old borne by the hereditary Heads of the Clan Ross; THAT by Writ of Nomination re Chiefship of the Clan Ross by the said Miss Rosa Ross Williamson Ross of that Ilk and Pitcalnie, hereditary Chief of the Name and Head of the Clan Ross, of date 3rd April 1957 (recorded in Lyon Court Books 8th July 1957) the Petitioner was nominated to succeed, as Chief of the Clan Ross and to the relative Armorial Bearings after the said Miss Rosa and her sisters, and so constituted Tanister to the said Hereditary Chiefship and Arms demonstrative thereof, in name or title of Ross of that Ilk, (as distinct from the representation or chieftaincy of the House of Ross of Pitcalnie as a House within and under the stem of the race, Name, and Clan of Ross; AND the Petitioner having prayed that the aforesaid Ensigns Armorial might be matriculated of new in his own name without difference and with the addition of such Supporters and Crest as of old pertained to Chiefs of Clan Ross but with brisure appropriate to him as Tanister until his succession to the Chiefship the Lord Lyon King of Arms by Interlocutor of date 6th March 1961 FOUND (1) That the Petitioner had been lawfully and effectually nominated by the De[...] Lyon of date 8th July 1957 by Miss Rosa Ross Williamson Ross of that Ilk and Pitcalnie, present Hereditary Chief of the Clan Ross, to be successor to her in the undifferenced arms and appropriate Crest and Supporters of Ross of that Ilk (as distinct from the arms pertaining to the representationship of the arms of Ross of Pitcalnie) so that the Petitioner is now Tanister of the Clan Ross; (2) That the Petitioner is accordingly entitled to bear the shield without brisure or mark of cadency and external additaments of and appropriate to Ross of that Ilk and to the name and style Ross of that Ilk on being so, defeasibly, matriculated in the said arms with the difference due to a Tanister or heir-presumptive are or until any recall by the said Miss Rosa Ross Williamson Ross of that Ilk and Pitcalnie of the said nominating; (3) That Ensigns Armorial, including crest and supporters, are graven at Balnagowan Castle and in the Memorial to the Barons of Balnagown, Chiefs of the Clan Ross, of a date of which parts of the same would appear to be about or anterior to the year 1672; and Granted Warrant to the Lyon Clerk to matriculate in the Public Register of All Arms and Bearings in Scotland in name of the Petitioner as Charles Campbell Ross of that Ilk, Tanister of the Clan Ross, the following Ensigns Armorial, videlicet:- Gules, three lions rampant Argent, armed and langued Azure, a label of three points Or for difference; Above the Shield is placed an Helm befitting his degree with a Mantling Gules doubled Argent, and on a Wreath of the Liveries is set for Crest a hand holding a garland of juniper proper, and in an Escrol over the same this Motto "SPEM SUCCESSUS ALIT"; On a Compartment below the Shield, embellished of juniper plants fructed proper, being the proper plant of the Clan Ross, are set for Supporters two savages, wreathed about the head with oak and loins with juniper all proper, that on the dexter holding in his exterior hand a club Gules resting on his shoulder proper, that on the sinister holding a branch of juniper fructed proper in his exterior hand and also resting on his shoulder, the said Crest and Supporters being also debruised by a label of three points Or as in the Shield all which labels are to be borne by the Petitioner during his Tanistership; He bears for Badge a sprig of juniper fructed proper, which is depicted in 2nd & 4th compartments along with the Crest in the first and third Compartments, of a Standard four yards in length with end split, the arms of Ross of that Ilk in the hoist, of these Liveries Argent and Gules, along with this Motto "SPEM · SUCCESSUS · ALIT" in letters Argent upon three transverse bands Azure, which Standard during his Tanistership is to be raised for Miss Rosa Ross Williamson Ross of that Ilk and Pitcalnie, present Hereditary Chief of the Clan Ross. Matriculated the 6th day of June 1961. Extracted furth of the twenty-first and twenty-second page in Vol 46 of the Public Register of All Arms and Bearings in Scotland, eodie.

H A B Lawson
Lyon Clerk Keeper of the Records

Matriculation Certificate of
Sheriff Charles Campbell Ross of that Ilk Yr.
Tanister of the Clan Ross.
Presented by the Lord Lyon King of Arms, March 1961.

# 5. CLAN ROSS IN THE NEW WORLD

## FAILURE IN NOVA SCOTIA

One of the earliest attempts at settlement of the New World in which Scotsmen took part was organized in 1622 under the auspices of Sir William Alexander, Earl of Stirling. King James VI of Scotland (who was to become James I of England), and later his son Charles I gave the Earl large grants of land or "Land Charters" in the new world to establish a crown colony. These grants included Acadia, New Brunswick, Prince Edward Island, and Cape Breton; as well as parts of Quebec, Maine, New Hampshire, and Vermont; and the greater part of the states of Pennsylvania and New York. This made the Earl of Stirling probably one of the most extensive landowners the world has ever known.

Sir William was born at Menstrie[1], a small village east of Stirling, but spent most of his later years at "Argyll's Lodging" in the old royal city of Stirling. He had already made a name for himself as a poet and courtier when he assumed the role of colonizer.

The shipload of emigrants he persuaded to settle in Nova Scotia, (New Scotland) was driven to Newfoundland by a storm. Some of these people finally reached Nova Scotia, but severe hardship caused most of them to return to Britain the next year. The majority of these emigrants were said to be from Kircudbright on the Solway Firth.

In 1623 the Earl of Stirling and his son Lord Alexander visited Canada. They had received a royal patent for thirty-one years "for the

[1] The old castle at Menstrie where Sir William was born has recently been completely renovated, and on one wall of the Commemoration Room are displayed the heraldic shields of the Baronets of Nova Scotia, surrounding a portrait of Charles I. The carefully drawn and decorated heraldic shields are the work of Ian Ross of Glasgow.

sole trade in all and singular regions, countries and dominions and all places adjacent to the River and Gulf of Canada, and the sole traffic from thence, and places adjoining, for beaver skins, and wool, and all other skins of wild beasts." Strenuous but unsuccessful efforts were made to procure more colonists who would be willing to bring their families to the new world. Then it was proposed that a number of leading Scottish gentlemen be invited to become members of a new order of "Baronets of Nova Scotia", with each of the Baronets providing a certain number of settlers in return for his title.

The historic method of creating these Baronets is well known. An area of soil of Castlehill at Edinburgh Castle was declared by royal mandate to be part of the territory of Nova Scotia, and it was on this ground that the titles were conferred. Sir William Alexander, Viscount of Canada, created 64 baronets in the next 25 years. From each he received £166, in return for which he transferred to each new Lord a tract of six square miles of land in the new world, with the right of "pit and gallows" thereon.

The first baronet was Sir Robert Gordon in 1625; the last was Craigie of Gainsay in 1707.

In 1628 seventy colonists were duly settled in Acadia at Port Royal, but nearly half of them died the first winter from hardships and sickness. Among those remaining a small fur trading company was set up. In 1632 Acadia was restored to France and the Scots settlers were brought back to Britain.

Lord Stirling next attempted to establish a settlement further south along the coast of Maine. For the most part this colonizing experiment also ended in failure, although a few of the colonists, by dint of hard labour and perseverance were able to survive.

## The Rosses in New England

In searching the records of the old Massachusetts Bay Colony, we find that the earliest of the Rosses to arrive were nine men of that ilk who came to Charlestown, Mass., in the latter part of the year 1652. Of these, three were listed as John Ross, two as James Ross, and one each as Dan Ross, Jonas Ross, Alester Ross, and David Ross. The last four names do not appear again on any record yet found; either they left no descendants, or their names became so changed that they could not be recognized.

In studying the old records of this section of New England, it must be remembered that the clerks or scribes were occasionally careless in recording and in spelling names. The name Ross often became confused with other family names, such as Rolfe, Rose, Russ and Roff.

In 1652 the ship *John and Sarah* arrived in Boston harbour with 272 Scotsmen who had been taken prisoner by Oliver Cromwell in the battle of Worchester,[1] 1651. It will be recalled that David twelfth Chief of Balnagowan and the survivors of his regiment were among the prisoners taken in that disastrous battle. A few of these Ross-shire volunteers along with their families were put aboard the *John and Sarah* as colonists for the new land. Given their freedom on arrival, they settled down in the vicinity of Boston.

After 1652 the names of other Ross families appear on the records. James Ross of Sudbury, 1654; James Ross of Falmouth, Maine, about 1657; John Ross of Kittery, Maine, about 1660; John Ross of Ipswich, Mass. 1662; John Ross of Malden, 1662; John Ross of Boston, 1658; Thomas Ross of Cambridge, 1656; Killicross Ross of Ipswich, 1654; Fennell Ross of Ipswich, 1662; and John Ross of Plymouth, Mass., 1658. These Highland soldiers formed the nucleus of the New England Rosses in the seventeenth century.

The births of 52 children of these ten men are recorded, and of this number, ten were sons who lived to manhood and whose names appear in the record books of the several towns in which they lived. Many of the Ross families in Massachusetts today find their ancestors among these pioneers.

Four of these pioneer Rosses have left a large number of descendants who have become scattered to various sections of New England. Of one family, that of James Ross of Sudbury, more than two thousand descendants who retain the name of Ross have been traced; they have lived in Sudbury, Lancaster, Sterling, Bolton, Deerfield, Newton, Templeton, and several other towns in Massachusetts, as well as in Jaffrey, N.H., and in St. Johnsbury, V. Descendants of John Ross of Ipswich are found in large numbers in Windham Country, Conn. Thomas Ross of Cambridge removed to Billerica, Mass., where his descendants were well known for more than two hundred years. They chiefly settled in the towns of Concord, Lancaster and Petersham, in Massachusetts. Killicross Ross of Ipswich left descendants, who were recorded on the town's books and numbered more than 150 in 1880. A few of these remain residents of the old town, while others have settled in Maine and New Hampshire.

From the year 1662 until about 1705, apparently no immigrant Scottish settlers by the name of Ross came into the Massachusetts area. About this latter date many Scotch and Scotch-Irish came to America, among them Reverend George Ross of Balblair, and John Ross, from Sligo, Ireland. The latter settled in the town of Berwick, Maine where

[1] For further reference see page 74.

his descendants can still be traced. Later Alexander Ross and his brother James, born in Stroma Scotland, about 1750, settled in Maine, Alexander in Portland and James in Gorham, both leaving a large number of descendants.

The Scots emigrated to the New England States in larger numbers in the late 1700's and early 1800's. In 1773 four hundred Highlanders from Glengarry, Glen Morrison, Glen Urquhart and Strathglass sailed for America in the *Pearl*, a frigate of the Royal Navy, and landed at the port of New York. This expedition was organized by three brothers named MacDonell and it included many other MacDonells as well as Camerons, Grants, Chisholms, MacIntyres, Fergusons, and Rosses. The party had been in communication with Sir William Johnson who owned a large tract of land in the Mohawk Valley, and he gave the Highlanders permission to settle on these lands, where they prospered. Many of the present families in Massachusetts, New Hampshire and Vermont may trace their origins to these early Scotch and Scotch-Irish colonists.

## THE BALBLAIR ROSSES, EARLY AMERICAN COLONISTS 1651-1911

Many of the Rosses of Balblair, a cadet branch of Clan Ross, descended from Hugh fourth Chief of Balnagowan, became outstanding citizens both in Scotland and in America, where some of them emigrated in the early years of the eighteenth century. An American historian has truly said that this family of Rosses was probably the most noted of their day, in the American colonies. The *Reverend George Ross* of the family of Balblair was one of the fathers of the Church of England in America in the early eighteenth century. His grandson *Colonel George Ross* was one of the signatories of the American Declaration of Independence and afterwards became Chief Justice of Delaware. *Betsy Ross,* widow of Col. George Ross's brother John, made the first American flag, which was later approved by the Congress of the United States. Other Balblair Rosses became distinguished soldiers in the war between the North and the South, and one, a lawyer, became Vice-President of the State of Pennsylvania. Two Balblair Rosses became outstanding medical doctors. The biographies of only a few of the members of this important family are given.

### *Andrew Ross, first laird of Balblair*

He was a younger son of George Ross, fifth laird of Balmuchy. He was twelfth in lineal descent from Hugh of Rarichies, first Baron of Balnagowan, Chief of the ancient Clan Ross, and heir male to the Earldom of Ross. Andrew Ross's descent was by the Rosses of Balnagowan, through William of Little Allan, Shandwick and Balmuchy. See chart page 62.

*David Ross, second of Balblair*

He was the eldest son of Andrew Ross, had as issue: (1) Andrew Ross, (2) George Ross, (3) Hugh Ross, and (4) Elizabeth, who married David Munro.

*Andrew Ross, third of Balblair*

He was the eldest son of David, was succeeded by his only son, Andrew.

*Dr. Andrew Ross, fourth laird*

Dr. Ross practiced medicine in Jamaica where he died without issue and was succeeded by his uncle George, second son of David.

*Rev. George Ross, fifth of Balblair*

He was born at the Balblair homestead in 1679. Since this laird was one of the most important of the Balblair Rosses who carried the clan line to the new world, a few facts about him are in order. A precocious boy, he attended grammar school at an early age, determined to be a "scholar". He took his M.A. in Edinburgh in 1700 and three years after that graduated from the Divinity School. At this point he broke with his Scottish tradition and entered the Church of England. From London he secured a position as chaplain in the Royal Navy. He then applied to the "Royal Society for Propagating the Gospel in Foreign Parts" and was sent, in 1705, as a missionary to New Castle on the Delaware, in Pennsylvania. There he founded the Parish of New Castle and was its rector until his death in 1753.

George Ross visited Scotland in 1710, and while returning to America the following year, he was taken prisoner at sea by a French man-of-war, and kept under custody in France for a time. After his release he returned to America and became one of the fathers of the Church of England in America. In this service he had a long and honourable career.

The Reverend George Ross married first, Joanna Williams of Delaware in 1706, and by her had six children: (1) David Ross, who married Sarah Rolfe (he predeceased his father), (2) Margaret Ross, (3) Hon. John Ross, who married Elizabeth Morgan, (4) Rev. Aneas Ross, who married Sarah Leach, (5) Susanna Ross, and (6) Dr. Jacob Ross, who married Jane Sayre. All these children had issue.

George Ross married, secondly, Catherine Van Gezel of Delaware, granddaughter of Cornelius Van Gezel, a Dutchman, who was the nephew and secretary of Jacob Alricks, the Governor of the Dutch colony on the Delaware. By her he had five children: (1) Colonel George Ross, who married Ann Lawler, (2) Gertrude Ross, (3) Catherine Ross, who married General William Thompson, (4) Elizabeth Ross, (5) Mary Ross. All of these children also had issue.

Brief biographies of some of the distinguished children of the Rev. George Ross are given.

*Hon. John Ross, 1711-1776,* educated by his father, studied law and established himself in practice in Philadelphia, where he became known as one of the ablest attorneys in the colonies, and amassed a large fortune. He was at one time the legal representative of the Penns, and Attorney-General for the lower counties on the Delaware. His sympathies were with the King's party at the outbreak of the Revolution, but he felt the colonies had some just reasons for complaint. He died early in 1776, too early in the struggle for liberty, for us to form any conclusions as to what stand he would have taken. John Adams of Massachusetts in his diary (September 25, 1775) speaks of him as "a lawyer of great eloquence and an extensive practice, a great Tory, but now they say beginning to be converted" (to the viewpoint of the colonies).

In 1764, Hugh Ross, laird of Shandwick, in writing to the Hon. John Ross of Philadelphia, said: "My house of Little Allan and Shandwick is two hundred and ninety years from the Earls of Ross and Barony of Rarichies and Balnagowan. You John stand cadet of the decayed house of Ballamuchy. The Balblair Estates were purchased by my brother, as it was part of his house originally. Your uncle, Andrew Ross of Balblair, long since dead, left an only son, Andrew Ross, Doctor of Medicine at Kingston in Jamaica, also dead there without heirs. So that I think you must be the male representative of that house (Balblair), and as I find that your house of Balblair is descended from mine of Shandwick, I send you an account thereof, herewith, not inferior to any extent as your father truly tells you. My eldest brother dying a bachelor, you shall find me his heir, as the Historiographer of Scotland's deductions show".

*Margaret Ross* second child of Rev. George Ross married first the Rev. Walter Hackett and secondly the Rev. William Currie. Both were well-known Church of England clergyman of Scottish birth, they served in America in the "Society for Propagating the Gospel in Foreign Parts".

*Rev. Aneas Ross* followed his father in the ministry of the Church of England, and succeeded him as Rector of the church at New Castle, where he remained until his death. His son, John, married a young Quakeress named Elizabeth Griscom in 1774, and left her a childless widow in 1776, having lost his life during a defence of Philadelphia. It was John's widow, *Betsy Ross,* who made for the Congress the first Stars and Stripes.

*Colonel George Ross (1730-1779)* was another of the sons of the Reverend George Ross fifth laird of Balblair. At Philadelphia he studied law under his half brother John and in 1751 he moved to Lancaster where he began a career in law.

He was appointed Crown Prosecutor for Lancaster and other interior counties of the Province of Pennsylvania, and very soon established a reputation as an able attorney. Judge Ross was then elected a member of the Pennsylvania Assembly and continued to take a leading part in its proceedings until it was dissolved after the beginning of the Revolution. He was elected to the first Continental Congress in 1774, and held his seat until 1777, when ill health compelled him to retire. At this time the citizens of Lancaster voted him a piece of silver plate to cost £150, but he declined it on the ground that "it was the duty of each man, especially of every representative of the people to contribute by every means within his power to the welfare of his country without expecting pecuniary reward". In 1776 Colonel George Ross was one of the fifty-six Americans who pledged their lives, their fortunes, and their sacred honour in the historic document, the *Declaration of Independence.* In 1779 he was appointed Judge of the Court of Admiralty of Pennsylvania but died suddenly a few months later at his country seat near Philadelphia.

*Gertrude Ross,* a daughter of the Reverend George Ross, married Thomas Till, Esq., son of a leading citizen of Pennsylvania; and after his death she married Hon. George Read of Delaware, one of the foremost statesmen of his day. He succeeded her brother, John, as Attorney-General under the Crown for the lower counties on Delaware, and sat in the first and second Continental Congresses. The Hon. George Read was also one of the signers of the Declaration of Independence. He was one of the very few American Statesmen who signed all three of the great State papers on which the Government rests: the original petition of Congress to the King in 1774, the Declaration of Independence, and the Constitution of the United States. He was Judge of the United States Court of Appeals in Admiralty, Chief Justice of Delaware, and one of the first Senators of the United States.

*Elizabeth Ross* married Colonel Edward Riddle, a lawyer by profession, a soldier in the French and Indian Wars, member of, and last speaker of the Pennsylvania Assembly, and member of the first and second Congresses of the United States. Because of ill-health, Colonel Riddle resigned from Congress in the latter part of June, 1776, just before the Declaration of Independence was signed, and thus lost the great honour of signing it. He was again elected to Congress in 1778 and 1779, but his bad health prevented him taking his seat, and he died in September of the latter year.

*Susanna Ross* married Rev. William Thomson, D.D., cousin of General Thompson, although he spelled his name without the "p". He was educated in England and entered the Church. After his ordination by the Bishop of London he joined the "Society for Propagating the Gospel in Foreign Parts", was sent to America, and became first Rector of the Parish of Carlisle, Pennsylvania. He espoused the cause of the colonies and was a very well-known Churchman until his death in 1786.

*Mary Ross* married Colonel Mark Bird of Birdsboro, one of Pennsylvania's early ironmasters. He was a public-spirited citizen, a member of the Pennsylvania Assembly, Chairman of its Committee of Safety during the Revolution, and a Colonel of Pennsylvanian troops during that struggle. He served as Assistant Quartermaster-General of the Continental Army under Major-General Thomas Mifflin, and advanced much money for the cause from his private purse.

*Dr. Jacob Ross* another son of the Reverend George Ross was a well-known and highly respected doctor of medicine in Delaware in the later half of the 18th century.

The following three United States Senators were also descendants of the Rosses of Balblair.

*James Ross,* Senator of Pennsylvania, was a friend and advisor of President Washington, and one of the foremost men in the early life of the American nation. *Edmund Gibson Ross* of Kansas was a member of the Senate during the administration of President Andrew Johnson. His deciding vote in the impeachment proceedings saved President Johnson from expulsion from office. *Jonathan Ross* of Vermont, Chief Justice of the Supreme Court of that State, took his seat in the Senate during President McKinley's administration, and was a controlling force in shaping the national policy in the matter of annexation of conquered territory.

Senator James Ross died in 1847. In that year, Edmund Gibson Ross and Jonathan Ross were each entering upon their twenty-first year. While these last two Senators were born in the same year (1826), their terms in the United States Senate were nearly forty years apart. James Ross died at the age of 85; Edmund Gibson Ross at 81, and Jonathan Ross at 79. The lives of these statesmen, their sacrifices and accomplishments form an interesting chapter in the annals of Clan Ross in America.

*Elizabeth Ross,* better known as Betsy, was born in Philadelphia, January 1, 1752 to Samuel and Rebecca Griscom. She was destined to play an important role in American history. Her father, a member of the

Society of Friends, was a noted builder, having assisted in the erection of Independence Hall.

Betsy was fond of embroidery, and other artistic and delicate needle work. After her marriage in 1773 to John Ross, a nephew of Hon. George Ross, they started an upholstery business in Philadelphia. They conducted this business until January 1776, when John Ross died from an injury received while guarding military stores at Philadelphia.

The young widow continued the business alone. In June 1776, Congress appointed a committee to design a suitable flag for the young nation. This committee consisted of General Washington, Robert Morris and Hon. George Ross. At the suggestion of Col. Ross, the committee went to the shop of Betsy Ross, at 239 Arch Street, and engaged her to make the flag from a design that had been drawn up by Washington and Colonel Ross. The drawing represented the outlines of a flag of thirteen stripes and thirteen six-pointed stars. Mrs. Ross suggested changing the stars from six to five points, because one could cut them out so much easier. She illustrated this by deftly folding a piece of paper, and producing a five-pointed star with a single snip of the scissors. Her sample flag was accepted by the committee, and adopted as the national flag by Congress, June 14, 1777.

After this Betsy Ross received the contract to make all government flags and held it for many years. Her daughter, Mrs. Clarissa Wilson, continued the business until 1857. Mrs. Ross was married for the second time to Captain Ashburn, and for the third time to John Claypole. She died in Philadelphia, January 30, 1836.

## The Rosses of Bladensburg

Another distinguished family of Rosses who saw military service in the United States were the Rosses of Bladensburg. Two of the more illustrious members will be briefly discussed here.

### *Major-General Robert Ross of Bladensburg 1741-1814*

Major-General Robert Ross had a very distinguished military career during the war of 1812. The Duke of Wellington placed him in command of the British troops who were sent to America in 1814, after Napoleon's defeat in Europe. Their mission was to converge on Washington, and in this way to relieve the military pressure which was being exerted on Canada. The troops numbering 4,500 disembarked at Chesapeake Bay and marched toward Washington, where they were met by the American Army at Bladensburg about five miles north of the capital. The British won the battle and the American militia fled in disorder. General Ross then proceeded to Washington where he burned part of the White House, in reprisal for the conduct of the American militia in Canada. In the following month the British attempted to land at Baltimore but they were defeated and General Ross was killed.

Like many other actions in the war of 1812, however, the Chesapeake campaign had very little serious effect on the final outcome, as it was considered mainly a diverting action.

General Ross will long be remembered as a brave and fearless soldier. In place of the contempt for the British which had grown up in America after the War of Independence, he is credited with fostering a new admiration for the British soldier, and for the military tactics of their generals. A year after his death his widow and descendants were granted the addition of "Bladensburg" to their name as a reward for his loyalty, ability, and valour. A granite column was raised to the memory of General Ross at Rostrevor, his birthplace in County Down, North Ireland. His heraldic shield is shown on page 175.

*Lt.Col. Sir John Ross of Bladensburg, K.C.B., K.C.V.O. 1848-1927*

Sir John was a grandson of Major-General Robert Ross. He was born in 1848 and educated at Radley, where he rowed in the School Eight in 1865. He went to Woolwich and joined the Royal Artillery, transferring to the Coldstream Guards in 1873. His essay on "The Causes which have led to the Pre-eminence of Nations in War" won the Gold Medal of the Royal United Services Institution. He wrote the history of the Coldstream Guards from 1815 to 1885 and shortly before he died in 1927 he completed the history of the regiment during the First World War. In 1903 he was created K.C.B. and in 1911 K.C.V.O.

Sir John Ross was also a noted horticulturist. He was an authority on trees, shrubs, and rare tropical plants of many varieties. His large garden at Rostrevor, Ireland, covered an area of about seventy acres and contained rare and beautiful flowering plants which he had collected from many parts of the world. His knowledge and skill enabled him to obtain results which were often envied by the gardeners at Kew and attracted enthusiasts from distant lands. According to his biographer, Brigadier-General H. W. Studd, Sir John will be remembered as a great Guardsman, a great horticulturist, and a great gentleman.

## EARLY COLONIZATION IN CANADA

Britain gained Acadia and the Hudson's Bay territory in North America by the treaty of 1713 that ended the War of the Spanish Succession. The way was thus opened again for an attempt at settlement by British emigrants, and in the later years of the eighteenth century two strong causes operated to stimulate a real effort at colonization on the Atlantic sea-board.

The first was the failure of the Stuart cause in the Rebellions of 1715 and 1745. After 1745 the English Government took strong measures to subdue the Scots. By the third Disarming Act they were compelled to surrender all their arms, and were forbidden to wear the kilt or speak Gaelic. The old clan system and the heritable jurisdiction were broken up. This Act, more effectively enforced than the first two, brought an end to the old feuds and quarrels, but it left many proud and war-like Scots feeling angry and humiliated, and in no mood to settle down to a farmer's life. They saw in the New World a new outlet for their energies.

The second impetus developed with the Clearances (or Enclosure) Acts. Local squires got the government to pass legislation by which they could buy up and then fence in the village lands for their own development. This meant that the peasants lost their own small and scattered holdings, as well as their use of the "common". The evil applied to Scotland, where some of the Highland chiefs began to copy the southern mode of farming. They ejected the small crofters who had from time immemorial cultivated the land in small glebes, or occupied the fields with small herds of cattle, and threw the whole extent of their possessions into large sheep-grazing farms, under management of agents from the south. This change was the ruin of the peasants. Many men entered the army; others turned to the New World, financed partly by public assistance and partly by their own savings.

The enforced clearing of the lands in Ross and the Isles for sheep-walks proved a great stimulus to emigration. Sir John Lockhart-Ross of Balnagowan as previously mentioned had the questionable honour of being the first to introduce the sheep into the county of Ross in 1762. On his return from the navy with the rank of Vice-Admiral, he decided to try sheep farming in order to increase the revenue of his farms, and thought that the glens of Ross-shire would be admirably suited for grazing. Sir John placed his lands in the charge of a lowlander with considerable experience, and imported a number of Cheviot sheep. The first trials proved successful and other lairds followed his example. Sheep farming soon spread through Easter Ross and northward to Caithness, but in its path it brought great hardship and distress to many of the tenants of the larger estates who were evicted, sometimes quietly, but frequently brutally, by the proprietors.

Many of these evicted crofters were forced to board the ships waiting in the harbours on the west coast, by the Factors who were deputized to execute the writs of removal. The Highland Emigration Society assisted the lairds in clearing their lands and in supplying the emigrant ships. Much suffering and hardship was endured by many of the tenants when they were forced to leave their homes and witness their destruction by the Factor and his men. Some homes were burned and others were levelled to the ground. The reasons and excuses frequently given by the proprietors for the removal of their tenants were non-payment of rent, or poor use of the land.

After the evictions many of the glens and straths of Ross were completely deserted. In later years the Scots accepted the removals as a consequence of progress, even after much of the land that was once their heritage was given over to the deer and sporting reserves.

The first emigrant ship to sail for Nova Scotia after the clearances was the *Hector,* in 1773. The owner of the ship, John Pagan, with a Dr. Witherspoon and other members of the Philadelphia Company, purchased land in Pictou, Nova Scotia, and prepared to settle the new land with Scottish immigrants. They employed a Mr. John Ross as agent to procure settlers. Under the contract, the settlers were to receive a free passage on the *Hector* and a free tract of land in Pictou.

The *Hector* sailed from Loch Broom in Ross-shire where 33 families and 25 single men embarked for the new land. Fifteen of the passengers were Rosses, one of the families being that of Alexander Ross, his wife and two children. Just before sailing a piper came aboard, who had not engaged his passage. The captain ordered him ashore, but the other passengers pleaded with him to allow the piper to remain, and during the long passage of eleven weeks he proved a great boon to the weary colonists, with his cheerful Highland tunes.

All told there were 189 who sailed from Ross-shire in July 1773 with their few belongings, to start a new life in Canada. The crossing was not without its sombre days, however, as smallpox and dysentery broke out on board. Eighteen passengers died on the voyage, most of them children.

The newcomers took up land near the shores of Nova Scotia and hurriedly built their log cabins. The first winter they suffered severely from lack of food and supplies, as many of these necessities had to be brought from the settlement at Truro through miles of forest. The little settlement at Pictou became well established, however, and they soon built a log church at the new Loch Broom in Pictou County where the services were conducted in Gaelic.

### *Scots Settlements at Pictou, Antigonish, and Prince Edward Island*

The good reports sent home to their friends in Scotland by these pioneer families soon brought more ship loads of Scots to Pictou. In 1801, three vessels arrived with 1500 more emigrants from the north of Scotland and soon the entire county of Pictou was occupied by Gaelic-speaking people.

The following passage is quoted from McGregor: "The town and whole district of Pictou are decidedly Scottish. In the streets, within the houses, in the shops and on board the vessels, we hear little but Gaelic and broad Scotch spoken. The Highland dress, the bagpipes and Scotch music are general in this part of the country, while the red gowns of the students, which we see waving here and there, bring the colleges of Aberdeen and Glasgow, with their associations, into recollection."

In 1774 a Scottish settlement began on Ile St. Jean (Prince Edward Island). However, a plague of locusts forced them to remove to Pictou county the following year. After the peace of 1783 many Scots from the 82nd or Hamilton Regiment, who had been on duty at Halifax under General McLean, were disbanded at Halifax and given a grant of land in Pictou called the 82nd grant. Here these Highland and Lowland families settled. The little settlement of Pictou soon began a shipbuilding industry, and in 1798 the *Harriet*, a sturdy vessel of six hundred tons, was launched, —a credit to the Scots who built her.

Early in the 19th century immigration received another great impetus. The Scottish crofters opened up a settlement at Millbrook in Pictou county, and thence the Rosses, Macdonalds and Gordons worked their way to the Middle River. In 1801, large numbers of Highlanders arrived, most of whom finally settled down in Antigonish and to the east. The Mount Thom settlement had names such as Stewart, McLean, McLeod, Urquhart, Macdonald, Fraser, Cameron and so on. During the early years of the century large numbers of Highland settlers were found in this district of Nova Scotia. These settlers came from Sutherland, the parish of Lairg, from Stornaway in Lewis, and the Northwest Highlands. Descendants of these old families are found among the citizens of Halifax, Montreal, Toronto and other Canadian cities and towns. Whole villages were Celtic in origin, and as late as the 1880's the Gaelic tongue could be heard almost as purely among the Canadian pines as in the glens of Inverness-shire or among the boatmen of green Islay itself. Scottish theology had been imported as well as Scottish love of education and habits of self-denial and thrift.

In 1801 the ship *Nora* sailed from Fort William on Loch Linnhe to Pictou, Nova Scotia, with 500 emigrants, after a passage of sixteen weeks. In 1803 the *Favourite* of Kirkaldy arrived from Ullapool with another 500 emigrants. Many hardships were endured by these early settlers. They had neither horses nor oxen, and they themselves were obliged to haul the logs for their houses from the forest. While wheat grew remarkably well, it was very difficult to get it ground into flour. The closest mill was at Guysborough, twenty eight miles from Pictou, and a bushel or two of grain was all that one man could carry on his back.

One method of obtaining colonists for America in these early days is demonstrated by the following damaged document from the Tain archives: 1767 Trial on the Island of Lewis . . . "that upon information by Rev. George Balfour, minister at Tarbat that I was guilty of Bigamy . . . I was committed prisoner by the Tolbooth of Tain . . . under extreme hardship for want of subsistance . . . I am willing and desirous . . . to be banished . . . will save the court trouble and expense. . . . Since petitioner at bar acknowledges the petition . . . personally consents. . . . Sheriff . . . deems the said Donald . . . to any of his Majesty's plantations in America. . . . If he shall return to Ross or Cromarty . . . be put in the pillory and scourged . . . and recommitted to jail until . . . occasion . . . transporting him again."

*John Ross* and *Alexander Ross* were two of the earliest settlers in the Big Brook area (now called Lorne), and the Glengarry area of Pictou, arriving about 1809. The town of Rossfield in Pictou still bears the name of the early settlers. Alexander Ross came to Pictou County from Tain in Ross-shire. His homestead in Lorne was part of the land granted to Charles MacLean in 1810. Ross and his wife, Betty Gunn, had a son, John Ross, who was born in 1846. The Rev. D. K. Ross and the Rev. Wm. A. Ross, early residents of Nova Scotia were descendants of this family. The former clergyman has published a careful genealogy of these early families of Pictou.

One of the earliest settlers in the West River area of Nova Scotia was the *Rev. Duncan Ross.* He was born at Tarbert, Ross-shire, and was educated at Edinburgh University. He was ordained as a missionary to Nova Scotia in 1795 and was in charge of the parish of West River for nearly forty years, until he died in 1834. He was the author of a number of pamphlets dealing with such religious subjects as the modes of baptism. *James Ross,* his son, was born at West River, Nova Scotia in 1811. In 1835 he was ordained a minister of the Presbyterian Church and later became principal of the Presbyterian Theological Seminary at West River, and afterwards at Truro. When this college was merged with Dalhousie College in 1863 he was appointed principal of Dalhousie, and professor of ethics and political economy. He died at Dartmouth, Nova Scotia, in 1886.

At the time of the revolution in the United States whole bands of Loyalists crossed the border to live in Nova Scotia. Restigouche was almost wholly a Scottish County and the names of many of its townships,

Glenelg, Glenliver, Dundee and Campbelltown indicate the districts of Scotland from which the earliest settlers had come.

Once a year in the Canadian maritime settlement, the whole Scottish community would meet to transact business, and then the scene was like a gathering of the clans. The convivial habits and rough hospitality of these Scots was much the same as that of their Highland ancestors, and the Highland dancing in kilts and sporans, to the tunes of the bagpipes, was a rousing sight in the clearings.

A public notice of the first stage coach to operate in Nova Scotia is preserved in the Citadel Archives at Halifax. This notice, dated 1829, announces that "The Eastern Stage Coach will carry passengers from Halifax to Truro and return, three days a week, the fare being five dollars." This notice is signed by the Committee of Management N. Beck, William Corbet and John Ross.

In 1802 the sailing ship *Neptune* with over 700 Scots aboard left Scotland on the long voyage across the Atlantic. These settlers decided to proceed further up the St. Lawrence River, and after docking at Quebec some of them finally settled at Williamstown and others at Glengarry. They were for the most part farmers from Glenelg and Kintail in Ross-shire, hardy stock who were accustomed to farming under adverse conditions. The crossing took four months. Among the hazards of such long voyages, apart from storms and weather, were such diseases as scurvy, which occurred sporadically from lack of fresh vegetables and fruit, and smallpox which occasionally broke out aboard ship, as well as other infectious diseases such as typhoid and cholera.

The *Neptune* arrived at Quebec and the Highland families aboard decided to make a settlement on the slopes of Mount Johnson (later called Chambley Mountain). After a great deal of toil and privation in clearing the land for small farm plots, they found in the following seasons that the land they had chosen was too wet for growing such crops as potatoes and corn, and sixty of the families decided to move to the vicinity of Williamstown, on the south shore of the St. Lawrence River. Here they founded a "Scottish Settlement" in 1816.

### *The Glengarry Settlement*

When the American Revolutionary war broke out large numbers of Highlanders formed the King's Royal Regiment of New York and the 84th Royal Highland Emigrants. At the close of the war these soldiers were offered grants of land in the British territory to the north. As United Empire Loyalists many of them made their way with their wives and children, through the wilderness to the north shore of the St. Lawrence River, just east of the city of Cornwall, Upper Canada, in the present county of Glengarry. They settled in this densely wooded area, building log cabins and hewing out small farms in the rich soil. There were fourteen hundred of these veterans and their families, and among them were twenty families of Rosses. On arrival they contacted the government land agent, and drew lots for their land grants. The government provided food and clothing for three years, as well as seed grain. Saws, axes, and ploughs were also provided, and one cow was alloted for two families.

Friends and relatives back in the Highlands heard of this new and prosperous settlement, and in 1785, five hundred emigrants from Knoydart on the Sound of Sleat arrived in Quebec, aboard the *McDonald,* bound for Glengarry. Other waves of Scottish emigrants followed from Glenelg and Kintail, from Strathglass and the Isle of Skye. Thus in Glengarry in Upper Canada (now Ontario) there grew up a transplanted part of the Highlands, Gaelic in speech and Scottish in custom. Here they could freely wear their native dress and carry arms without restraint.

Many of the Glengarry Highlanders who emigrated to Upper Canada with their wives and families were descendants of the Glengarry Fencible Corps in Scotland. The Fencibles were a Corps for the internal defence of the kingdom. When the regiment was disbanded in 1802, the government decided to send the soldiers and their families as colonists to the island of Trinidad, which had just been ceded to Great Britain. Their chaplain, the Rev. M. Macdonald, had other plans for them, however, and went to London to negotiate with the government for assistance to enable them to emigrate to Upper Canada. He finally secured from the Lieutenant-Governor of Upper Canada a commitment to grant two hundred acres of land to every Highlander who should arrive.

In spite of strong protests which were made by the members of Parliament for Inverness-shire, and other Highland gentlemen, as well as by the Prince of Wales, who was induced to try and dissuade them from leaving Scotland, the greater part of the Glengarry Fencibles emigrated with their wives and families to Upper Canada. They settled in the Glengarry Settlement, calling the district after the name of their native glen. Every head of a family also named his plot of land after the farm he had possessed in Glengarry. Among these pioneers were a few families of Rosses.

In 1812 the *fiery cross* was used to summon the Glengarry Highlanders to repel an American raid on their settlement. This is believed to be the last time the Scots have invoked this old clan custom.

A number of families of Rosses settled in the vicinity of Lancaster in the township of Glengarry, still others settled further inland in the vicinity of Alexandria. In the census of 1852 there were 139 Rosses in the Glengarry settlement.

Peter Ross in 1889 stated: "The places in the Maritime provinces where the Gaelic language prevails or is still largely spoken are the counties of Pictou and Antigonish, Earltown in the county of Colchester, the Island of Cape Breton, Prince Edward Island and some settlements along the Bay of Chaleur in New Brunswick. In Glengarry county in Ontario, Gaelic still continues to be the language of the people and is there spoken as purely as it is in Dingwall or Lewis".

*The Scots Settlement at Red River, Manitoba*

Lord Selkirk's effort to colonize central Canada in the days of the fur traders is a partly thrilling and partly tragic story of hardship and adventure for the Highland Scots who decided to become Canadians. Among these early settlers Clan Ross was represented by a few families.

The great philanthropist and colonizer Lord Selkirk first visited Canada in 1803. On this visit he became so impressed with the possibilities for agricultural and industrial development, that he was soon taking active steps to encourage Scottish families to emigrate to Canada. From the Hudson's Bay Company officials he had reports of the vast central prairie region of Canada with its excellent soil and climate; it seemed an ideal area for Highland crofters.

Lord Selkirk purchased from the Hudson's Bay Company a tract of land, 116,000 square miles in area, in the vicinity of the Red River at the southern end of Lake Winnipeg. Colonists were recruited from Ross-shire, the Islands of Lewis and Skye, Stromness in the Orkney Islands, and Glasgow.

The colonists sailed in the *Edward and Ann*, accompanied by two Hudson's Bay Company ships, the *Prince of Wales* and the *Eddystone*, which carried employees and supplies for the Canadian fur trade.

In June 1811 the three ships set sail from Stromness on the historic voyage. There were in all only seventy colonists, as some deserted the ships just before sailing. The voyage took sixty-one days from Stornaway, on the east coast of Lewis in Ross-shire, which was the last calling port to pick up the passengers, to York Factory, the trading post on the coast of Hudson's Bay, between the Nelson River and the Hayes River.

The Hudson's Bay Company had a few log buildings for the fur trading operations at this post. As cold weather was approaching, it was decided that the colonists should winter at York Factory rather than attempt the hazardous journey overland to the Red River. Ice was beginning to form on the Bay when the three ships sailed away again, for the return voyage to Scotland on the fifth of October. New log buildings to house the colonists against the severe cold of winter were immediately built. Scurvy broke out during the winter from the lack of fresh vegetables but the Islanders were told to drink a brew made from the sap of spruce trees and this controlled the outbreak. This "spruce beer", which was none too palatable, had to be taken throughout the winter.

Lord Selkirk had chosen Miles Macdonnell, a United Empire Loyalist from Glengarry in Upper Canada, to conduct his colonists from York Factory on Hudson's Bay, to the Red River settlement. Governor Macdonnell kept the colonists employed during the long winter months building four river boats for the journey to the Red River. Food was in short supply but towards spring the local Indians supplied the colonists with venison, a great improvement over the salt meat rations which they had brought with them.

When the spring ice broke in the rivers, the party took off in their "York boats". They rowed up the Hayes and Steel Rivers to the Hill River, then via the Jacktent River to Knee Lake. To portage these heavy, awkward boats past the many rapids and falls on the rivers was a long and arduous task. The difficult Fall Portage on the Trout River was a great trial to the colonists, but after passing the height of land, travelling became easier as the rivers flowed south toward their destination at Red River.

After about two months the colonists reached the Hudson's Bay Fort of Norway House, at the northern end of Lake Winnipeg; this first sign of civilization greatly encouraged them. The weary band finally arrived at the Pembina River where it joins the Red, and chose a site for a fort.

Governor Macdonnell sent a report to Lord Selkirk that as soon as the settlement at Pembina took form, a flag staff was erected on the fort and it was named Fort Daer.

The farm plots of the settlers were situated on cleared land, three miles from the Pembina Colony; this caused considerable inconvenience to the colonists, but they soon had a thriving little community established.

Buffalo meat was in good supply and was brought to the settlement by friendly Indians and French-Canadian trappers.

In 1813 a second band of settlers was sent out by Lord Selkirk. After a hazardous journey on the *Prince of Wales* where ship fever broke out; and after the overland trip of more than one hundred miles from Fort Churchill on Hudson's Bay where they disembarked, they finally arrived at York Factory. The heroic band then proceeded to Red River where they received a royal welcome. They had arrived in time to plant potatoes for themselves and the other colonists, who did not have sufficient seed crops for the coming season.

During the second winter the colonists experienced considerable opposition from the North-West Fur Company. The fur traders, who were also living at Pembina, began to show hostility to the new settlers. The hostility grew to such a pitch that after a conclave at their headquarters at Fort William, the Nor'-Westers decided to break up the Red River Settlement and disperse its members. Duncan Cameron, a persuasive U.E. Loyalist who had become a Nor'-Wester, was prevailed upon to try and move the whole Scottish settlement back east to Upper Canada. He pretended to be very friendly with the colonists and ingratiated himself in their good graces with his Gaelic speech. Cameron actually persuaded one hundred and fifty of the two hundred colonists at the Red River Settlement to set out for the Holland River, and the St. Thomas area, in Upper Canada, a distance of nearly a thousand miles. They took the old fur trader's route to Fort William, then made their way along the north shore of Lake Superior to Sault Ste. Marie, and continued along the shore of Lake Huron to Penetanguishene on Georgian Bay. Here winter overtook them, and their Indian guides showed them how to build windbreaks and shelters. After three and a half months on the journey through the wilderness, they followed the new military road the government had built from Penetanguishene to Holland Landing. The weary Scots finally halted at Holland Landing, some forty miles north of Toronto, in the year 1815. The government gave a number of them grants of land in the Holland River Valley and provided them with sufficient clothing, provisions, and farming implements, for one year. Other colonists moved on to West Gwillimbury Township, where they received grants of land in the Talbot settlement near St. Thomas.

At the Red River, meanwhile, the Nor'-Westers had burned down the settlement, but under the leadership of John McLeod, the remaining colonists successfully drove off their enemies, and started re-building the fort and log cabins. It is not known whether any Rosses were amongst the twenty settlers who were killed by the North-West Company's traders at the massacre of Seven Oaks. In 1817 Lord Selkirk travelled all the way from his home on St. Mary's Isle on Solway Firth and visited his colonists at Red River. He did all he could to encourage them to stand their ground, and promised to send other colonists to help build up the settlement. Among the settlers who met Lord Selkirk at the Red River was George Ross from Kildonan.

Further hardships were in store for these Red River colonists. In July 1818, a plague of grasshoppers destroyed all the wheat, oat, and barley crops, and the unfortunate settlers were left without seed grain for the following year, as well as a shortage of cereal grain for daily consumption. To obtain these essentials, a party of the Highlanders had to travel all the way to an American settlement in Minnesota.

A system of government was set up by Governor Simpson for the colonists at Red River and Sheriff Alexander Ross was one of the men appointed to the council of Assiniboia. This Council, appointed in 1835, booked legislation which was most beneficial to the Red River community. In 1821, the two fur trading companies had amalgamated under the name of the Hudson Bay Company, thus ending the rivalry which had so bedeviled the colony. Alexander Ross a very colourful Scot was the chief spokesman for the community at this time. He was born in Nairnshire, Scotland, in 1783 and in 1805 was one of the Highlanders who first emigrated to the settlement in Glengarry, near Cornwall. He remained only a short time at Glengarry, when he joined Astor's expedition to Oregon in 1810. He sailed around Cape Horn, and finally arrived at British Columbia. Here he joined the Hudson's Bay Company as a fur trader and soon rose to be an officer in the Company. He married the daughter of an Indian chief at Okanagan, travelled across the Rocky Mountains with his young wife, and finally arrived at the Red River settlement. He was given a free gift of a farm by Sir George Simpson, the governor, which is said to have been situated in the vicinity of Ross Street in present-day Winnipeg. Ross had considerable literary ability; he has vividly described life at the settlement, the buffalo hunt, the Red River carts, and other features of prairie life.

The little community was greatly distressed, particularly at times when marriages, births, and deaths occurred, to be without the services of an ordained minister of the Scottish Presbyterian Church. After many letters had been sent by Alexander Ross and others to Scotland, the Reverend John Black finally arrived at Red River in 1857, and stayed at the hospitable home of Alexander Ross until his own house could be built. The next year, the colonists erected the first Presbyterian Church of Kildonan, which still stands. Rev. Black afterwards married Alexander Ross's daughter.

A James Ross was Chairman of the Red River settlement in 1863; he presented a brief to the Canadian Government urging the building of a railway from Fort William to the settlement. He suggested that this railway should follow the regular fur trade route that the Nor'-Westers and the Hudson's Bay Company had used for many years.

*Members of Clan Ross in the Hudson's Bay Company and in the Nor'Westers*

Six Highland Rosses were among the early pioneers and fur traders with the Hudson's Bay Company. *Malcolm Ross* explored and trapped for the Hudson's Bay Company at Cumberland House as early as 1774.

He was a member of the party that, under great hardship, explored the Athabaska territory. This exploration over long portages, such as the thirteen-mile portage of Portage La Loche, tested to the utmost the strength and stamina of the "Voyageurs" in their long canoes. These expeditions have been perpetuated in many early Canadian folk songs and stories of the West. Malcolm was originally a tacksman from Ross-shire.

*John Ross* was one of the earliest of the Canadian fur traders. His name first appears in the fur trade licences in Canada in 1779 when he was placed in charge of the Athabaska district. He was killed in a fight with some men of the North-West Company in 1787.

*William Ross* was also a fur trader with the Hudson's Bay Company. He was born in Ross-shire, about 1780 and served with the Eleventh Regiment of Foot for some years. After entering the service of the Hudson's Bay Company, he was placed in charge of the post at Oxford House. Later he took charge of Nelson House and finally presided at Fort Churchill. He died at Ottawa in 1855.

*Charles Ross*, was born at Kingcraig, Inverness-shire, Scotland. He was a clerk with the North-West Company in 1818 and was stationed at Norway House. After the union of the North-West and Hudson's Bay Companies, he was stationed at Rainy Lake. In 1824 he was transferred to New Caledonia and appointed chief trader in 1831. Charles Ross was put in charge of the building of Fort Victoria in 1843 and died there the following year.

*Donald Ross* was Chief Factor for the Hudson's Bay Company at Norway House in 1841, where he contributed greatly in building up successful fur trade in this area.

Another member of the Clan Ross in the employ of the Hudson's Bay Company was Mr. *B. R. Ross*. He became a trusted executive and was Chief Factor at Fort Simpson in 1850. The Ross River, a tributary of the Anderson River, was named in his honour.

## CLAN ROSS SOCIETY IN AMERICA

In 1910 a number of prominent American and Canadian citizens were assembled at an inaugural meeting in New York City to establish the *Clan Ross in America*. Sir George William Ross LLD., Premier of Ontario, was elected the first president. Alexander Ross MacMahon of Devon, Pennsylvania was secretary and historian, and Raymond S. Ross of Elizabeth, New Jersey was Treasurer.

Sir George Ross died in 1914 and at the second meeting of the Clan two years before a slate of distinguished officers were elected.

Alexander Ross MacMahon, the secretary, published a very comprehensive year book in 1914, in which he outlined the early history of Clan Ross in Scotland and gave short summaries of the genealogy, and positions held by the officers of the Clan in the United States and Canada. In an interesting section of the Clan Ross Year Book, MacMahon quotes some of the early statistics of the Old Massachusetts Bay Colony for the year 1651. "In the first census taken in this area there are ten families listed under the name of Ross. Four of these pioneer Rosses of 1651 have left a large number of descendants, who settled in various cities in New England.

"Many families of the Rosses of Balblair who emigrated from Scotland to America before the disastrous battle of Worcester, or who were sent to America as colonist prisoners by Cromwell after the battle joined the Massachusetts Bay Colony, and their descendants in later years formed the nucleus of Clan Ross in America."

Short accounts of the two Presidents and three of the Vice-Presidents of Clan Ross in America are given. The accomplishments of these distinguished officers reflect a proud record of achievement, and bring honour to the descendants of the Rosses of Balblair and to the clan at large.

### Senator Sir George William Ross, K.B., LL.D.
### (1841 - 1914)

*First President of Clan Ross in America*

Sir George William Ross LL.D., Premier of Ontario and Liberal leader in the Dominion Senate, had a many sided personality. He was, in the early days, a zealous educationalist; later he became a diligent legislator, a forceful debater and a far-seeing statesman. He was born near Nairn, Middlesex County, Ontario in 1841. His father was James Ross and his mother's maiden name was Ellen McKinnon. They were natives of Ross-shire, and came to Canada in 1832. In 1879, at an age when most men are settling down to the routine of middle life, he returned to college and took his matriculation in Law at Albert College, Belleville, and was graduated from that institution in 1883 with the degree of LL.B. In 1883, Mr. Ross was sworn in as Minister of Education in the Government of Sir Oliver Mowat.

Sir George Ross was the author of several important works including, *A History of the School System of Ontario, A Report of the Schools of England and Germany, The Making of the Canadian Constitution,* and *The Historical Significance of the Plains of Abraham.*

He was elected Vice-President of the British Association for the Advancement of Science and was one of the founders of the Canadian Educational Association. He was elected a Fellow of the Royal Society

## OFFICERS OF CLAN ROSS IN AMERICA 1911-1914

*Honorary Chieftain*
Sir Charles Ross of Balnagowan, Baronet.
Balnagowan Castle, Ross-shire, Scotland.

*First President*
Senator Sir George W. Ross,
Premier of Ontario.

*Second President*
Hon. Leonard Warren Ross,
Boston, Massachusetts.

*Vice-Presidents*
Commodore James Ross, C. E.
Montreal, Canada.

Senator William Ross,
Halifax, Nova Scotia.

Rear Admiral Albert Ross,
United States Navy,
Clarion, Pa.

Hon. David H. Ross,
Philadelphia, Pa.

Captain-Commandant Worth Gwynn Ross
New Bedford, Mass.

Judge Nesbitt S. Ross,
Superior Court,
York, P.A.

Hon. William Roderick Ross, M.P.P.
Minister of Lands
Victoria, B.C., Canada.

Samuel Ross,
Washington, D.C.

Edwin James Ross,
East Orange, N.J.

Dr. Arthur E. Ross, M.P.P.,
Provincial Legislature,
Toronto, Canada.

Hon. Duncan Campbell Ross, M.P.
Ottawa, Canada

Judge William M. Ross,
Supreme Court,
State of New York.

*Secretary and Historian*
Alexander Ross MacMahon,
Devon, Pa.

*Treasurer*
Raymond S. Ross,
Elizabeth, N.J.

of Canada in 1896. Knighthood was conferred upon him by King George in 1910. He was the recipient of the honorary degree of Doctor of Laws from a number of Universities including St. Andrews, (Scotland), University of Toronto, and Queen's University.

Sir George was survived by Lady Ross, whose maiden name was Mildred Peel, sister of the eminent painter, Paul Peel. In addition to his two sons, Mr. D. C. Ross, M.P. and Dr. G. W. Ross, Sir George was survived by five daughters. Dr. G. W. Ross worked for some time in the research laboratories of The University of Toronto with Sir Frederick Banting, endeavouring to find a serum for the cure of tuberculosis.

At the funeral of Sir George Ross, Colonel Sir Henry Pellatt officially represented the Duke of Connaught. Among other notables of Church and State who attended the funeral were the Sons of Scotland, the Gaelic Society and the Clan Ross in America. All paid tribute to this great statesman.

Following is a letter from Sir George Ross, First President of Clan Ross in America, to the Secretary of the Clan:—

My dear Clansman;

Office of the Premier
Ontario
May 6th, 1913

I am delighted to learn of your successful efforts in organizing our fellow-clansmen in the United States and Canada. The patriotic spirit which the Scottish race exhibits in all parts of the world, comes, in my opinion, from the traditional feeling that no matter where they reside, they are still clansmen and feel in their veins the emotions of devotion to each other which were necessary in the early history of the race. To be a clansman in the true sense of the word means a sense of brotherhood, ready in any emergency to repell an invader, to protect the weak, and assist a fellow clansman in adversity or need. This feeling of brotherhood is an inheritance to be prized and is a never failing fountain of loyalty which is calculated to promote unity in national affairs and a spirit of kindness and citizenship in all its forms and duties. In bringing together the members of the Clan Ross you are promoting this unity and connecting a new land with the traditions of a race whose skill in arms and art and song have given them a place in the history of the world, of which our fellow clansmen, I am sure, are proud. In this history the Clan Ross has played its part. To recall the story of their achievements and of the race to which they belong is the object of our Association. What has made Scotland great will make your country and my country great. Energy of character, integrity of purpose, nobility of ideals and a conscience void of offense before God and man, are qualifications for the citizenship which is our desire to cultivate, and if these qualities prevail and maintain the ascendency, no future declaration of independence will be necessary to perpetuate the honour and glory of either country.

Yours truly,
GEORGE W. ROSS PRES.

## COMMODORE JAMES ROSS, C.E. 1858-1913
*First Vice-President of Clan Ross in America*

James Ross was born at Cromarty, Scotland. His father was Captain John Ross, shipowner and merchant. James received his early education in engineering at Inverness Academy and in England. After spending some years in railway construction and harbour work in Great Britain, he came to America in 1870 and was appointed chief engineer of the Delaware Railway.

His efficency as a railroad engineer became known to many other companies and he was soon appointed to other staff positions. He was made general manager of the Victoria Railway in 1878 and at the same time he was consulting engineer for the Ontario and Quebec Railway. Since it seemed that his field of operations was to be largely in Canada, he moved his home to Montreal.

James Ross's crowning achievement occurred in 1883 when he was given the contract for the construction of the Canadian Pacific Railway west of Winnipeg, and in the short space of two years completed the line over the Rocky Mountains to Vancouver.

Mr. Ross was associated with many outstanding Canadians in his vast railroading enterprises. He was a lifelong friend of Sir Sanford Fleming and had intimate dealings with Sir William Van Horne, Sir Thomas Shaughnessy, and Donald Smith, later Lord Strathcona.

After taking up residence in Montreal in 1888 he contracted and built the Regina and Long Lake Railway and in 1889 he supervised the construction of the Calgary and Edmonton Railway.

In 1892 James Ross directed his energies to the street railways of Toronto and Montreal. He and Sir William Mackenzie purchased the Toronto Street Railway which then consisted of small, horse-driven open cars, running on tracks. He converted these to the electric system. Ross then made the same change-over for the Montreal Street Railway and later for the street car services of Winnipeg, Man., and St. John, N.B.

In 1896, Mr Ross again joined Sir William Mackenzie in the purchase of the tramway systems of Birmingham, England and formed the City of Birmingham Tramways Company for the operation of the road under an electric system. This was followed by a charter from the Government of Jamaica to built electric tramways on the island.

In later years James Ross took an active interest in the coal and iron industries of Cape Breton Island, where he foresaw great possibilities in the development of these natural resources. He became Vice-President of the Dominion Coal Company and managing director of the Dominion Iron and Steel Company in 1901. He sold his interests in the Coal Company for over four and one half million dollars in 1909.

As Commodore, Ross took an active interest in yachting and was the owner of the *Glencairn,* which won the Seawanhaka-Corinthian Cup in American waters in 1896. He was Commodore of the Royal St. Lawrence Yacht Club for many years. He also owned a handsome sea-going yacht in which he sailed to the Mediterranean on his vacations.

James Ross married Annie Ker of Kingston, New York, and had one son, J. K. L. Ross. He was an adherent of the Presbyterian Church in Montreal.

Commodore James Ross considered it a great honour when he was elected Vice-President of Clan Ross in America. After his death the annual gathering of the Society, held at New York City, May 23rd., 1914 passed the following resolution:

"James Ross was a man, useful to his fellow beings, energetic, effective and enormously capable in all his undertakings; a true captain of industry; a nation builder, loved and honoured and respected by all with whom he came in contact; resourceful of mind and powerful in execution of the greatest constructive enterprises of his day. Born in the Highlands of old Scotland, he early learned the value of industry and thrift. Honourable in all his dealings he inspired the confidence of the ablest and greatest men in his chosen field of activity. It is not strange that he advanced with giant strides to the zenith of business and industrial accomplishment; yet, amidst all this, the sweet, tender instincts of his nature found abundant expression in art, music and education, and in wholesome sport and recreation. A great man has gone, and Clan Ross gratefully acknowledges its appreciation of his connection with, and interest in, our cause. We most deeply and keenly feel our loss, and sincerely record our appreciation of his long and useful life".

### Hon. Leonard Ross (1856-1917)
*Second President of Clan Ross in America*

The Hon. Leonard Warren Ross, the son of William Johnson and Maria (Loring) Ross, was born at Worcester, Mass., October 5th, 1856. He received his early education in public schools and by private tuition.

At the age of nineteen he moved to Boston, and devoted his energies to landscape architecture, horticulture, forestry and kindred subjects, giving special attention to the development of modern parks. A notable achievement was the reclamation of the vast sand dunes of Cape Cod. In 1898 he was elected to the Massachusetts House of Representatives, and was reelected in 1899. In 1900 he was elected to the Massachusetts State Senate. He served on important committees, and was especially active in railroad, transportation, municipal government, park and public reservations and land title questions.

Mr. Ross was married in 1886 to Florence Adelaide Pierce, of Dorchester, Mass., a lineal descendant of the English colonial family of that name, which came to Boston in 1631. His son, Winthrop Pierce Ross, born in 1893, studied law at Dartmouth College. Mr. Ross was a Republican in political affiliation, and a Scottish and York Rite Mason.

The Hon. Leonard Ross's ancestor was James Ross, one of the many Highland prisoners taken by Cromwell at the battle of Worcester in 1651. Sent out to America as colonists, he and his family settled at Sudbury, Massachusetts.

### Senator William Ross of Halifax, N.S. (1825-1913)
*Vice-President of Clan Ross in America 1911-1912*

Senator Ross was the son of John and Robina Ross and was born at Boulardie Island, Nova Scotia, 1825. John Ross, his father, was a native of Ross-shire, Scotland, and came to Nova Scotia on the sailing vessel *Aurora* in 1816.

William Ross was elected to the House of Assembly in 1859 after winning his first election at Victoria. In 1867 and 1872 he was elected by acclamation to the House of Commons at Ottawa, and was appointed Minister of Militia in the MacKenzie Government in 1873. In the following year he was appointed Collector of Customs at the port of Halifax. He was called to the Dominion Senate in 1906.

In 1855 he married Eliza Moore of North Sydney; they had four sons and a daughter: Peter H. Ross of Lunenburg, Hugh W. Ross of Vancouver, Daniel H. Ross, Canadian Trade Commissioner at Melbourne, Australia, and Dr. James Ross of Halifax. His daughter was Annie H. Ross of Halifax.

Senator Ross remained remarkably vigorous as he grew older, and was a very familiar figure on the streets of Halifax and at public meetings in the city. He had been a Lieutenant-Colonel in the Cape Breton Militia Battalion of Nova Scotia prior to Confederation. One of his notable accomplishments as Minister of Militia was the introduction of the bill for the founding of the Royal Military College at Kingston.

At the second Annual Gathering of the Clan Ross in America, at New York, the following resolution was passed on the death of Senator William Ross of Nova Scotia, who had been elected Vice-President in 1911:

"Therefore be it resolved, that in his death Clan Ross in America has lost a devoted, earnest member and official; one who has given of his best thought, eminating from a rich experience in advancing interests, and who has looked forward to the Clan development with pleasurable anticipation.

Resolved that this resolution be entered in full upon the records of this Gathering, and a copy sent to the bereaved family of the late Senator Ross."

### Hon. David H. Ross (1844-1914)
*Vice-President of Clan Ross in America*

David H. Ross of Philadelphia, one of the most active members of Clan Ross Society since its foundation, was born at Dervock, Co. Antrim, Ireland, in 1844. His parents, John and Jean (Thompson) Ross, were of Scotch-Irish ancestry. Mr. Ross was the seventh of a family of eight sons. In 1860 at the age of sixteen he came to America. He entered the Philadelphia College of Pharmacy, where he was graduated in 1878.

A devout Presbyterian, Mr. Ross took an active interest in the work of the church, and held the place of ruling elder for over forty years. A man of sterling integrity, with the courage to express his convictions on any occasion, Mr. Ross's services and support were always in demand. For years he was staunch supporter of the reform cause in municipal politics, and in 1911 was prevailed upon to become a candidate for Council. He was elected and served his constituents faithfully.

Mr. Ross was a former secretary and treasurer of the Philadelphia Drug Company, and at the time of his death was treasurer of the Druggists' Building and Loan Association.

### Commander J. K. L. Ross of Montreal (1876-1951)

Another Canadian member of Clan Ross in America was James Kenneth Levenson Ross. He was born at Lindsay, Ontario, in 1876, son of Commodore James Ross, the Scottish engineer, whose biography is given in the previous section.

J. K. L. Ross was educated first at the exclusive Bishop's College

School, in English-type private school at Lennoxville, Quebec. In 1893 he entered McGill University, where he showed good academic ability; he also was a star linesman on McGill's 1896 champion football team. He graduated with a Bachelor of Science degree in 1899 and the following year his father sent him to England for further apprenticeship. He returned to Montreal in 1901 and gradually took over the management of a number of his father's extensive business enterprises.

Ross married Ethel Matthews, daughter of a Toronto financier W. D. Matthews, and shortly after his father made him assistant General Manager of the Dominion Coal Company, with mines near Sidney, Nova Scotia.

In 1913 when Ross was thirty-seven years of age his father died and left him almost his entire fortune. Ross ordered a new one hundred foot motor yacht, the *Albacore*, intending to take extended cruises. The outbreak of the First World War changed his plans, however, and he loaned the yacht to the Canadian Navy as a patrol vessel. J. K. L. Ross also purchased the large steam yacht *Tarantula* from the American millionaire W. K. Vanderbilt and gave her to the Canadian Navy as an outright gift. A few months later he bought the steam yacht *Winchester* from a wealthy Englishman, and gave her also to the Navy. He was apparently endeavouring to build up the Canadian Navy patrol boat service as a one man venture. The Navy changed the name of the *Winchester* to the *Grilse*, commissioned Ross as a reserve Lieutenant and gave him command of the vessel. He was at sea in the *Grilse* for two years during the First World War on patrol between Halifax and Bermuda. He did not see naval action while on duty but was twice mentioned in despatches for the seamanlike way he handled her in winter storms and a hurricane. In 1917 the Navy, in recognition of his war services, promoted him to Commander.

On his fortieth birthday Commander Ross inherited the sixteen million dollar balance of his father's fortune. He promptly donated a million dollars to the Royal Victoria Hospital, Montreal, for a new wing in memory of his father. He also donated a large sum to his old school, Bishop's College, and gave substantial amounts to other worthy causes. He became interested in horse-racing and breeding, and built up a breeding farm at Vercheres on the St. Lawrence. For the next few years Commander Ross raced his thoroughbreds, and in 1919, his horse Sir Barton won the Kentucky Derby at Churchill Downs, the Preakness Stakes and Belmont Stakes. This was the first time a Canadian owned horse had ever won these famous races.

Commander Ross and his wife and son James entertained lavishly in their mansion on Peel Street in Mount Royal, Montreal. He also owned an estate in Jamaica with a house that was one of the showplaces of the island. He died in 1951 but the memory of this great sportsman and philanthropist is still fresh in the minds of many Canadians.

Clan Ross in America made plans for a third ceilidh which was to be held at Toronto in 1915, but this meeting had to be cancelled because of the outbreak of the war in Europe.

# 6. OUTSTANDING MEMBERS OF CLAN ROSS

## In Britain

This section is devoted to brief accounts of the lives of other individuals of the Clan Ross from the seventeenth to the twentieth century. It is only possible to include a few of those who have attained positions of distinction not only in Scotland and England, but also in the United States, in the tropics, in Australia and New Zealand, at the Poles, and in Canada.

### *Rev. Alexander Ross: a King's Chaplain (1602-1654)*

Alexander Ross left his native Aberdeenshire to live in London, because of his adherence to Episcopacy. It is conjectured that he was descended from a cadet branch of the Rosses of Balmuchy, the first of whom was Hugh, a younger son of Walter Ross, first of Shandwick.

The Reverend Alexander Ross was appointed chaplain to King Charles I, by Archbishop Laud. While in London he wrote many learned treatises on Christian doctrine, history, mythology and other related subjects. He also was appointed master in the Grammar School at Southampton. Of his many publications he is best known for *Mel Heliconium* or *Poetical Honey from the Weeds of Parnassus* which was published in London in 1642. Other publications were *The Phylosophical Touchstone,* and *Medicus Medicatus* or *The Physician's Religion Cured.* In 1652 he published *The History of the World* in six volumes, which augmented the concurrently published *History of the World* by Sir Walter Raleigh.

Towards the end of his life, Alexander Ross lived at Bramshill with his friend, Sir Andrew Henley. He died in 1654 and was buried in the Chapel of Eversley Church. He had prepared his sepulchre before he died and placed at each corner of the stone a shield bearing, not the three

Lions of the Earls of Ross, but the chevron checky, azure argent, between three water bouqets sable.

The English translation of the epitaph which is engraved in Latin on the stone is as follows:

> "Stop stranger, view this dust, and taught, you'll see
> What I am now, what have been, what shall be.
> I have been dew, and dust, shall be a shade,
> The dew is gone, dust scattered, fled the shade.
> What thyself art, hence learn, what all things are,
> What are all things in human nature here,
> That they are all what I now am, be taught
> They're dust, are dew, are ashes, shadow, nought."

*Hugh Ross of Balmuchy (1614-1662)*

Hugh Ross, fifth of the Rosses of Balmuchy, served for a number of years under King Charles I as his European agent in France. His duty was to obtain the freedom of the British subjects imprisoned in Flanders by the King of Spain. In this service he expended large sums of his own money, for which he received no compensation from King Charles.

In 1640 he petitioned the King to grant him relief, but his petition was forwarded to the Lords in Parliament for their consideration. It appears that nothing was done on his behalf. In a later petition (1642) he asked King Charles to give him protection against being arrested for debt until his business affairs were settled.

Lieutenant Hugh Ross served for some years with the "Scots Regiment". In the history of this famous regiment published in 1637 by Major General Robert Munro it is recorded that they served first under the King of Denmark, and later under the King of Sweden. From this historic document the following note is extracted:

> "At our going to the post, the enemies Cannon played continually on the colors, which were torne with the Cannon. Also to my greife, my Camerade Lieutenant Hugh Ross, was the first that felt the smart of the Cannon Bullet, being shot in the leg, who falling, not fainting at his losse, did call courageously, 'Go on bravely, Comerades, and I wish I had a Treene (wooden leg) for your sakes.' In this instant of time and I believe, with one Bullet, the leg was also shot from David Rosse, sonne to Rosse of Gannis."

Another passage in this document states:

> "At our first drawing up in battell a worthy gent. called Robert Ross, one of our Regt. was killed with the Cannon, being blowing of Tobacco before the Regt. fought in battell, died instantly and was transported to Letts, where he was honourable buried in the church, whose last words were 'Lord, receive my soule'."

It would appear that even in these early days the smoking of tobacco could result in serious consequences.

*Alexander Ross (1699-1784)*

One of old Scotland's bards who has been too much neglected is Alexander Ross. He was the son of an Aberdeenshire farmer who, after graduating with the M.A. degree from Marischal College Aberdeen, became a teacher. He settled as the parish schoolmaster at Lochlee, Forfarshire, where he was headmaster for fifty-one years.

Alexander Ross is best known for his pastoral poem *Helenore the Fortunate Sheperdess,* which was written in 1768 in the quaint Aberdeenshire dialect. The poem became quite popular in the north of Scotland. Ross also wrote a number of witty and vivacious songs about the many phases of domestic life of the times. Two of the better known of these are *The Rock and the Wee Pickle Tow; Wooed and Married and A'.*

At Balhangie, the ruins of the churchyard can still be seen where Alexander Ross is buried. The foundations of his house and the old Lochlee schoolhouse may also be seen in the beautiful glen nearby.

*General Charles Ross of Invercharron (1729-1797)*

This distinguished officer was the second son of David Ross ninth of Invercharron. He was commissioned as ensign in the Thirty-second Regiment of Foot in 1747. He advanced steadily in rank until the year 1781, when, with the rank of Major General, he was given command of his regiment, the 72nd Foot or Royal Manchester Volunteers, who were at the time stationed at Gibraltar. On November 27 he commanded a force of about 2,000 men in a sortie from the garrison at Gibraltar and succeeded in destroying the enemy's advanced batteries.

General Ross returned to England and was elected member of parliament for Wick Burghs, and appointment which he held until 1784. He became a Lieutenant General in 1793 and died unmarried in 1797.

*William Ross, Gaelic Bard of the Highlands (1762-1790)*

William Ross, the Skye bard, is generally considered to be one of the greatest of the Gaelic poets, and it is with pride that we claim him as a member of the great Clan Ross. He was born at Broadford on the Isle of Skye in 1762. His father, John Ross, was a native of the island, and his mother came from Gairloch in Ross-shire. She was a daughter of John MacKay, the blind poet who was piper to the family of Gairloch.

Young William Ross showed great aptitude in his studies and completed his education at the Grammar School at Forres. The family then moved to Gairloch and built a house on Aird Bhad-a-Chrotha, where William, at the age of twenty-four years, was appointed schoolmaster in the Clachan of Gairloch, a position which he held with distinction. As a scholar Ross excelled in both Latin and Greek, as well as being the best Gaelic scholar of his day. He was the author of a number of Gaelic poems of great sensitivity and charm which were long recited in the Highlands. He travelled extensively through the northern parts of Scotland, in order to become acquainted with the different dialects of the Gaelic language. He claimed that the purest and most genuine Gaelic was to be found among the inhabitants of the west side of the Isle of Skye. A number of his songs and poetry have unfortunately been lost to posterity. Ross was also quite musical and sang many of his songs to the accompaniment of the violin, which he played with considerable skill.

William Ross died at the early age of twenty-eight from tuberculosis, but in his short life he had made a permanent name for himself.

A stone pillar was erected by his countrymen in 1850, in the churchyard at Gairloch, with an inscription declaring their respect and admiration for his extraordinary genius and great talent.

Few of our Highland bards have acquired the celebrity of William Ross and fewer still possessed his true poetic powers. A number of his poems and songs were collected and ably translated by John Mackenzie and Dr. George Calder, of the University of Glasgow, in 1937.

Two verses of one of his poems are here give in the Gaelic with the English translation.

*Moladh Na-H-Oighe Gaidhlich*

A nighean bhoidheach
An or-fhuilt bhachalaich,
Nan gorm-shul miogach,
'S nam min bhas sneachda-gheal,
Gu'n siubhlainn reidhleach
A's sleibhtean Bhreatainn leat,
Fo earradh sgaoilte
De dh' aodach breacain orm.

'S e sud an t-eideadh
Ri 'n eireadh m'aigne-sa,
'S mo nighean Ghaidhleach,
Aluinn agam ann;
O bheul na h-oidhche
Gu soills' na madainne,
Gu'm b' ait nar sugradh
Gun duiseal cadail oirnn.

*Highland Maid*

My pretty Highland maiden,
With tresses golden bright,
And blue eyes softly shading,
And soft hands snowy white;
O'er Scotland's hills and plains
With thee I fain would go,
Wrapped in our native tartan plaids
That in the breezes flow.

Give me my Highland dress,
'Tis grand beyond compare;
Give me my Highland maid,
Sweet, smiling, young and fair;
Then banish sleep and care,
From eve to rosy morn,
In happy love beneath our plaid,
The proudest dress that's worn.

### *Hercules and Horatio Ross of Rossie and Certain Members of this Family*

*Hercules Ross* amassed a small fortune in Jamaica in 1761 and became a great friend of Lord Nelson. He returned to Glasgow in 1782 and built the Rossie Castle on his estate, near Montrose. He was the son of John Ross, Excise Officer for the Port of Glasgow in the early eighteenth century.

*Horatio Ross* was the only son of Hercules Ross and his wife, Henrietta Parish, and was born at Rossie Castle in 1801. Lord Nelson was his godfather and he expressed a wish that the child should bear his name. Horatio became known in later life as the "King of the Sportsmen." His prowess with gun and rifle and his many records in grouse-shooting and deer-stalking, a number of them in Wyvis Forest in Ross-shire, were long remembered and related among Scottish sportsmen. Horatio served with the 14th Light Dragoons in early life and in 1831 was a member of Parliament for the Burghs of Aberdeen, Berrie and Montrose. He died in 1873, leaving his wife, and six sons.

*Dr. Alexander Charles Ross* is numbered among the distinguished descendants of this family. He held the post of Inspector-General of Hospitals in the Army Medical Corps.

Another descendant of Hercules Ross of Rossie was *Rear-Admiral George Parish Ross, C.B.*, of the Royal Navy. He was the youngest son of Horatio John Ross of the Bengal Civil Service. He served on H.M.S. *Raleigh* at the Cape of Good Hope Station in 1894 and in the Gamilia expedition, where he received the West African Medal with clasp. He was Commander-in-Chief on the Mediterranean dispatch vessel H.M.S. *Surprise* from 1896-1901. He commanded H.M.S. *Teutonic* and the 10th Crusier Squadron in the great blockade between the Orkney Islands, Iceland and Norway during the First World War. Captain (later Rear-Admiral) George Ross received the Most Honourable Order of the Bath for his war services and also received the Russian Order of St. Anne, 2nd Class with Crossed Swords, for services at the Battle of Jutland.

### *David Ross of Dingwall and certain members of his family*

*David Ross,* son of Donald Ross of Ross-shire, was born in Morayshire, and was elected Provost of Dingwall, in 1884.

He received his early training in banking and law, and in 1868 was appointed County Collector for Ross and Cromarty and later was made a Justice of the Peace, and Hon. Sheriff-Substitute for the County. He married Margaret Macbean, daughter of the Rev. Alexander Macbean, minister of Kincardine, and had a family of one son and three daughters.

David's son, *Donald Alexander Macbean Ross,* was the London manager of the Commonwealth Bank of Scotland. There were three distinguished doctors in his family.

(1) *Dr. James Ness Macbean Ross,* Fellow of the Royal College of Surgeons, distinguished himself in both military and civilian life, winning the Military Cross and Bar, and the Croix de Guerre. (2) *Dr. Elizabeth Ness Ross* practised in Persia, Serbia, China, and other remote areas. Her book, *A Lady Doctor in Bakhtiari Land,* was published after her death. She died of Typhus fever in 1915, while treating her patients at the Typhus Hospital at Kraqujevatz. (3) *Dr. Lucy Macbean Ross* studied Public Health Medicine at Glasgow and practised in York.

*Alexander Ross of Inverness (1834-1897)*

Alexander Ross, LL.D., a noted architect, was born at Brechin in 1834. He succeeded to his father's architectural practice in 1853 and is responsible for drawing plans for many important buildings in the Highlands during the succeeding decades. He drew up the plans for three castles which were rebuilt or renovated in the middle years of the nineteenth century: Andross Castle, Duncraig Castle, and Skibo Castle. He also drew up the plans for St. Andrew's Cathedral, Inverness, the Bishop's Palace, the General Post Office, the Royal Academy and many other buildings.

Dr. Ross was elected Provost of Inverness in 1889 and fostered many local organizations and industries. He also served in the Volunteer Corps and retired with the rank of Lieutenant-Colonel of the Inverness Artillery Volunteers. He was a life-long student of archeology, geology, and the antiquities of Scotland, and made important contributions to the transactions of the Inverness Scientific and Field Club, on these and related subjects.

*Dr. John M. Ross (1833-1918)*

This eminent Scottish historian and educator was born at Kilmarnock in the Highlands and received his education at Glasgow University. After graduation he was appointed English master at the High School. He later became an elder and lay minister in the Scottish Presbyterian Church. In 1874 the University of Glasgow recognizing his professional eminence conferred on him the degree of LL.D.

Dr. Ross published his *Scottish History and Literature* in 1884, which is one of the important documentaries of that time dealing with early Scottish historical events.

*David Ross, Shakespearean Actor, (1728-1790)*

Son of Alexander Ross, Master of the Rolls, London. David Ross has been referred to as the "Father of the Scottish Theatre". He brought the first official Play to the legitimate stage in Edinburgh. When he decided to make his career on the stage he was cut off by his father with the proverbial shilling which his sister was instructed to give him annually. With his sister's help he took his case to the House of Lords and won £6,000 from his father's estate. His portrait as Hamlet, by Zoffany, hangs in the Garrick Club, London.

David was buried at St. James, Piccadilly, and James Boswell, Dr. Johnson's biograher, was one of the chief mourners.

*Kenneth Ross (1800-1846)*

This Scotch Presbyterian Layman from the island of Lewis is worthy of a place among the noted men of the Clan. He was one of the "Men" of the Church, so called because they preached the gospel and took an active part in the services, but were not ordained ministers.

Kenneth Ross was known throughout the islands as a man of sterling character, and a true Christian gentleman. The Highlanders in Ross-shire spoke of him in superlatives. He was born in Crobeg, Lochs, in 1800 and decided to take up the duties of a lay-minister under the preaching stimulus of the Rev. Finlay Cook. He was soon appointed catechist at Lochs, and later appointed lay missionary and catechist at Carloway. Here he carried on his ministry for fourteen years, as there was no ordained minister in this area. He was urged by his parishioners to apply for ordination but he refused, saying that he felt inadequate for this high calling.

*Sir William Charles Ross, Royal Academy, (1794-1860)*

The last of the great Miniature Portrait painters, Sir William painted more than 2,000 miniatures in his lifetime, including Queen Victoria, the Prince Consort, and their children. Sir William was appointed miniature painter to the Queen in 1837 and there is a fine collection of originals painted by him at Windsor Castle.

Mr. Graham Reynolds in his book, "English Portrait Miniatures", says of Sir William: "In time there can be no doubt that he will be regarded as being as much the leader of Miniature Painting in the Nineteenth Century as was Hilliard in the Sixteenth Century, Cooper in the Seventeenth Century, and Cosway in the Eighteenth Century."

In 1837 the technique of photography was perfected. In France that year Louis Daguerre became the first man to fix permanently the image of the camera obscura, and in 1841 Richard Beard opened in London the first public photographic studio in Britain. By 1861 there were over 200 Studios.

On his deathbed the last of the important Miniaturists, Sir William Ross, lamented that the days of Miniature Painting were over and his prophecy proved correct. The delicate art of painting on ivory had to give way to science in the form of the camera.

*Sir John Ross (1838-1932)*

Sir John Ross, LL.D., a notable member of the Clan, died at his residence at Dunfermline, in his ninety-fourth year. He was the first chairman of the Carnegie Dunfermline Trust, the Carnegie Hero Fund, and the Carnegie United Kingdom Trust.

Sir John was born in Edinburgh on July 28, 1838, having in his veins a happy blend of Highland and Lowland blood. His parents were in comparatively modest circumstances and he had few advantages in the matter of education, though for a short time he attended classes in Edinburgh University. He began life as a boy messenger and later was a clerk in the offices of the famous temperance advocate, Mr. John Hope. In December 1867, he moved to Dunfermline. There, his strong personality and his aptitude for hard work were important factors in his rise to the head of the firm of solicitors known as Messrs. Ross and Connell. His rapid success was strikingly shown by the readiness with which his friends came to his aid and when he was all but ruined in 1878 by the sudden collapse of the City of Glasgow Bank, of which he was local agent. His widely acknowledged ability and character brought him immediate assistance; with remarkable fortitude, he not only rebuilt his fortunes in a short period of years, but also reimbursed those of his clients who had suffered in the same disaster.

In later years, Sir John devoted his time, his intellectual gifts, his wide experience and his organizing ability to the administration of the four British Trusts founded by Andrew Carnegie. He was confidential adviser to Carnegie at the inception of all four.

A friend at his death said, "Sir John stood out in every company as a true gentleman of the old school. He had the grace of manner and phraseology which comes only from the innate chivalry of the cultured man. Considering the very elementary nature of his early education, his knowledge of literature, and the grace and accuracy of his own style were perhaps the most striking of his many attainments."

The honour of knighthood was conferred upon him in January 1921, and in the same year, he was made a Vice-President of the British Association.

## In The Tropics

### *George Clunies Ross (1796-1847)*

Here is an unusually romantic story of a Ross from the Orkney Islands. Because of the difficulties in making a living on these rocky isles, young George, one of a large family, was allowed to go to sea. In a remarkably short time he had become captain on a merchantman of the East India Company. From that time his fortunes may be traced in the records of the East India Company, and those of his descendants may be followed to the present day in the reports of the British Foreign Office.

An English expedition had seized the island of Java. Sir Stamford Raffles was in charge of the expedition and Captain George Ross was his second in command. A report which outlined the wonderful natural resources of the island was compiled by Raffles and Ross and was sent off to England via Calcutta. At Calcutta this report was pigeon-holed by an undersecretary and never reached London. The result was that the British Government, unaware of the wealth of the island, traded Java to the Dutch for a pittance.

We can well imagine the feeling of Ross and Sir Stamford Raffles over the blunder. Captain Ross was at Java at the time superintending the construction of a four-master for the East India Company. News reached him that if the vessel was not launched before a certain date, it would become the property of the Dutch. Ross worked his men day and night to prevent the vessel from falling into the hands of the Dutch. On the night of the twelfth the hull of the vessel was so far completed as to permit her to be towed out of the harbour and beyond the Dutch jurisdiction. The Dutch took possession of Java on the thirteenth.

On the open seas her masts and rigging were put in place, and Ross sailed away to Calcutta. Here disaster awaited him; the East India Company had failed and Sir Stamford Raffles was a ruined man. The company owed Ross a sum of £20,000, and despairing of any settlement, Ross agreed to take the vessel he had built in payment. Manning the ship with a crew of Malays and Lascars, Captain Ross again put out to sea.

In the year 1820, Capt. George Clunies Ross made his great discovery. While cruising off the coast of Java in the Indian Ocean, he sighted an uncharted and uninhabited group of seven islands. He landed and took formal possession in the name of George Ross, "Sailor of Fortune." The following day, probably as an afterthought, he hoisted the British flag and again took possession, this time in the name of His Majesty George III of England. It was well that he did this. A few days later a Russian man-of-war entered the lagoon and ran up the Russian flag. Ross convinced the Russians of the priority of his claim and the disappointed Russians departed. From that time onward the Clunies-Ross family became virtual kings of the Cocos Islands, a designation that soon became surrounded with a halo of romance.

Not long after, Capt. Ross decided to visit his home in Scotland. Embarking in his vessel he sailed southwest around the Cape of Good Hope, then northward, and reached Liverpool six months after leaving his newly discovered islands. He called on the Colonial Office at London, made known the nature of his discovery, and was later confirmed in his possession of the islands by the British Government. These coral islands had previously been discovered by a Captain William Keeling, but had remained uninhabited and uncharted. Ross then sailed up the Scottish coast to his old homestead in the Orkneys, and received from his family and clan a rousing welcome.

When Capt. Ross again lifted anchor a few weeks later to return to his islands, he carried with him upwards of two score of his relatives and clansmen.

On reaching the "Ross" islands he was confronted with his second disappointment. During his year's absence a man named Hare, whom he had previously known in Java, had put in at the islands and had made a settlement with some natives, whom he was holding as slaves. Ross dealt with this new development in characteristic fashion. The newcomer was ordered to leave, bag and baggage. When he refused to comply, Ross began hostilities. Hare's followers deserted to Ross on the neighbouring island of Pulu Selma, and Hare himself made his escape.

Captain Ross now set about putting his "kingdom" in order. From Java he imported five hundred natives and put them to the task of turning his island paradise into a paying proposition, treating them not as slaves but as paid employees. Many coconut palms were planted, and soon the islands were regularly exporting the finest grade of copra and oil to the ports of India.

Captain Ross had married late in life and had one son whom he sent to Aberdeen University. After graduation, the boy returned to the islands, and on his father's death succeeded to the proprietoreship.

*John George Clunies Ross the 2nd, and his descendants*

John Ross spent his time perfecting the island laws originally made by his father. He also had some medical ability, for tradition says that he cured many of the island sick, and laid down rules of hygiene which prevented much illness. His eldest son, *George Ross the 3rd,* was a good counterpart of his grandfather, the original founder of the islands. Capable and energetic, he governed the islands with a kind but firm hand. He encouraged industry, thrift, and sobriety among the islanders who had increased in number until there were now more than two thousand, not including the large number of white descendants of the clansmen brought from Scotland by the first proprietor. George Ross 3rd, died while on a visit to England in 1912 and was succeeded by his son *John Sidney Clunies Ross,* fourth in line of descent from Captain George Clunies Ross. In the records of the Colonial office he is listed as "Proprietor and Chief of the Cocos Keeling Islands".

The official designation of the islands is the Cocos Keeling Islands, but to the sailors in the Indian Ocean they are the "Ross Islands," and many are the stories still afloat concerning the man who, more than a century ago, made himself a kingdom on these unknown and uncharted islands.

During World War I, the German warship *Emden* landed sailors on the island with instructions to wreck the wireless station, and to commandeer Mr. Ross's private yacht *Ayesha* which was lying at anchor in the harbour. Later Captain Von Mueller was forced to surrender by the Australian battleship *Sydney* which was cruising nearby. The fight occurred in full view of the islanders gathered upon the shore.

Queen Elizabeth II and Prince Philip visited the islands on their world cruise to Sydney in 1952, and received a rousing welcome from the Scots and native islanders.

## In Australia and New Zealand

### *Sir John Ross of New Zealand (1857-1930)*

This Scot was born in the village of Halkirk, Caithness, and emigrated to New Zealand in early life. Here he founded the firm of Ross and Glendening and embarked on a very successful wholesale business employing upward of 1,500 men.

Some years later, seeing the need for enlarged facilities for college students in New Zealand, he founded and endowed Knox College, Dunedin, a residential college for divinity and medical students. Sir John was later appointed Governor of Otago University, and was knighted for his many achievements in advancing the academic as well as the financial status of New Zealand at that time. Sir John died in his ninety-third year at Dunedin in 1930.

### *David Ross (1850-1912)*

This scientist and banker was the youngest son of John Ross of Ardgay, Ross-shire, where he was born in 1850. After leaving Tain Academy, David Ross was trained as a banker, and from his boyhood showed an aptitude for both business and science. He emigrated to Australia and soon became manager of the National Bank of Australia. Here he made a special study and a hobby of the science of astronomy. When he retired from the managership of the National Bank he devoted all his energies to this science, and built an observatory on the highest point of the Christmas hills. He constructed his telescope from plans which he drew himself, and with this instrument he was able to make his remarkable observations, discovering two comets—Ross's Comet, and a second Comet in 1906. His observatory was visited by many of the foremost professors of astronomy, who found his telescope remarkable for its magnifying power and the delicacy of its adjustments. David Ross made many contributions to the literature of Astronomical Science, and is still regarded as one of the outstanding astronomers of his day.

*David Alexander Ross (1883-1938)*

Another noted Australian astronomer and philosopher was born in Glasgow in 1883. He was the son of Dr. David Ross of Glasgow, and following his undergraduate training in Scotland he also emigrated to Australia where he became Professor of Mathematics and Physics at the University of Western Australia in 1912. He was appointed President of the British Astronomical Association, Scottish Branch, in 1913, and President of the Royal Society of West Australia in 1916. He was President of the West Australia Astronomical Society from 1915 to 1917, and was a member of the Crocker Solar Eclipse Expedition of the Lick Observatory in 1922.

David Alexander Ross published many important treatises on magnetism, spectroscopy, astrophysics, and other subjects, and will be remembered for his contributions to the advancement of scientific knowledge in these fields.

## At The Poles

*Sir John Ross, Arctic Explorer (1777-1856)*

In the early years of the nineteenth century a new breed of Arctic explorers emerged. One of these, Sir John Ross, was born in 1777 at Balsarroch in Wigtownshire, Scotland. He entered the Royal Navy in 1786 at the age of nine. After service in the French Revolutionary and Napoleonic Wars, he was assigned to search for the North-West passage in 1818. He set sail in the *Isabella*, accompanied by Lt. Parry in the *Alexander*. After crossing the north Atlantic, the ships passed through Davis Strait, Baffin Bay and sailed for a distance of fifty miles into Lancaster Sound. This sound was later found to be the eastern entrance to the North-West Passage. Captain John Ross did not realize this, however, and turned back when he observed a range of mountains ahead which seemed to impede further progress.

His first officer on this expedition, William Edward Parry, flatly contradicted his superior, declaring that no such barrier existed. Parry was successful in proving this contention when he himself led an expedition in the following year, and sailed through Lancaster Sound as far as Melville Island before his ships became frozen fast in the Arctic ice.

In 1829 Captain John Ross vindicated himself by sailing again in the *Victory* to the Arctic, "stimulated by the desire to secure for his country, Great Britain, the honour of settling the long-agitated question of a North-West Passage". The vessel and equipment for this expedition were provided by the generosity of the Sheriff of London, Sir Felix Booth. Captain Ross firmly believed that ocean going ships should have a steam engine to supplement the sails; but the engine he had installed in the *Victory* did not perform satisfactorily and had to be discarded long before he reached the Arctic regions.

For his navigator and first officer on the voyage, Captain Ross selected his nephew, Commander James Clark Ross, who had sailed on previous expeditions to the Arctic Seas, and was very experienced and capable.

The expedition remained in the arctic regions for four years and the crew endured great hardships and privations. Capt. Ross discovered and named the gulf and isthmus of Boothia in honour of Sir Felix Booth.

While wintering in this area with their ship frozen in pack ice, Commander James Ross the navigator made a series of explorations on foot with some of the crew, and was successful in discovering the exact location of the *Magnetic Pole.* In a letter to the Admiralty, Commander Ross states that he had placed the name of his sovereign, on the true position of the Magnetic Pole. After their ship became damaged and lost in the Arctic ice the Captain, officers and crew came upon the *Isabella,* which had been frozen in pack ice since his first polar voyage in 1819, and in the *Isabella* they returned safely to England in 1833.

Captain Ross was called to appear before a board of inquiry of the House of Commons to report the discoveries he and his navigator had made, and to determine what compensation he should be given, if any, since both he and Commander Ross had not received any wages for the four years of his sojourn in the Arctic. The Committee stated in their report that "Although the expedition was undertaken as a private venture, the Committee appreciates the valuable additions to magnetic science, meteorology and geographical knowledge which this expedition has supplied. The Committee cannot overlook the public service which is rendered to a maritime country, by deeds of daring, enterprise and patient endurance of hardship, which excite the public sympathy, and enlist the general feeling in favour of maritime adventure".

So in 1834, Captain John Ross received the honour of knighthood and a grant of £5,000 from Parliament. In 1835 he published an interesting account of his second voyage, and his long residence in the Arctic regions, with special reference to the discovery of the North Magnetic Pole by Commander James Ross who was later given the title Sir James

Ross. Captain Sir John Ross also wrote an important treatise on *Navigation by Steam,* even though his first steam engine proved to be a complete failure.

Sir John made his last expedition to the Arctic in 1850, when he sailed in the *Felix,* on a vain search for Sir John Franklin, the famous explorer who had also endeavoured to find the North-West Passage. The following year he was made a Rear-Admiral; he died in 1856 in London.

Sir John and Sir James Ross were also signally honoured by the Lord Lyon when they received permission to augment their personal Ross arms with the addition to the upper section of the shield, of a portion of the northern hemisphere depicting the arctic regions. There was also a double crest, one was the dexter hand with garland of juniper, and the other new crest was a rock with the Union Jack flying above it and showing the date of discovery of the magnetic pole June 1, 1831.

*Sir James Clark Ross, Antartic Explorer (1800-1862)*

Sir James Ross was born in London in 1800 and entered the Royal Navy in his twelfth year. As mentioned above, he had accompanied his uncle Captain John Ross on his first voyage to the Arctic regions in 1818. During the next five years he accompanied Sir W. Parry on his four expeditions in search of the passage. In 1829 he again engaged to sail as Commander with Captain John Ross in the *Victory* on his arctic voyage. Commander James Ross was given full recognition by the Admiralty for having discovered the location of the North Magnetic Pole on this voyage.

In 1839 Captain Ross commanded two sailing vessels in a voyage of discovery to the Antarctic Regions, hitherto unvisited. Sailing south with the *Erebus* and the *Terror,* he crossed the Antarctic Circle on January 1st, 1841 and entered the pack ice. Five days later he passed into open water and sighted a chain of mountains rising from the coast line which ran due south. This land was formally claimed for Queen Victoria and the ships continued southward along the coast line of Victoria Land for a distance of about 450 miles until an island with twin peaks was sighted. This was later named *Ross Island,* and the peaks are called *Erebus* and *Terror.* (See map on back cover.)

On the southern extremity of Ross Island, two observatory stations are now located. Scott Station is maintained by New Zealand and McMurdo Station by the United States.

Captain Ross then sailed back to Hobart but returned in November of the same year to the Antarctic waters. Steering southeast from New Zealand, he passed through the pack ice, and in 1842 established a new "farthest south" of 78°10' near the Bay of Whales on Ross Sea. At this point he had again reached the Ross Ice Shelf, a huge level-surfaced ice formation about 600 to 1,000 feet thick. Large flat icebergs break away from the seaward edge as the ice shelf moves northward and out to sea at the rate of about four feet per day. This is the largest floating ice shelf in the Antarctic and is roughly the size of France. The inner end of the ice shelf is held fast to the continent of Antarctica by glaciers which act as feeders, and by shoals close to the actual coast which anchor it. This ice shelf later proved to be the easiest route for the discovery of the South Pole.

On his return from these voyages in 1843, Sir James Ross was knighted, and in 1847 he published *A Voyage of Discovery and Research in the Southern and Antarctic Regions during the years 1839-43.*

STANDARD OF CHIEF DAVID CAMPBELL ROSS OF SHANDWICK

# APPENDIX I

## CADET BRANCHES OF CLAN ROSS

Most of the cadet branches of the clan who inherited estates in Ross-shire, have no living descendants at the present time. Two of the later cadets, the Kindeace and Cromarty branches probably have living heirs but these have not been traced. Short summaries of the following cadets are given: the Rosses of Invercharron, the Rosses of Braelanqwell, Easter Fearn and Ankerville, the Rosses of Achnacloich, the Rosses of Kindeace, the Rosses of Invercastley, the Rosses of Calrossie, the Rosses of Aldie, the Rosses of Pitkerrie and Cromarty, (see page 62.)

The genealogy of these families was derived from History of the Clan Ross by Alexander M. Ross.

### The Rosses of Invercharron

*William Ross, first of Invercharron,* was formerly William Ross of Ardgay, second son of Sir David Ross, seventh of Balnagowan, by his wife Helen Keith of Inverguie. In 1528 he acquired from the Crown the lands of Strathoickell, in the Parish of Kincardine. He married a daughter of Alexander Mackenzie of Davochmaluag. The ruins of Davochmaluag can still be traced on the estate of Tulloch, in the Strathpeffer valley.

Of this marriage there was a family of three sons and a daughter: (1) Alexander, who succeeded (2) Hugh (3) John (4) Effie. The last named married Hector Munro, first Presbyterian minister of Edderton after the Reformation. Beside being minister of the parish he was also proprietor of the small estate of Meikle Daan, in the parish of Edderton.

*Alexander Ross, second of Invercharron,* succeeded to the property in 1593. The only event for which he is remembered is a raid which he and the men of Ross made upon the lands of Vass Lochslin in Easter

Ross. Considerable booty was taken. He was married twice: first to Margaret Innes of Calrossie, secondly to Isobel, daughter of William Ross of Priesthill. By both marriages he had a large family of boys. The following can be traced: (1) William, who succeeded (2) Nicholas (3) David (4) Alexander, who is designated "of Drumgillie" (5) George (6) Walter (7) Thomas.

*William Ross, third of Invercharron,* married Catherine, daughter of Hugh Munro of Assynt, and has as issue: (1) Walter, who succeeded (2) Hugh (3) Robert, founder of the family of Rosses of Ankerville and of Easter Fearn (4) Alexander (5) Ada, who married William Ross of Priesthill.

*Walter Ross, fourth of Invercharron,* married first Isobel, widow of James Innes of Calrossie and second Margaret, daughter of David Munro of Culnauld. James VI had granted to David Munro the escheat of all the goods upon the quarter lands of Meikle Allan, which had been forfeited by John Leslie, Bishop, of Ross, for treason. The treason consisted in his attempt to have Queen Mary married to the Duke of Norfolk. The Bishop was imprisoned in the Tower for three years.

By the first marriage (of Walter Ross and Isobel Innes) there were born (1) Sir David Broadfoord, Knight of Malta, (2) William, who succeeded his father (3) Janet, who married first, Thomas Ross of Priesthill, and secondly, as his second wife, Kenneth Mackenzie, first of Scatwell. Her two sons were Alexander, and Kenneth, fourth of Scatwell, who was created a Baronet of Nova Scotia in 1703. (4) Catherine, who married Hugh Macleod of Cambuscurry, a son of Donald Macleod, seventh of Assynt, by Catherine, daughter of Nicholas Ross of Pitcalnie, an ancestor of the Macleods of Cadboll. There does not appear to have been a family by the second marriage.

*William Ross, fifth of Invercharron,* was styled "of Grunzeard" (Greensward) previous to his accession to the family property. He married Janet, daughter of Walter Innes of Inverbreakie (Invergordon) and had as issue: (1) Walter, who succeeded (2) William, (3) *Hugh, who became first of Braelangwell* (4) David (5) Isabel, who married Andrew Ross of Shandwick (6) Janet, who married George Baillie of the family of Dunain.

In Brodie's Diary under the date 22nd May, 1671, which must therefore apply to the fifth proprietor of Invercharron, the following entry is made: "I heard of the abomination committed by Ross of Invercharron . . . that he hanged a man, and lived in adultery".

On 30th December 1661, William granted a charter of Invercharron to his son Walter and his spouse Margaret Gray, widow of George Gray of Calrossie.

*Walter Ross, sixth of Invercharron,* died without issue.

*William Ross, seventh of Invercharron,* succeeded his brother Walter.

*Walter Ross, eighth of Invercharron,* eldest surviving son of William Ross, seventh of Invercharron. He married Christina, daughter of Malcolm Ross of Kindeace. She married as her second husband John Ross.

*David Ross, ninth of Invercharron,* succeeded his father in the property. He married Isobel, daughter of Hugh Ross of Achnacloich, and left a family of two sons and three daughters. Charles Ross, the second son, had a distinguished military career at Gibraltar.[1]

*William Ross, tenth of Invercharron,* succeeded his father as last proprietor of the old family. He married Ann, daughter of David Ross. While there was a family of two sons and two daughters, the sons became soldiers and died without leaving issue. The estate was judicially sold and the Invercharron line of Clan Ross came to an end.

It is quite probable that there are living descendants of Alexander Ross, second of Invercharron who had a large family of seven boys, but the descendants have not been traced.

## THE ROSSES OF BRAELANGWELL, 1661-1710

*Hugh Ross, first of Braelangwell* This Cadet branch of the Ross family acquired the lands of Braelangwell some two hundred and fifty years ago. The founder of this family was Hugh Ross, youngest son of William Ross, fifth of Invercharron. He was married to Helen, daughter of David Dunbar of Dumphail, a Deputy-Lieutenant of Morayshire.

Hugh Ross was a zealous Hanoverian as were most of the other Rosses, and when the Government of King George determined to suppress the rebellious spirit of the Highlanders by the Disarming Act, making it a criminal offence to wear the Highland dress, David Dunbar was one of those entrusted with enforcing the Act in the County of Elgin.

Of the marriage there was a family of a son and two daughters: (1) Hugh, who became second of Braelangwell (2) Ann, who married John Gordon, and (3) Helen, who married her cousin William Ross, eighth of Invercharron.

*Hugh Ross, second of Braelangwell* He was twice married, but the name of the first wife cannot be ascertained. It was known, however, that by this union at least one child, a son, was born. Hugh was married, secondly, to Elizabeth daughter of William Ross of Aldie, his wife being Sibil, Mackenzie. By this marriage there was a family of two sons and seven daughters: (1) William and (2) Simon. All the daughters

[1] For further reference to Charles Ross see page 80.

were married; one Georgine, married the Rev. John Macdonald, D.D., "The Apostle of the North." The estate of Aldie was settled on the sons of the second marriage. Nothing further is known of this family of Rosses.

## Branch of Ankerville

*Alexander Ross, first of Ankerville.* Robert Ross, second son of William Ross, third of Invercharron, left two sons: (i) William (ii) Alexander, who became first of Easter Fearn, in the Parish of Kincardine.

William, the eldest, had a son named Alexander, who became first of Ankerville. He acquired the land by purchase, after amassing a fortune in commerce as a merchant in Cracow. Pocock, in his *Tour through Scotland* refers to this Alexander Ross as follows: "Alexander Ross, first of Ankerville, was in the service of Augustus, King of Poland, became a Commissary, came away with plunder in the war for the Crown of Poland, purchased this estate of one hundred pounds a year, built and lived too greatly for it, and died much reduced." He was married and left two sons, but it is not known what became of them.

## Rosses of Easter Fearn, 1655-1735

*Alexander Ross, first of Easter Fearn,* was the second son of Robert Ross, the progenitor of Ross of Ankerville previously referred to. He had two sons: (1) William, who succeeded him in the property, and (2) Walter.

*William Ross, second of Easter Fearn,* was married to Isabella Ross. They had a family of two sons: (1) Hugh, who succeeded to the property, and (2) William.

*Hugh Ross, third of Easter Fearn, married Isabella,* daughter of Walter Ross Morangie, and had two sons, Hugh and Alexander. The former succeeded his father in the property.

*Hugh Ross, fourth of Eastern Fearn,* was married and left a son named Thomas, and a daughter, Helen, who married Frances Robertson in Balcony Castle. The son Thomas died young, and the property reverted to Alexander, fifth of Easter Fearn.

*Alexander Ross, fifth of Easter Fearn* Besides owning these lands, he was the proprietor of Kirksheath. He was married to Janet, daughter of Gilbert Robertson, second of Kindeace. Of the marriage there was a large family, and the following can be accounted for: (1) William, who succeeded to the property (2) Alexander Ross of Little Daan, (3) Robert Ross, a Baillie in Tain.

*William Ross, sixth of Easter Fearn,* on his father's death, succeeded to the property. William was a strong anti-Jaconite, and was one of those appointed by the government to uplift the rents of estates after the '15 Rebellion. One of the properties attained was that of Seaforth. His tenants, adhered loyally to their proprietor, and refused to pay rent to the representatives of the Crown.

William left a family of three sons and two daughters. The eldest (1) Alexander, succeeded his father in the property (2) Edward became a merchant in Inverness (3) Walter, the third son, was mortally wounded in the Murchison battle and was interred at Beauly. One of the daughters married Thomas Ross of Calrossie.

*Alexander Ross, seventh of Easter Fearn,* succeeded to the property after his father's death. He received the appointment of Commissary Clerk for the County of Ross. It would appear that Alexander became involved in debt and the estate of Easter Fearn had to be judicially sold in 1735.

## The Rosses of Achnacloich, 1490-1759

*Hugh Ross, first of Achnacloich,* was the youngest son of Sir David Ross, seventh of the old family of Balnagowan. He was granted the lands of Achnacloich by King James V on the annual payment of twelve pounds. In the Kalendar of Fearn he is described as "ane honorabil man".

*Hugh Ross, second of Achnacloich,* succeeded his father as second proprietor. He was married to a daughter of George Munro, fourth of Milntown. They had a son, Hugh, who became the third of Achnaloich.

*Hugh Ross, third of Achnacloich,* is referred to in the Register of Privy Council in connection with a complaint against him by the Crown for seizing a man named John Ross without a proper warrant, and carrying him prisoner to Balnagowan Castle. It would appear that he and the contemporary laird of Balnagowan were on the best of terms for, according to Reid's *Earls of Ross,* David Ross, eleventh of Balnagowan granted to Hugh of Achnacloich, and to his eldest son, the office of Forestry Friwater. This gentleman, it seems came to a very sad end, as may be inferred from the following extract from *Memorials of the Troubles in Scotland,* a Spalding Club publication: "Ypone Wednesday the first Februar 1643 thair cam to the place of Cromartie, quhair the ladie was Hutcheon Ross of Auchincloche, with two vether gentilmen, whair they weir maid welcum, coupit mirrilie, but reckleslie gat ane colltioun (poison cup) whiche was prepaired for ane vether, and was all thrie found died in their bedis on the morn".

Hugh Ross married a daughter of John Mackenzie, first of Inveraul, and had a family of two sons and a daughter.

Of the fourth proprietor, nothing is known.

*John Ross, fifth of Achnacloich,* married Margaret, daughter of Colin Mackenzie, first of Kincraig—"A distinguished warrior, who took a prominent part in the frequent encounters between the Mackenzies and the Macdonalds of Glengarry, and often commanded the Clan Ross on these occasions". Margaret was the widow of Gilbert Robertson, second of Kindeace, a merchant of Inverness. Their son inherited the property.

*John Ross, sixth of Achnacloich,* took a leading part in the county affairs, being a Commissioner of Supply and a Sheriff-Deputy of Ross. He married Margaret Balfour, daughter of a magistrate of the town of Inverness. They had a family of at least two sons and a daughter. The latter married Hugh Munro of Kiltearn, minister of Tain. She is noted as being the first annuitant on the Ministers' Widows' Fund. Her husband, the Rev. Mr. Munro, according to Taylor's *History of Tain,* "seems to have been a good and able man, and the Presbytery attached importance to his translation to Tain from Tarbat which took place in 1700, much to the displeasure of the people of Tarbat, who strenuously resisted the transfer. . . . A party from Tain, it is said went to Tarbat, and actually taking the minister out of the pulpit, carried him in triumph to Tain, where they placed him in the Regent Murray's pulpit to preach the sermon he was to have preached in Tarbat".

*Hugh, Ross, seventh of Achnacloich,* succeeded his father in the property. He must have been of courageous mould, for at the time of the first Jacobite Rebellion (1715) he was selected by the Magistrates of Tain to command a band of the townspeople to guard the interests of the burgh against any possible invasion. As the people of Tain had shown themselves, in the sixteenth century, zealous for the Reformation, and in the seventeenth for the freedom of the Church and its government, so in the eighteenth century, they were found decidedly in favour of the Revolution Settlement, and of the Orange and Hanoverian Government.

Captain Hugh Ross, it would appear, was killed in a duel by Bailie Hugh Ross of Shandwick, 1721. Taylor's reference to this tragic event is to the following effect: "There is a sandhill in the Fendom, which is connected with the tradition of a duel fought between two neighbouring proprietors, Ross of Shandwick and Ross of Achnacloich, who are said to have quarrelled at the time of a market. Captain Ross of Achnacloich was killed and Ross of Shandwick, escaping on horseback, expiated himself in Sweden. The impression this event made on the popular mind is said to be evidenced by the careful preservation and renewal, generation after generation, of the footprints of the combatants at the spot where they fought, and the prints of the hoofs of the fugitive's horse on the moist ground as he galloped over, what has ever since been known as Duel Hill".

Captain Ross was married to Janet, sister of Sir William Gordon of Invergordon, and left a son and a daughter. The son died unmarried. The daughter, Isabella Ross, married (1) as her first husband, David Ross of Invercharron, and (2) Robert Munro.

*Robert Ross, eighth of Achnacloich,* was the second son of John, sixth of Achnacloich. He was married to Catherine Mackenzie, daughter of John Mackenzie, second of Highfield. He in turn was succeeded by his son.

*John Ross, ninth of Achnacloich,* was a Captain in the army. In 1759 he acquired the lands of Wester Cadboll, now known as Balintore. He apparently died unmarried, and this line of the Clan Ross became extinct.

THE ROSSES OF KINDEACE, 1624-1835

The Rosses of Kindeace were descended from the Rosses of Pitcalnie. The first of the name was Malcolm, who was the third son of David Ross, second of Pitcalnie. Kindeace, from which this branch of the Clan Ross took its name, is situated in the Parish of Nigg, and is now known as Bayfield. In 1788 the estate of Kindeace was sold to John Mackenzie, Commander of the "Prince Keunitz", who was responsible for the change of name, and although the property is now owned by another family, it is still known as Bayfield. Descendants of this family emigrated to Ireland, then to Canada in the early nineteenth century.

*Malcolm Ross, first of Kindeace,* appears to have occupied land in the Parish of Tarbat. In a sasine dated 12th July, 1624, he is described as "in Gany" (Geanies). He obtained a charter from John Corbet of Little Rainie, of part of the lands of Mid-Geanies, formerly Fearn Abbey lands, in favour of himself and his wife, Catherine Corbet. In the Valuation Roll of the County of Ross for 1644, preserved in *Antiquarian Notes,* John Corbet of Little Rainie's property valuation is returned at £233/6 shillings, and 8 pence Scots. In the Valuation Roll referred to, the property of Little Tarrel is returned as being in the possession of Hugh Rose, but, in those days, in Ross-shire, the surnames of Rose and Ross were frequently interchanged.

It would appear that this Malcolm associated himself with the anti-Papal party and was fined in the sum of £600. He was married (1) to Catherine Corbet, presumably daughter of John Corbet of Little Rainie, and had issue (1) William (see below), (2) David, who became the founder of the Rosses of Invercastley (3) Malcolm, who became a merchant in Inverness (4) Thomas, who founded the Rosses of Calrossie (5) Catherine, who married (1) William Ross, seventh of Invercharron, and (2) John Ross of Guinards. Malcolm, first of Kindeace, married as his second wife, Jean, daughter of Thomas McCulloch, Provost of Tain, with issue a son, Alexander.

William, eldest son of Malcolm, was a burgess of Tain in 1660. He was infefted by his father in the estates of Kindeace on the 25th September, 1664. The property of Invercastley was also given to him by his father. He married Jane Dunbar, daughter of Sir James Dunbar of Syderhall, Sutherland.

In 1668, William was murdered by the second Lord Duffus, who owed him a sum of money. According to one authority the foul deed took place while the men were walking together from Balnagowan to Inverbrakie (Invergordon). Ross apparently demanded payment, which so angered Lord Duffus that he ran his creditor through with his sword. Lord Duffus fled to England and remained there until his friends purchased a remission from the Crown.

Lord Duffus's wife was Margaret, daughter of Kenneth, third Earl of Seaforth, who used every influence within her power to have the criminal letters against her husband withdrawn, at the insistence of David Ross of Balnagowan. In *Antiquarian Notes* the author, commenting on this tragedy, takes the following extract from one of the papers for the prosecution: "And besides that, John Sutherland, bag-butler to my Lord Duffus, and William Mitchell, his footman, are his menial servants; it is offered to be proven that the said John Sutherland did act as a party in said slaughter by pursuing the said William Ross with his gun, of full purpose to shoot him, and having come his length, he saw him drop dead from his horse, having been mortally wounded".

William Ross's family consisted of a son and daughter, David and Catherine. On the 17th March, 1706, Catherine married George Mackay of Boghouse, Sutherland. The crest of Kindeace is the fox.

*David Ross, second of Kindeace,* son of William Ross (who was murdered) was served as heir to his grandfather. He was a burgess of Tain in 1709, and of Dingwall in 1732. In 1728, he received the appointment of Chamberlain for the purpose of receiving the revenues of the Ross estates. He married Cresilda, seventh daughter of Duncan Forbes of Culloden, and had issue: (1) Duncan Forbes Ross, who became third of Kindeace (2) John Ross (3) Mary, who married Bernard Mackenzie (4) Jean Dunbar, who married Donald Mackenzie of Orloch Hill and (5) Catherine, who married Provost Ross of Fortrose.

*Duncan Forbes Ross, third of Kindeace* succeeded to the property on his father's death. He was married to Jean, daughter of Hugh Rose, thirteenth Baron of Kilravock, who represented the County of Ross in Parliament for seven years. Duncan died in November, 1769 and his wife in 1776. Their family consisted of: (1) David, who became fourth of Kindeace (2) Hugh, a lieutenant in the army (3) John (4) Jean, who married Joseph Taylor, minister of Carnlee, Fife (5) Ann (6) Grace (7) Caroline. None of these last three were married.

*David Ross, fourth of Kindeace,* was not married. He disposed of the property to John Mackenzie, who changed the name of the estates to Bayfield, as noted above. John, the third son, is styled "of Kindeace". He was Lieutenant-Colonel in the 42nd Regiment, and died at Bath in 1819. He was married to Lititia Brown, fourth daughter of the first Lord Kilmain, and left a family of one son and two daughters. The two daughters died young. The son, Lieutenant James Munro Ross, died unmarried in India in 1834.

Another branch of this family who emigrated to Canada have been traced.

John Ross the second son of David Ross second of Kindeace had a son also called John who married and emigrated from Bayfield to County Monaghan, Ireland. His only son Alexander Ross was born in 1803. Alexander married Eliza Kinnier in 1835 and the young couple moved to Canada where they settled in Innisfil township, Upper Canada.

THE ROSSES OF INVERCASTLEY, 1671-1836

*David Ross, first of Invercastley* This family of Rosses acquired the lands of Invercastley in 1671. The first of the name to own these lands was David Ross, second son by his first marriage of Malcolm Ross, first of Kindeace. In a previous chapter, note was taken of the fact that David Ross, thirteenth of Balnagowan, granted a charter of the lands of Invercastley to Malcolm Ross. In consequence of the murder of his elder brother William, David was appointed Tutor of Kindeace. In 1692 he was in business in Edinburgh as a "Writer" or lawyer, and took an active part in county affairs. He was a Commissioner of Supply, and for several years a Sheriff-Designate of Ross-shire. He was twice married: (1) to Catherine, daughter of Hugh Munro, second of Newmore, and (2) to Mary, daughter of Andrew Ross, sixth of Shandwick.

By his first marriage he had two sons: (1) David, who became second of Invercastley (2) Malcolm.

By the second marriage he left a daughter, who married, and left issue. He died at Tarlogie, near Tain, in 1723, and was buried at Tain.

*David Ross, second of Invercastley* In 1726 he acquired the additional lands of Easter and Wester Morangie from George Ross. In the same year he purchased the property of Dibidale. He was twice married: (1) to Elspet, daughter of James Sutherland of Clyne, (2) to Ann Ross. By the first union he left a large family which included the following: (i) David Ross, who became third of Invercastley (ii) Charles, who rose to the rank of General in the army, became owner of Invercharron, but died unmarried (iii) James, who became an officer in the Scots Fusiliers (iv) Jean, who married Roderick McCulloch of Glastullich, (v) Isobel, wife of William Ross, ninth of Invercharron (vi) Mary.

By his second marriage he left a family (vii) John, who died in India (viii) Mary Ann, who married Captain Charles Monro of Culrain. Their grandson became Sir Charles Monro, Baronet.

David, second of Invercastley, died at Tarlogie in 1764, and was buried at Tain.

*David Ross, Lord Ankerville, third of Invercastley*. Lord Ankerville, succeeded to the property in 1756. He was born in 1727, became a prominent member of society, and exercised great influence in the community. He was a member of the Town Council of Fortrose. His object in occupying such a position is obvious. Before the days of Parliamentary Reform, a town council had a leading share in the election of a member of Parliament, and in order to have a vote, a seat on the Board of a town council was much prized. At that time, Sir Alexander Grant of Dalvey was the sitting member for the Inverness District of Burghs, but by a smart stratagem on the part of Sir Hector Munro of Novar, Sir Alexander Grant was unseated. Bribery and corruption were alleged, and a prolonged inquiry took place. David Ross was one of the defenders, and took an active part in refuting the allegation brought against Sir Hector Munro.

His first public office of note was that of Principal Clerk of Session, which he attained in 1763. In 1776, he was elevated to the Bench, and assumed the title of Lord Ankerville, a name by which part of his property was known. There is a farm in the Parish of Nigg called Ankerville, and a street in Tain called Ankerville Street. The Tain Royal Academy is built upon land gifted to the Trustees by his Lordship.

In 1786, he sold the estates of Shandwick, Culliss, and Ankerville to William Ross of Shandwick for £17,600 but retained possession of Tarlogie, Morangie and Aldie.

Lord Ankerville married Margaret, daughter of John Cochrane of Ravelring, and died at Tarlogie on 16th August, 1805. He left two sons and three daughters: (i) David (ii) Charles (iii) Margaret, who married

James Baillie of Ardmore, a Captain in the 7th Fusiliers (iv) Elizabeth, and (v) Jane, both of whom died unmarried. Lord Ankerville was succeeded by his eldest son David.

*David, fourth of Invercastley* In 1777 he entered the banking house of Messrs. Coutts & Drummond. He married Marion, daughter of Colonel Gall, Military Secretary to Warren Hastings. After the death of her first husband, she married Lord Reay. By her first marriage she had a family of three sons and three daughters. The sons entered the Bengal Army, and died without issue, so that the family in that line became extinct. One of the daughters, Marion, married Colonel Cramer Roberts, and by the union two sons were born. John the eldest, became heir of the line of Invercastley, but died without issue about 1836. Of the other son nothing is known.

THE ROSSSES OF CALROSSIE, 1709-1790

*Thomas Ross*, the first of the name to own the lands of Calrossie, was the fourth son of Malcolm Ross, first of Kindeace. Previous to possessing Calrossie he owned portions of other lands in Easter Ross, but their exact location is beyond identification.

Most of the Rosses of Calrossie engaged in military careers and gained distinction both in Scotland and in Canada.

It was from David Polson of Kimmylies near Inverness that Thomas Ross acquired the lands of Calrossie. This is shown in a sasine dated 11th July, 1709, which states that the lands of Calrossie, in the Parish of Logie-Easter, were made over by the said David Polson in favour of Thomas Ross of Knockan. Thomas Ross was married and had a son also named Thomas.

*Thomas Ross* became second of Calrossie. Living in the neighbourhood of the town of Tain, he naturally took an interest in the management of its affairs. He was its treasurer in 1736, and became Sherrif-Substitute of Ross in 1750. He was married to Isobel, daughter of William Ross, sixth of Eastern Fearn. He disposed of the lands of Pitnellies, in the Parish of Tain, to his wife on the 21st October, 1749; Thomas, their eldest son was a witness to the transaction. By the marriage they had three sons and two daughters.

(i) Thomas Ross the eldest son became an officer and served in Canada under General Wolfe at the capture of Quebec. He was a Captain with Fraser's Highland Regiment, and sailed with his regiment from Greenock to Halifax in June 1757. During the next winter it was proposed to change the uniform of the regiment, as Highland garb was judged unfit for the severe winters and hot summers in North America.

The officers and soldiers however were so vehemently opposed to abandoning the kilt that the plan was relinquished.

The regiment, together with Montgomery's Highlanders, had twenty-five sailing ships of the line, eighteen frigates and a number of fire ships. General Wolfe and Admiral Boscowen were in command and after successfully capturing the garrison at Louisbourg, they proceeded up the St. Lawrence with nine other regiments to the conquest of Quebec. Captain Thomas Ross of Calrossie died with his General on the plains of Abraham in 1759.

(ii) Alexander, the second son was also a soldier, and on his father's death, became third of Calrossie (iii) John, who was accidently poisoned in Ireland (iv) Elizabeth (v) Catherine, who married John Munro, second of Culcairn, and died at Newton, Novar, in 1757. Of Catherine's marriage there was a family of three sons and a daughter.

*Alexander Ross*, third Laird of Calrossie, adopted the army as a profession, and rose to the rank of Lieutenant-Colonel. He died in 1790 unmarried, the last male descendant of this branch of the Clan Ross.

The Rosses of Calrossie still continue however, in the female descent, as the present family of *Rosses of Cromarty*. Catherine Munro, the younger daughter of Thomas Ross, lived with her family at Cromarty. Her husband John Munro took a leading part in the defence of the country during the troublous times in the latter part of the eighteenth century.

## The Rosses of Aldie, 1628-1756

*John Ross, first of Aldie*. The first of the Clan Ross to possess the property of Aldie, in the vicinity of Tain, was *John Ross*, who was a merchant in the town. He acquired the land from Robert Munro in 1628. John, Bishop of Ross, confirmed the transfer by charter. John Ross was married to a daughter of John Ferguson, one of the magistrates of Tain, with issue. He was succeeded by his eldest son.

*John Ross, second of Aldie* He was married to a daughter of William Ross of Tain, and had two sons, William and John Ross.

*William Ross, third of Aldie* The property descended to the eldest son, William, who was a Commissioner of Supply for the county of Ross in 1689-90. The estate during his time was entailed. In the Register of Sasines at Inverness, there is entered the following: "Entail of Aldie, under great seal in favour of Simon Ross of Rosehill, son of William Ross of Aldie; . . . of the lands and mill of Aldie". This document bears date 26th July, 1723. William married Sibilla, daughter of Sir Kenneth Mackenzie of Coul, and secondly he married a daughter of Thomas

Mackenzie of Inverall. Sir Kenneth was in great favour with Charles II, who bestowed on him a baronetcy, with succession to the heirs male of his body, dated 1673.

William Ross had a family of several sons and daughters, including (i) Simon, who became fourth of Aldie; (ii) David, who became an eminent physician in Bristol (iii) Elizabeth, who married Hugh Ross of Braelangwell and (iv) Ann, who married John Sutherland of Little Torboll.

*Simon Ross, fourth of Aldie* He succeeded to the property on his father's death. He was married to Ann, second daughter of George Munro of Newmore, and had four sons. The eldest, William, inherited the property of Newmore which was willed to him by his uncle, Lieutenant-Colonel John Munro. The property was entailed by Colonel Munro on himself and his heirs whomsoever; whom, failing, on *David Ross, third of Invercastley.* Colonel Munro died without leaving issue, and the property went to David Ross, Lord Ankerville.

Simon, had three other sons—Duncan, Robert and David. When William succeeded to Newmore, Duncan claimed the estate of Aldie, but he died before his claim was allowed. His cousin, John Middleton, son of Dr. Middleton, carried on the suit. Captain Simon Mackenzie, second son of Kenether Mackenzie, eventually inherited Aldie, and added the name of Ross to his own.

The estate of Aldie has, like so many other Highland properties, passed out of the hands of its ancient possessors, and was recently owned by Mr. Finlay Macgillivary, the noted breeder of shorthorns. Before this it was in the possession of the late Mr. John Gunn, who spent a large sum of money on improvements.

THE ROSSES OF PITKERRIE

*Alexander* was the first of the line of Rosses of Pitkerrie, a son of John Ross of Little Tarrell. Rev. Alexander Ross was at one time a Minister of Tain. He married Janet, daughter of Andrew Munro of Limorn, and left a family of three sons. He was succeeded by his second son.

*Andrew,* second of Pitkerrie, was Minister of Tarbat Kirk. He married Elizabeth Bruce, and left two sons.

*Alexander,* third of Pitkerrie, married a daughter of William Cockburn, a major in the army, and left two sons, Benjamin and Andrew.

*Andrew* succeeded to the property. He was married to Catherine, daughter of Duncan Fraser of Achnagairn, seventh of Skibo. Catherine married, secondly, George Gray. By the first marriage she had a son, George and a daughter, Jean, who married Robert Kirk, minister of Dornoch. By the second marriage Mrs. Kirk had a daughter Catherine, who married Duncan Munro.

*George, fifth of Pitkerrie,* and first of Cromarty.

THE CROMARTY ROSSES, 1700-1924

*George Ross, fifth of Pitkerrie,* became *first of Cromarty* by his purchase of this estate in 1772. Born in 1700, he was an army agent during the reign of George II, and acquired a great fortune. He also purchased the Barony of Kimmylies, near Inverness, and made extensive improvements. This land was afterwards sold to the family of its present owner, Colonel J. E. B. Baillie of Dochfour.

When quite a young man George Ross, full of energy and enterprise, went south to seek his fortune. In London he enjoyed the friendship of many of the notable men of the period. "The good laird," was immortalised by "Junius," who, in one of his *Letters* referring to some transactions by Duke of Grafton, says that the person employed in the negotiations was George Ross, the Scotch Agent, the confidant of Lord Mansfield.

In 1772, George Ross purchased the estate and the whole town of Cromarty. He at once commenced to improve the estate, and it would appear that there was much need. "The country," writes Hugh Miller, "was dead. There was no manufacturing, no knowledge of agriculture, no consciousness that matters were ill, and consequently no desire to make them better." He established in the town of Cromarty an extensive factory for hempen cloth, which employed 200 persons within its walls. He next built an ale brewery, which became the largest in the North of Scotland. He constructed a harbour, established a nail and stake factory, brought women from England to instruct the young girls of Cromarty in the art of making lace, presented the town with a Council Chamber and Courthouse, and built the Gaelic chapel. He had an only son who predeceased his father by several years.

George Ross was M.P. for Cromartyshire from 1780 to 1784. He died on the 7th April, 1786, and the estate passed to George Gray, son of his half-brother, Alexander Gray of Skibo, who assumed the name of Ross. He, too, died without issue, and the property passed to Catherine Munro, niece of George Ross.

Catherine married Hugh Rose of Glastullich, who also assumed the name Ross, and had a family of two daughters and a son: (i) Catherine, who married Thomas Knox Hobson, and English barrister (ii) Arabella who married Duncan Davidson, of Tulloch (iii) George William Holmes Ross.

*Hugh Rose Ross, second of Cromarty,* amassed a fortune in the West Indies, and purchased Glastullich, Calrossie, Tarlogie, and Culcain. He greatly improved his properties, planted extensively, and in Mitchell's *Reminiscences* it is stated that Rose was "a great promoter of roads and public works" in and around Cromarty "and a keen litigant."

It is interesting to record, as an indication of old-time life and courtesies of the shire, that this Hugh fought a duel, the last known in Ross-shire, with Duncan Davidson of Tulloch, in January 1841. No untoward event happened, both men firing into the air in satisfaction of honour. Hugh Rose-Ross died in 1866 in his eightieth year. His eventful life was not without many good deeds to his credit. By his enterprise and generosity many worthy causes received benefit, and various local industries were encouraged. It was mainly through his help in raising a sum of ten thousand pounds that the Royal Academy of Tain was established and endowed. Hugh Ross was for some years Provost of the burgh of Tain, he was buried in its ancient church of St. Duthac.

*Colonel George William Holmes Ross, third of Cromarty,* son of the foregoing, succeeded to the Cromarty estate on the death of his mother in 1852. He entered the army and received his commission as ensign in the 92nd Highlanders. In 1854 he was gazetted Captain in the Ross-shire Militia (later 3rd Battalion Seaforth Highlanders), and rose to the position of Commander of that regiment.

It appears that Colonel Ross was prohibited by the terms of his ancestor's entail from bearing any other name that that of Ross. In 1878, however, he petitioned the Lord Lyon, and was granted permission to bear the crest and motto of the Munros with the Ross arms.

In 1852, Colonel Ross unsuccessfully contested Ross-shire against Sir James Matheson. He was married in 1849 to Adelaide Lucy, daughter of Duncan Davidson of Tulloch, and had a family of three sons and four daughters: (i) Duncan Munro Ross, who was born on the 29th September, 1851, and when quite young entered the Royal Navy. (ii) Hugh Ross, who became a lieutenant in the Royal Artillery. On the outbreak of war in Afghanistan in 1878 he went to the front but died at Quetta in 1879. (iii) Walter Charteris Ross, who succeeded to the estate.

*Sir "Watty" Ross, fourth of Cromarty,* was born on August 5, 1857. Following in his brother Hugh's footsteps Walter also joined the army and held rank in the Durham Light Infantry. He served in the Afghan War along with his brother, and was decorated for his services. He served in the South African War, 1899-1900, and was three times mentioned in dispatches. He received the Queen's Medal with five clasps, and was awarded his C.B. It is of interest to note that in the South African (Boer) War, General Ross was A.D.C. to General Sir Hector Macdonald, a Black Isle Laird, and a Black Isle smallholder's son, a fact honourable to both and of which both were mutually proud, understanding each other and sharing in the hardships and dangers during the most exacting period of the campaign. It was in course of his despatch duties that General Ross received a serious wound in the face, a Boer sharpshooter's bullet passing through his mouth, but fortunately he made a good recovery. Although retired, General Ross offered for the First World War in 1914, and was appointed to the Middle East Front, with a Brigadier-General's command in Salonika. Here he passed through strenuous hardships and some severe fighting. His services were recognized in despatches, and he was awarded the K.B.E. and C.M.G.

After the Armistice of 1918, General Ross took up his estate duties and interested himself in the public life of the county, taking special interest in farming. He was keenly interested in the cultivation of sugar beet as a likely assistance for the agricultural industry in the north of Scotland. Several farmers found it profitable, but the distance to the nearest sugar factory proved to be a great handicap and farmers lost interest. He was appointed Secretary to the Territorial Association of Ross and Cromarty, Sutherland and Caithness, Inverness and Nairn, and, with his staff did valued work in popularising the Territorial services in northern counties. He was secretary to the Moray Firth Salmon Fishing Association, chairman of the Harbour Trustees, chairman of the Cromarty Cottage Hospital, and of the Lifeboat Committee. An active member of the Black Isle Farmers' Society, he was one of its most valued members. His interest in the Northern Games was also well known, and his familiar figure in Highland dress, as one of the stewards and judges, was seldom absent from the games. His keen interest in Highland sports was inherited, and he was always happy when judging prowess at any of the Highland gatherings.

Personally, General Ross was one of the most genial of men. Naturally shy and diffident, despite his dash and courage as a soldier, his geniality was of the quiet and kindly type, and when in the mood, especially when making a speech at a farmers' dinner, or presiding at any social function, he had a sparkling humour that was always as apt as it was kindly. His death on February 9, 1928, was deeply regretted by everyone in his native Ross-shire.

General "Watty" Ross was twice married. In 1887, to May, a daughter of Field-Marshal Sir Donald Stewart, and in 1897, to Gertrude May Gathorne, daughter of Mr. Charles Hill of Clevedon Hall, Somerset. He was survived by two sons and four daughters. The eldest son,

George Duncan Noel Ross, like his father, chose a military career, entering the Royal Military Academy, and on January 30, 1924, the year of his coming of age, he was commissioned to the 1st Battalion The Seaforth Highlanders. Other members of this family of Rosses of Cromarty are believed to be living in Ross-shire but have not been identified.

Armorial Shield of
Major General Robert Ross
of Bladensburg 1814

# APPENDIX II

## KING ROBERT STEWART II OF SCOTLAND (1316 - 1390) AND CLAN ROSS

During the reign of King Robert II the Clan was closely associated with royalty.

It is not easy to have a mental picture of this early Scottish King who married Euphemia Ross, some time in the year 1355.

For both it was a second marriage, as Euphemia, daughter of Hugh 4th Earl of Ross, had already been married to Randolph Earl of Moray, comrade-in-arms and friend of Robert. Robert's first marriage had been with Elizabeth Mure of Rowallan in 1336.

Euphemia Ross's father had also been married twice. By his first marriage to Bruce's sister Maud he had three children, and by his second marriage to Margaret, daughter of Sir David Graham of Old Montrose, he had a son Hugh, who became founder of the Ross Clan as we know it to-day, and Euphemia who became Queen of Scotland in 1371.

To be accurate we should not call her Euphemia Ross or her brother Hugh Ross, as the use of the surname was not employed in Scotland until nearly two centuries later, but Euphemia, sister of Hugh of Rariches and Balnagowan, is too cumbersome for our purpose in this sketch.

Nearly everything recorded about Robert II is interesting and would make a good subject for biography.

He led the second division of the Scottish army at the battle of Halidon Hill in 1333, when only a lad of sixteen, and it was at this battle that his future father-in-law, Hugh the fourth Earl of Ross, was killed.

Robert had a fine appearance. Bower says: "He was beautiful beyond the sons of men, stalwart and tall, accessible to all, modest, liberal, cheerful and honest." The brilliance of his youth and the Stewart charm no doubt tended to spoil him, for he was a great favourite with the ladies, having at least twenty-two children, nine by Elizabeth Mure and four by Euphemia, and illegitimate ones by Lady Moram, Marion Cardeny, and Isobel Butler.

He lived at Dundonald Castle outside of Irvine, Ayrshire, and his summer residence was at Bute. Like all the Stewarts he was fond of the sea.

Let us turn for a moment to his birth and to the troubled state of Scotland at that time.

Robert was born by Caesarian section on the roadside near Renfrew —a mound of stones marks the spot to this day. His mother, Marjorie Bruce, was out hunting and fell from her horse, and later died from injuries received.

For the sake of the succession to the throne it was most important that Marjorie should have a son. Marjorie was Bruce's daughter, and had married the High Steward Walter, and up to the time of Robert's birth there was no male heir.

The Scottish Parliament had met at Ayr in 1315 and passed their first Act of Succession, whereby, failing male heirs, King Robert I (the Bruce) was to be succeeded by his brother Edward, who at one time was betrothed to Isabella Ross, sister of Hugh 4th Earl of Ross, and sister of Walter Ross killed at Bannockburn in 1314. Failing this match, the Crown was to go to Bruce's daughter Marjorie, who was married to Walter, but poor Marjorie died and Edward was killed in Ireland a few months later, so this Ayr Act did not come into effect.

The second Act of Succession at Scone in 1318 settled the Crown on Robert, but some years later Robert Bruce did eventually have a son David born in 1324.

The third Act of Succession in 1326 gave David precedence over his nephew Robert Stewart.

Bruce died of leprosy in 1329, to be succeeded by David II, age five, under the guardianship of Thomas Randolph Earl of Moray, who had led the left wing of the Scottish army at Bannockburn and who became father-in-law to Euphemia Ross. David was officially crowned in 1331. It was a bad time for Scotland as the old Comyn-Baliol faction (who had lost their estates because of their opposition to the Bruce family) were on the warpath again. The Earl of Athol was among them, as his mother was a daughter of Red John Comyn, whom Bruce had killed, and his aunt had been the wife of Edward Bruce, who had left after a quarrel.

Four Regents were killed, captured, or died within a year, and after Douglas the Regency was held jointly by John Randolph, son of the Earl of Moray and his friend Robert Stewart, who was eighteen at the time.

History does not relate how Euphemia Ross got on with that strong-minded sister of John Randolph. This was Agnes, Countess of March, who held the Castle of Dunbar for the first half of 1337. She sang insulting jingles to the besiegers and led her maids with dusters under fire to mock the results of Salisbury's mangonels. Black Agnes was almost starved out for the English had command of the sea, but the siege was raised by Ramsay of Dalhousie. Next morning Black Agnes sent Salisbury (who was also short of food) a gift of white bread and wine for she was a woman of spirit and sardonic humour. King Edward of England had young King David as his prisoner and we can look for a moment at Robert Stewart's domestic arrangements.

Elizabeth Mure bore him nine children. John, Walter, Robert, Alexander, Margaret, Marjorie, Elizabeth, Isabel, Jean; but after ten years Robert's enemies challenged the legality of the marriage on the grounds that the contracting parties were within the fourth degree of consanguinity—which meant that they were forty-second cousins. They applied to the Pope for a retrospective dispensation legitimising the children and this was granted in 1347. This matter is important to historians as it led directly to the murder of Robert Stewart's grandson, James I of Scotland, one of the best of the Stewart kings. Inded, the echoes of this legal squabble were to ring down the next two centuries till 1632, when the Earl of Monteith claimed the Earldom of Strathearn and the crown worn by Charles I.

Robert Stewart had to endure much in the reign of David II. At one time when the barons were stronger he and his sons were incarcerated in various strongholds. Robert and his fourth son Alexander Stewart were sent to Lochleven Castle, where Mary, Queen of Scots, was also held prisoner a long time after. (Alexander, the "Wolf of Badenock", his son, married another Euphemia who was Countess of Ross in her own right.)

It was a time of plague, flood, and famine. After David was ransomed from England, and as he had married Joan the English King's sister, he found life in England much more pleasant than ruling a bankrupt Scotland. He died in 1371, aged forty-seven, leaving Scotland in chaos, and his nephew Robert Stewart became king at the age of fifty-four. Meantime, during David's captivity, Elizabeth Mure had died and Robert had married Euphemia Ross in 1355. She bore him four children: David, made Earl of Strathearn, Walter, made Earl of Athol, Egidia, who was a real beauty and might have become Queen of France had she not chosen a love match with Sir William Douglas, and Katherine who married the first Earl of Crawford.

Queen Euphemia was crowned separately from her husband in the summer of 1371, and she must have had a busy time arranging suitable matches for her large family. The heir John, Earl of Carrik, married Annabel the niece of Queen Margaret; Walter married Isabel Countess of Fife, in her own right; Robert, the ablest son, who became the Regent Albany, married (as her fourth husband) Margaret Graham, Countess of Monteith, then Muriel Keith, daughter of the Marischal. Another daughter Margaret married John, 1st Lord of the Isles, Elizabeth married Thomas Hay, the Constable, and Jean, last of the children of the first marriage married John Keith, heir of the Marischal. On his death Jean married Sir John Lyon of Glamis, the Chamberlain, who was murdered by his nephew. Jean is therefore ancestress of our most noble Queen Elizabeth II whom God preserve. There were other children by the left hand: John Sheriff of Bute, ancestor of the present Marquis, Thomas, Archdeacon of St. Andrews, John the Red Stewart of Dundonald, all full brothers as sons of Lady Moran, three more by Marion Cardney, and two by Isabel Butler.

Meantime Robert the King worked hard to repair the ruin of the country caused by David's disastrous reign, but he was in failing health, growing deaf and nearly blind. His old age saddened by infirmity and disillusion. He died at Dundonald on the 13th May, 1390, and was buried at Scone.

He was succeeded by his son John, now over fifty, who changed his name to Robert III. He had been badly kicked by a horse when young and grew up a sad melancholic invalid, with no vitality nor liking for the difficult job of keeping the turbulent nobles in order, and his reign barely saw out the century. He had been King for four years when Queen Annabel bore James, who was to be murdered, just as he was giving an indication that he was everything that his father was not. Not a propitious start for the Stewart dynasty.

# APPENDIX III

## THE SEVEN EUPHEMIAS

The name Euphemia (in Gaelic Eighrig) chimes like a silver bell through the saga of the early Earls of Ross, but without a genealogical table it is difficult to give each a local habitation and a name. The Euphemias however are the most important women in Clan Ross history.

Our first Euphemia was a daughter of the great Farquhar, first Earl of Ross, and was a sister of William the second Earl, who died in 1274. She married Sir Walter Moray, Lord of Duffus, but we have no records of her family after that. Our second Euphemia married William, the third Earl of Ross, who died in 1322; we do not know her antecedents, but she must have been a remarkable woman. When her husband fell foul of the king and was confined to the Tower of London from 1296 to 1303, she took the long road to London and so worked on the affections of King Edward I that she got William released and given the position of Warden of Scotland beyond the Spey. In the course of his duties Earl William arrested Bruce's wife and daughter, who had sought refuge in St. Duthac's Chapel, Tain, and handed them over to the custody of the English King. This action violated the sanctuary of the Church and forever afterwards was held against him. In spite of this Euphemia managed to arrange a marriage between her eldest son, Hugh, and Lady Maud Bruce, sister of Robert the Bruce. Hugh became fourth Earl of Ross, and was killed at Halidon Hill in 1333.

Hugh was married twice, and by his second marriage to Margaret Graham he had one son, Hugh, progenitor of the Ross Clan, and one daughter, Euphemia. Euphemia (third) married Randolph, Earl of Moray, who was co-regent with Robert Stewart, his friend and comrade in arms, when the latter was only eighteen. Some two years later Robert married

Elizabeth Mure of Rowallan, by whom he had nine children. When John Randolph died, his widow, Euphemia, married Robert Stewart in 1355, Elizabeth Mure having died also. Euphemia bore the King four children, David, Walter, Egidia and Katherine. David II died in 1371, after a disastrous reign, and Robert became King Robert II of Scotland. *Euphemia was crowned Queen of Scotland* some months later and is chiefly notable for her skill as a matchmaker. She had twenty-two children of Robert's to arrange marriages for, and she did her work so well that Robert might well be called the Father of Scottish Aristocracy.

The fifth Earl of Ross was William Lord of Skye who married Mary, daughter of Angus Og. They had three children, Euphemia, William and Janet. This Euphemia (fourth) is perhaps the most interesting of all the Euphemias.

In 1346, William, her father, was on the way south with his clansmen to assist King David against the English.[1] They had a rendezvous with Reginald of the Isles and his men at Perth. During the evening William had a quarrel with his relative by marriage, and in the dead of night Earl William led a small party to the monastery where Reginald was quartered and slew him and seven of his clansmen. These were harsh and brutal times, but this foul deed brought about Earl William's downfall and the loss of all his vast possessions, for the men of Ross and the Isles returned home, instead of assisting the royal forces. King David pressed on regardless and met the English forces at Durham, where he was badly beaten, captured, and sent to the Tower of London; nor would Earl William contribute to the ransom of the King.

King David was not at all like his father (Robert the Bruce), being petulant and uncertain in all his dealings. Although he appears now to have been too harsh with Earl William, nevertheless, in this matter he had a certain justification. King David would not sanction William's proposal that his half-brother, Hugh of Rarichies should be declared heir to the Earldom.

He drew up a new charter for the Earldom of Ross and the Lordship of Skye and all the other lands to heirs male of the Earl's body, whom failing, to his daughter, Euphemia, and her husband, Sir Walter Leslie. Earl William's son died before his father. King David was succeeded by King Robert II. Earl William tried to get the new King to alter the judgement but William died on 9th February, 1372, and Earl William's daughter, Euphemia, succeeded as Countess of Ross in her own right, with Sir Walter Leslie calling himself the new Earl of Ross. By the claims of blood, though, this title should have gone to William 2nd of Balnagown.

[1] See page 44.

Euphemia was not happy with Sir Walter Leslie and on his death married Sir Alexander Stewart, fourth son of King Robert II by his first wife. He was the *Wolf of Badenoch,* a hard and ruthless type. This marriage is said to have been forced on her, perhaps by the other Euphemia, her aunt and Queen. In time, Euphemia (fourth) got a divorce from the "Wolf". She was in love with Alexander Mackenzie of Kintail, a fine man in every way. He, however, did not fancy her, so she captured him and took him to her castle at Dingwall as prisoner. While this was done quietly it was soon made known to all, and the powerful Mackenzie Clan rose up to rescue their chief. This led to a clan fight in the Glen of Peffery where, with much bloodshed, Alexander was rescued and Dingwall Castle was burned.

No doubt discouraged, the Countess of Ross took the veil and in time became Abbess of Elcho—at that very same monastery where her father had killed Reginald of the Isles. She became renowned for her good works and was buried at Fortrose. She was a tall gaunt woman with a long nose and a fine carriage.

Countess Euphemia had two children, Alexander Leslie and Mary (or Margaret) Leslie. Alexander married Isabella Stewart, daughter of Robert, Duke of Albany, the ablest of all King Robert II's sons. They had one daughter, Euphemia, (fifth) who had poor health. She took the veil at an early age, illegally renouncing all claim to her father's Earldom in favour of her mother's brother, John Stewart, Earl of Buchan. It was this renunciation by Euphemia that caused the battle of Harlaw in 1411, for her father's sister, Mary Leslie, had married Donald, Lord of the Isles, the best fighter in the north, and he had a strong claim to the Earldom of Ross through his wife.

To place the sixth and seventh Euphemias we must think of King Robert II and his second wife Euphemia (third).

The first son was David and the second Walter. Robert II made David Earl of Strathearn and Caithness. He left only one daughter Euphemia (sixth) who had married Sir Patrick Graham of Dundaff. There were two children of this marriage, Malise and Euphemia (seventh). Now Sir Patrick had a wild and unscrupulous younger brother Robert Graham who became involved in various plots and was finally arrested by James I in 1424, but was later released.

James I was happily married to Joan Beaufort of England and was murdered by Walter Earl of Athol and Robert Graham in a cellar beneath the Queen's bedroom in Perth. Both were beheaded for one of the most cruel and senseless murders in Scotland's troubled history. Young Malise was a hostage in England at the time.

His sister, our last Euphemia married the fifth Earl of Douglas. They had two sons, both executed in Edinburgh in 1440 by Sir William Cricton, to break the power of the Douglas family.

Scotland was a small nation and the principal characters in these early days were all closely related.

# APPENDIX IV

MOTTO: "THINK ON"

## GENEALOGY OF THE TWELFTH LORD ROSS OF HAWKHEAD

The first Geoffrey de Ros was Bailiff de Bonneville-sur-Touques in Lower Normandy, and he got a gift of the property of Hamlake in Yorkshire from Henry III.

His son, Robert de Ros, married Isabel, daughter of the Scottish King William the Lion and his Queen Ermengarde de Beaumont. This Robert de Ros, Guardian of North England got from the English King the Royal Manors of Sowerby, Carleton and Oulsby in Cumberland, and he built a Castle on a lovely site at Wark in Northumberland. Robert de Ros with two other English Knights was made Custodian, responsible to the English King for the safety and comfort of his young daughter Margaret, when she married King Alexander III of Scotland. In this matter Robert de Ros failed in his duty. Young Margaret complained to Reginald her physician that she was not allowed any freedom to see her husband in Edinburgh Castle. Reginald was mysteriously poisoned when he complained of the Queen's captivity, but before he died he managed to send word to the English King, who sent up the Earl of Gloucester and another to investigate, and Baron de Ros of Wark was heavily fined.

Isobel and Robert had one son William who had a son Robert, who in turn had a son Williams de Ros, who was one of the thirteen claimants for the Scottish Throne, ultimately given to Baliol.

This man's cousin was Sir Godfrey Ross who was Sheriff of Ayr in 1335. In or about the year 1367 he got a grant of the lands of Hawkhead in Renfrewshire from Malise, 8th Earl of Strathearn who had married Marjorie, sister of William, 5th of Ross. This transaction is surrounded in mystery. Both the Sheriff of Ayr and the Earl of Strathearn supported

King Baliol, but when Baliol was deposed by Bruce, the Sheriff was killed. Strathearn was held for treason and lost his Earldom to the Crown. But before this he had given certain lands to his kinsman Godfrey de Ros.

A Century later a descendant was made the *first Lord Ross of Hawkhead* and got the Lands of Stewartory and Melville by Charter dated 1489. The second Lord Ross was chosen with two others to fight three Burgundian Knights before James II. The third Lord Ross was killed at Flodden 1513. The fourth Lord Ross was juryman at trial of Bothwell 1567. The tenth Lord Ross was fined £3000 by Cromwell 1654. The eleventh Lord Ross married Lady Grizel Cochrane, Daughter of Lord Dundonald. The twelfth Lord Ross of Hawkhead lived from 1656 to 1738. It is he who received severe censure from the Rosses of Balnagowan for usurping their estates and the baronetsy while there was still a legitimate heir male. He was married four times, first to Anges Wilkie, by whom he had one son George, and one daughter Euphemia who married the third Earl of Kilmarnock. One daughter married the Duke of Atholl, another daughter Grizel married Sir James Lockhart.

His second marriage to a daughter of Philip Lord Warton had no issue; the third marriage was to Lady Hay, Daughter of Marquis of Tweedale, by whom he had one daughter Anne, who died unmarried. The fourth, to Henrietta had no issue.

The twelfth Lord Ross was sent to the Tower in 1690 for share in the Montgomery plot, he was fined and later pardoned. After the accession of Queen Anne in 1701 he was made Lord High Commissioner for the Church of Scotland at Edinburgh.

His greatest ambition was to become the Earl of Ross. Perhaps this was why he bought the Balnagowan estates, and it is curious that Strathearn who married the sister of the fifth Earl of Ross should have referred to Godfrey de Ros as a "Kinsman". The connection is not traceable, and the Earl of Cromartie was highly indignant at the suggestion that the Rosses of Hawkhead or their predecessors had any claim to Highland ancestry. None the less, though they were not of Highland blood, their blood was bluest of the blue. Could they not boast one Admiral John de Ros in the time of Edward II and another Admiral Sir John Lockhart Ross in Nelson's time?

# Clan Notes

BADGE

Juniper—*Aiteann* in Gaelic

MOTTO

*Spem successus alit.* Success nourishes hope.

CREST

A hand holding a garland of Juniper, proper.

COAT OF ARMOUR

Three lions rampant on shield.

PIPE MUSIC

Clan Ross has produced a number of excellent pipers. William Ross a native of Ross-shire has published a book of marches, strathspeys and reels, which has become a standard of Highland bagpipe music. It includes the march "The Ross-shire Volunteers".

The distinctive pipe music of Clan Ross is "The Earl of Ross's March —*Spaidsearachd Iarla Rois.*

PRECEDENCE OF SCOTTISH CLANS AND NAMES

In a list of hereditary precedence of Scottish Clans and Names[1] deriving from Baronage, Ross is first in precedence, dating from 1160.

TARTAN

In addition to the red Tartan of Ross, there is the Hunting Tartan in green.

[1] Frank Adam and Sir Thomas Innes of Learney, 4th Ed. 1952.

# Index


A

Abbey, Edderton, 18
Acadia, 113, 114
Achnacloich, Rosses of, 66, 90
Adams, John, 118
Aindreis, Clan, 1, 2, 4, 36
Alban, 15
Albacore, Ship, 141
Albany, Duke of, 51
Aldearn, 42
Aldie, Rosses of, 90, 170, 171
Alexander "Crotach" Macleod, 56
Alexander Lord, 13, 113
Alexander of the Isles, 13, 47, 49, 54
Alexander of Lochalsh, 13, 58
Alexander Ross, 126
Alexander Ross, King's Chaplain, 143
Alexander Ross, Scots Bard, 145
Alexander Ross of Inverness, 148
Alexander "the Upright" Mackenzie, 57
Alexander II, 38, 39
Alexander III, 5, 39, 40, 41
Alexander, Sir William, 113, 114
Alness, 17, 61, 80, 92
Alt a' Charrais, 3, 32, 35, 65, 66, 97
Alt-Grannda, 12, 21
American Flag (Betsy Ross), 116, 119
Andrew, 4
Angus Og, 47, 55, 57, 59
Ankerville, Lord, 168
Ankerville, Rosses of, 90, 102, 162
Antigonish, 124, 129
Applecross, 2, 15, 18, 36, 39
Ardtornish Castle, 10, 14, 50, 56
Ardtornish, treaty of, 56
Argyll, 4
Aros Castle, 15
Assiniboia, Council of, 132
Assint, 2, 91
Athole, Earl, 41
Aurora, the ship, 139
Avoch Castle, 10, 14

B

Badenoch, 9, 13, 50
Balblair Rosses, 102, 116, 118, 134
  Andrew Ross, 1st laird, 116
  David Ross, 2nd laird, 117
  Andrew Ross, 3rd laird, 117
  Dr. Andrew Ross, 4th laird, 117
  Rev. George Ross, 5th laird, 117
  Hon. John Ross, 118
  Rev. Aneas Ross, 118
  George Ross, Col., 119
  Gertrude Ross, 119
  Elizabeth Ross, 119
  Susanna Ross, 120
  Mary Ross, 120
  Dr. Jacob Ross, 120
  Hon. James Ross, 120
  Hon. Edmond Ross, 120
  Hon. Jonathan Ross, 120
  Elizabeth (Betsy) Ross, 120, 121
Balconie Boulder, 22
Balconie Castle, 10
Balconie, Lady of, 21
Balliol, King John, 41
Balloch, Donald, 56
Balnagowan, 2, 11, 60, 67, 68-72, 75, 81, 87
Balnagowan Castle, 2, 11, 12, 61, 68, 74-5, 80, 84, 85, 87, 88, 92, 93, 95, 96, 163

Balnagowan, Chiefs of
Hugh of Rarichies, 1st chief, 1, 43, 60, 61, 62, 94, 181
William, 2nd chief, 61, 62
Walter Ross, 3rd chief, 62, 64
Hugh Ross, 4th chief, 62, 63
John Ross, 5th chief, 62, 65
Alexander Ross, 6th chief, 62, 65
Sir David Ross, 7th chief, 62, 66, 163
Walter Ross, 8th chief, 62, 67
Alexander Ross, 9th chief, 63, 67
George Ross, 10th chief, 63, 70, 71
David Ross, 11th chief, 63, 72, 73, 163
David Ross, 12th chief, 63, 73, 74, 75
David Ross, 13th chief, 63, 75, 76
New Line of Succession of Balnagowan
Francis Stewart, 76, 77, 78
Lord Ross of Hawkhead, 77, 78, 79, 80
Lt. General Charles Ross, 77, 80
Col. Charles Ross, 77, 81
Lady Grizel Lockhart and Sir James, 77, 82, 83
Sir William-Lockhart-Ross, 77, 82
Sir James Lockhart, 77, 83
Sir George Lockhart, 77, 83
Admiral Sir John Lockhart-Ross, 77, 83, 84, 85
Sir Charles W.A. Lockhart-Ross, 77, 85
Sir Charles H.A.F. Lockhart-Ross, 77, 86, 87
Balnagowan, Historical Documents, 88, 89
Bannockburn, 6, 42, 177
Baronet of Nova Scotia, 83, 85, 87, 113-14, 160
Baronial alliances, 66
Battle of Bloody Bay, 57
Bernere, 9
Berwick, 115
Bird, Col. Mark, 120
Bishop of Ross, 15, 48, 97
Black Isle, 5, 15, 84, 174
Black plague, 44
Black, Rev. 132
Bladensburg Rosses, 121, 122
Major Gen. Robert Ross, 121, 122
Lt. Col. Sir John Ross, 122
Blair Castle, 56
Boece Hector, 5
Bolton U.S.A., 115
Bothwell, Earl of, 70
Braelangwell, Rosses of, 90, 160, 161
Brahan Castle, 9
Brochs, 19
Dun Borve, 19
Dun Cromore, 19
Cisteal Gruguig, 19
Broom, Loch, 124
Bruce, King Robert, 19, 42, 43, 177, 180
Buchan, Earl of, 61

C

Cadboll, 67, 68, 69, 79, 160
Cadets of Clan Ross, 90, 159 to 175
Caithness, Earl of, 70
Caithness, Earldom of, 6, 123
Caledonia, 27, 133
Caledonians, 4
Calrossie, Rosses of, 169, 170
Cambridge, U.S.A., 115
Cameron Duncan, 131
Cameron Clan, 2, 55, 116, 125
Campbell, Sir John, 72
Canmore, Malcolm, 5
Canadian Colonization, 113, 114, 122, 123, 124, 125, 126, 127
Carlisle, Parish of, 120
Carnegie, Andrew, 151
Castles—
Ardtornish Castle, 14, 50, 55
Aros Castle, 15
Argyll Castle, 13
Avoch Castle, 14
Balconie Castle, 12
Balnagowan Castle, 2, 11, 12, 61, 68, 74, 75, 80, 87, 88, 95, 96, 163
Blair Castle, 56
Brahan, 9
Cadboll Castle, 68
Cromartie, 88
Delny Castle, 13, 40, 43
Duart Castle, 9
Dingwall Castle, 10, 15, 42, 52, 57, 58
Dunbar Castle, 41, 178
Dundonald Castle, 177, 179
Eilean Donnain Castle, 39
Inverness Castle, 13, 54
Kildrummie Castle, 48
Leod Castle, 59
Loch-an-Eilean Castle, 13
Lochindorb Castle, 13
Lochleven Castle, 178
Redcastle, 15
Rossie Castle, 147
Ruthven Castle, 13
Skibo Castle, 148
Swin Castle, 14
Tantallon Castle, 55
Urquhart Castle, 12, 43, 56
Celestine, 58, 59

Celtic, 4, 6, 18, 20, 125
Celtic Cross, 20
Chamberlain of Ross, 10
Charles I, 17, 113, 144
Charles II, 59, 74, 171
Chattan, Clan, 27, 55, 73
Chisolm, 2, 116
Churchill, 130
Clan Aindreis, 1, 2, 4, 36
Clan Ross Septs, 3
Clan Ross Society in America, 133 to 142
  Sir George W. Ross, 133, 135
  Hon. Leonard W. Ross, 135, 138
  Commodore James Ross, 135, 137
  Senator William Ross, 135, 139
  Rear Admiral Albert Ross, 135
  Hon. David Ross, 135, 140
  Capt. Worth G. Ross, 135
  Judge Nesbitt S. Ross, 135
  Hon. Wm. R. Ross, 135
  Samuel Ross, 135
  Edwin James Ross, 135
  Dr. Arthur E. Ross, 135
  Hon. Duncan Ross, 135
  Judge Wm. N. Ross, 135
  Alexander Ross MacMahon, 133, 135
  Raymond S. Ross, 135
Clanship, 6, 7
Claverhouse, 75
Clunies Ross, George, 151, 152
  John, 2nd, 153
  George, 3rd, 153
  John Sidney, 4th, 153
Clearances, 84, 123, 124
Cocos Keeling Islands (Ross), 153
Colin of Aird, 2, 36
Comet, Ross's, 154
Comyns, 13, 177
Concord, U.S.A., 115
Congregations of Reformers, 67
Corbet, 3
Corm, Donald, 59
Cottars, 9
Countess of Ross, 45, 54, 55, 182
Coul, Earl of, 56
County of Ross, 5, 123
Covenanters, 17
Covetyce, 31
Craigie of Gainsay, 114
Crawford, Earl of, 56
Cromartie, Earl of, 78, 185
Cromartie, Rosses, 90, 172, 173
Cromwell, 74
Culbrain, Earl of, 79
Cullisse, 64
Culloden, 13
Cumberland House, 132
Custodiers, 58

D

Daer, Fort, 130
Dalriada, 4
Darnley, Lord, 59
David I, 5, 50
David II, King, 44-7, 50-1, 60, 61, 177-8
David Ross, chief, 11
David Ross, of Dingwall, 147
David Ross, Shakespearean Actor, 149
David Ross, Scientist, 154
David A. Ross, Astronomer, 155
Declaration of Independence, 119
Deerfield, U.S.A., 115
Deis-iuil, 22
Dekantar tribe, 4
Delaware, 116
Delny Castle, 10, 13, 40, 43, 46
DeMoleyns, Hon. Francis, 12
Denoon, 3
Diarmaid, 22
Dingwall, 3, 5, 16, 51-2, 84, 129
Dingwall Castle, 13, 15, 49, 56-7, 58
Dingwall, Lord, 10, 58
Diri Moir, 23
Disarming Act, 9, 123, 161
Donald Clan, 51
Donald Corm, 59
Donald, Lord of the Isles, 44, 49, 51-3
Dornock Firth, 18, 64
Dorchester, Mass., 139
Douglas, Earl of, 56
Drowning pool, 20
Druidism, 15
Dukedom of Ross, 59
Duke of Albany, 182
Duart Castle, 9
Dubh, Donald, 47, 59
Dun Borve Brock, 19
Dunbar, Castle, 41
Dunbar, John, 31
Duncan of the Isles, 55
Dun Cromare Broch, 19
Dundonald Castle, 10, 14
Dun of Creich, 64

E

Earldom of Ross, 10, 39, 57, 73, 79
Earls of Ross, 1, 2, 10, 11, 46, 47, 90, 97, 144
  Farquhar, 1st Earl, 10, 18, 36-9
  William, 2nd Earl, 40
  William, 3rd Earl, 10, 13, 41-2, 180

Hugh, 4th Earl, 43
William, 5th Earl, 1, 44-5, 181
Sir Walter Leslie, 6th Earl, 46-7, 182
Alexander Leslie, 7th Earl, 47
Sir John Stewart, 8th Earl, 47
Alexander (Macdonald), 9th Earl, 47
John (Macdonald), 10th Earl, 47
Easter Allan, 61
Easter Fearn, Rosses of, 90, 162
Edderton, 16, 19, 39, 86
Edderton Abbey, 18
Eddystone, ship, 129
Ederachillis, the wolf of, 23
Edward I, 13, 41, 42
Edward IV, 14, 56
Edward and Ann, ship, 129
Elcho Monastery, 48
Elgin Cathedral, 48
Erebus, the ship, 157
Euphemia Ross, 14, 15, 42, 46, 47-51, 94, 176, 177-8, 181-2
Euphemias, The seven, 180
Executioner, 83

F

Farquhar, Earl, 35-40
Favourite, the, 125
Fearn, 3, 70, 86, 100
Fearn, Abbot of, 16
Fearn Abbey, 18, 40, 73, 91, 97
Fergusons, 116
Fiery cross, 128
Fingal, 22
Finleigh, 22
Flodden, 58
Fontenoy, 81
Fort Churchill, 130
Fortrose, 168
Fort Simpson, 133
Fort William, 125
Foulis, Earl of, 57, 79
Fraser, 125, 169

G

Gaelic, 4, 5, 6, 36, 68, 124, 125, 129, 131
Gaelic bard, 145
Gairloch 4, 146
Gairloch, Earl of, 78
Galda, Sir Donald, 58
Galloway, 6
Gavel, 8
General Bond, 71
General Wolfe, 169
Gurkhas, 104
Gille Aindrias, 1
Gillanders, 3, 4
Glenelg, 127
Glengarry Fencible Corps, 128
Glengarry, 116, 128, 129, 132
Glengarry Settlement, 127, 128, 129, 132
Glen Morrison, 116
Glen Urquhart, 116
Golden Age, 39
Gordon, Sir Robert, 114
Gordon Clan, 125
Gorme Donald, 71
Graham, Sir David, 61
Grampians, 6
Grant Clan, 2, 12, 116
Griscom, Elizabeth, 118
Griscom, Rebecca, 120
Grove of Flight, 65

H

Haakon, King, 6, 24, 40, 41, 50
Hagbuttis, 71
Halidon Hill, 43, 61, 180
Hamilton Regiment, 125
Hanging Hill, 20
Hardyknute, 24-9
Harlaw, battle of, 48-9, 52-3, 182
Harriet, the Ship, 125
Hawkhead, Lord Ross of, 77-80, 92, 184-5
Hays River, 129
Hebrides, 6, 39
Hector, The Ship, 124
Hercules Ross of Rossie, 147
Highland Emigration Society, 123
Highlanders, 7, 52, 127, 128, 131, 132
Highland maid, 146
Horatio Ross of Rossie, 147
Hucheon Ross, Rev., 17
Hudson's Bay, 122, 130
Hudson's Bay Company, 8, 129, 130, 132
Hudson's Bay Co. and Clan Ross, 132
Malcolm Ross, 133
John Ross, 133
William Ross, 133
Charles Ross, 133
Donald Ross, 133
B.B. Ross, 133
Hugh of Rarichies, 45, 46
Hugh Ross, Lt., 97

I

Ile St. Jean, 125
Inchcolm monastery, 55
Invercharron, Rosses of, 66
Inscribed stones, 19
Invercastley, Rosses, 90, 159, 167

Inverness, 52, 54, 56, 73, 92
Inverness Castle, 10, 13
Inverness, governor of, 75
Isabella, The ship, 155, 156
Islay, 4

J

Jacktent River, 130
Jacobite Rising, 2, 80, 101
James, Duke of Ross, 59
James I, 13, 49, 54, 66
James II, 18
James III, 31, 56
James IV, 10, 12, 15, 19, 31, 56-7
James VI, 73, 82
James C. Ross, Sir, 156-7
John and Sarah, The ship, 115
John de Ross, 36, 43
John de Yle, 14
John, Lord of the Isles, 14, 50
John of Fowlis, 57
John Ross, Sir, Arctic Explorer, 156-7
Johnson, Sir William, 116
Jura, 4
Justiciar of Scotland, 44, 54

K

Kalendar of Fearn, 43, 67
Karnonaki tribe, 4
Keith, Sir Andrew, 58
Kelpie, 20
Kenneth Ross of Lewis, 79
Kerse and Skeldon, 101-3
Kincardine, 85, 86, 100, 159
Kincardine Kirk, 16
Kildonan, 131
Kildrummie Castle, 48
Kindeace, Rosses of, 90, 91, 165-6
Kilvarock, Earl of, 79
King's Bridge, 11
King's Royal Regiment, 127
Kintail, 48, 51, 127, 128, 182
Kintail, Lord of, 48, 72
Kintyre, 9, 24, 57
Kirkaldy, 125
Knox, John, 16

L

Lady Maud Bruce, 43
Lancaster, U.S.A., 115, 119
Largs, battle of, 24, 41, 50
Leod Castle, 59
Leslie, Alexander, 47, 49
Leslie, John, 15
Leslie, Sir Walter, 15, 45, 46, 47
Lewis, island of, 5, 19, 39, 41, 125, 129, 150
Linnhe, Loch, 125
Little Allan, 118
Livingstone, Lord, 61
Lochalsh, Alexander of, 13, 58
Loch-an-Eilean Castle, 13, 46
Lochbroom, 39
Locindorb Castle, 13, 46
Loch Scaven, 21
Lockhart Rosses, 77, 82-7
Lockhart Rosses, 12
  Sir James, 77, 82, 83
  Sir William, 77, 82
  Sir George, 77, 83
  Admiral Sir John, 77, 83, 84, 123
  Lady Grizel, 82, 83
  Lt. General Sir Charles, 77, 80
  Sir Charles W.A., 77, 85
  Sir Charles H.A.F., 12, 77, 86, 87
Lord Ankerville, 168
Lord Duffus, 166, 180
Lord Macdonell, 59
Lords of the Isles, 6, 14, 15, 47, 49, 57
  John, 1st Lord, 50
  Donald, 2nd Lord, 49
  Alexander, 3rd Lord, 13, 47, 49, 54
  John, 4th Lord, 47, 49, 65
Lord John of the Isles, 65
Lord Lovat, 67
Lord of Skye, 41, 45, 181
Lord Ross of Hawkhead, 77, 78
Lord Selkirk, 129, 130
Louis XIV, 80
Loyalists, 126
Lord Lyon, King of Arms, 3, 86, 88, 109, 112, 173

M

MacAlpin, Kenneth, 4
MacCulloch, 3, 65-6, 92-3
Macdonald Clan, 2, 13, 71, 125
Macdonells, 116
Macdonell, Aeneas, 59
Macdonnell, Miles, 130
Macintosh, 2, 52
Macintyre, 116
MacKay, Angus, 3
MacKay, Clan, 51, 65
MacKay, John Raibhaich, 65, 66
MacKenzie, Alexander, 2, 91, 182
Mackenzie Clan, 2, 3, 4, 13, 51, 65
MacKinnon, Donald, 36
MacLean, 52, 126
MacLeod, 2, 3, 125
MacLeod, Torquil, 65

Macrae, Clan, 2, 48
MacTaggart, 3
MacTear, 3
MacTire, Paul, 1, 2
MacTyre, 3, 64
Magnetic Pole, 156-7
Magnus IV, 6, 41
Malcolm Canmore, 5
Malcolm de Ross, 37
Malcolm III, 5
Manrent, 7, 66
Mary, Queen of Scots, 58, 67
Maolbride, 1
Mormaers, 1, 5, 6, 10
Mar, Earl of, 52
Mariota Athyn, 48
Massachusetts Bay Colony, 114, 134
Maud Bruce, Lady, 43, 44
Maud, Princess, 42
McLeod, Clan, 2, 3, 125, 131
McDonald, ship, 128
McKinley, President U.S.A., 120
McTyre, Paul, 64
Menstrie, 113
Mitchell, 3
Mohawk Valley, 116
Moleyns, Hon. Francis de, 12
Monastery of Ross, 18
Monteith, Earl, 41
Montrose, Earl of, 17
Moray, Earl of, 43, 76, 79, 177
Moray, 5, 6, 19
Moray Firth, 68
Mull, Sound of, 9
Munro Clan, 2, 3, 15, 17, 51
Munro, Donald, 3
Munro, Robert, 70
Murray, Earl of, 73

N

Naomi Ross, 78, 93
Nairnshire, 132
Nelson House, 133
Nelson River, 129
Neptune, ship, 127
New Castle, U.S.A., 117
New England, 114
New England Rosses, 114-15
Newton, U.S.A., 115
Nigg, 16, 64, 165, 168
Ninian, 18, 39
Nobel prize, 107
Nora, the ship, 125
Norse, 5, 28, 38, 39
Nova Scotia, 124, 125, 126, 139, 140
North Magnetic Pole, 156-7
Norway House, 130, 133
Nor-Westers, 131, 133
North West Passage, 155, 156

O

O'Beolain, 1, 36, 41, 60, 75-6, 90-1
Og, Angus, 47, 55, 57, 59, 180
Okanagan, 132
Olaf the Red, 50, 64, 69
Orkney Islands, 129, 151
Oykel River, 11, 65

P

Paisley Abbey, 57
Pagan John, 124
Parry, William Edward, 155
Pellatt, Sir H., 136
Pearl, The ship, 116
Peffery, Glen of, 48
Pembina Settlement, 130
Petersham, U.S.A., 115
Philroth, Lord of, 61
Picts, 4, 5, 15, 19, 27
Pictou, 124-6, 129
Pictou Settlement, 124, 125
Pit and gallows, 114
Pitkerrie, Rosses of, 90, 171
Pitcalnie Rosses, 90-3
Nicholas Ross, 1st laird, 91
David Ross, 2nd laird, 91
David Ross, 3rd laird, 91
Alexander Ross, 4th laird, 92
Malcolm Ross, 5th laird, 92
Alexander Ross, 6th laird, 93
Munro Ross, 7th laird, 94
Capt. James Ross, 8th laird, 94
James Ross, 9th laird, 94
George Ross, 10th laird, 95
George Williamson Ross, 11th laird, 95
Ethel Williamson Ross, 12th laird, 94, 95
Rosa Williamson Ross, 13th laird, 94, 95, 96, 110, 111,
Port Royal, 114
Priory of Forres, 48
Protestantism, 16
Prince Charlie, 92, 93
Prince of Wales, The ship, 129, 130

Q

Queen Elizabeth II, 154
Queen Euphemia Ross, 46

R

Raffles, Sir Stamford, 152

Ragnhildis, 50
Rarichies, Hugh of, 1, 43, 60-2, 94, 181
Rarichies, lands of, 43, 118
Read, George, 119
Redcastle, 15, 79
Red River, 129, 130, 131, 132
Red River Carts, 132
Red River Settlement, 129, 130, 131, 132
Reformation, 16, 17, 67, 91
Reginald of the Isles, 44, 181
Reinfeftment, 45
Religion in the Highlands, 15
Riddle, Edward, 119
Robert Stewart II, King, 13, 14, 43, 46, 57, 61, 176-9, 181-2
Robert the Bruce, 19, 42-3, 177, 180-1
Roderick of Bute, 44
Ronald of the Isles, 55
Rory of the Isles, 44
Rosemarkie, 15
Ross
  Ross, Albert, Admiral, 135
  Ross, Alester, 114
  Ross, Alexander, 89, 92, 115, 124, 126, 132, 143, 145, 147-8
  Ross and Cromarty, 174
  Ross, Andrew, 118
  Ross, Aneas, 117, 118
  Ross, Annie H., 139
  Ross, Arthur E., M.P.P., 135
  Ross, Betsy, 116, 119-21
  Ross, B.R., 133
  Ross, Charles, 80-2, 133, 145
  Ross, Charles Campbell (chief designate), 96, 108
  Ross, Sir Campbell, 104
  Ross, Sir Charles, 135
  Ross, County of, 5, 86
  Ross, Dan, 114
  Ross, Daniel H., 139
  Ross, D.C., M.P., 136
  Ross, David, 11, 91, 147, 149, 154-5
  Ross, David Campbell, Chief of Clan, 96
  Ross, Donald, 102, 133
  Ross, Duncan, 102, 126, 135
  Ross, Elizabeth, 118, 119
  Ross, Ethel F.S. Williamson, Chief, 88, 95, 110
  Ross, Euphemia, 14, 15, 42, 46, 47, 48, 49, 51, 94, 176-8, 181-2
  Ross, Fenell, 115
  Rossfield, 126
  Ross, Gwynn, 136
Ross, George, 115, 116, 118-20, 131, 172
Ross, George Clunies, 151-3
Ross, Sir George, 134
Ross, Gertrude, 118, 119
Ross of Hawkhead, 12th Lord, 77-80
Ross, Hercules and Horatio of Rossie, 147
Ross, Hugh of Rarichies, 43, 45-6, 94, 118
Ross, Hugh, 139, 144, 173
Ross, Hutcheon, 16, 17, 68
Ross Institute, 96
Ross Islands, 153, 157
Ross, James, Commodore, 135, 137
Ross, James, Senator, U.S.A., 120
Ross, Jacob, 117, 120
Ross, James, 114-16, 120, 126, 132, 135
Ross, Dr. James, 139
Ross, Commander James Clark, 156, 157
Ross, Hon. John, 117, 118
Ross, John, 43, 69, 71-2, 114, 115, 118, 126, 127, 133, 150-1, 153-4
Ross, John M., 5, 148
Ross, Sir John, 155-7
Ross, Jonathan, 120
Ross, Jonas, 114
Ross, Commander J.K.L., 140
Ross, Katherine, 83
Ross, Keneth, 150
Ross, Killicross, 115
Ross, Lady, 76, 78, 80, 87
Ross, Leonard Warren, 135, 138
Ross, Malcolm, 78, 92, 93, 132
Ross, Margaret, 117
Ross, Naomi, 93
Ross, Nesbitt S., Judge, 135
Ross, Nicholas, 68
Ross, Nicholas of Pitcalnie, 91
Ross, Peter, 129
Ross, Peter H., 139
Ross, Raymond S., 135
Ross Rifle, 82, 86-7
Ross River, 133
Ross, Robert, 17, 121
Ross, Sir Ronald, 96, 105-8
Ross, Rosa Williamson, Chief, 77, 94-6, 110, 111
Ross, Samuel, 135
Ross, Sir Watty, 173
Ross, Susanna, 117, 119
Ross, Thomas, Capt., 170
Ross, William, 145, 150
Ross, Thomas, 17, 64, 115
Ross, Sir Walter de, 42

Ross, William, 64, 65, 133, 135
Ross, Wm. A., 126
Ross, William M., Judge, 135
Ross, William R., Hon., 135
Rostrevor, 122
Royal Highland Emigrants, 127
Royal Military College, 140
Royal Victoria Hospital, 141
Ruthven, Castle, 9, 10, 13, 46, 56

S

Scots, 6, 66, 116, 123-5
Scottish Presbyterian Church, 16
Scotwell, Earl of, 79
Scrymeogur, Sir James, 52
Sculptured stones, 20
Seaforth, Earl of, 72, 79
Selkirk, Lord, 129, 131
Septs of Clan Ross, 3
Seven Oaks, battle of, 131
Shandwick Rosses, 96, 98
Walter Ross, 1st laird, 97, 98
Donald Ross, 2nd laird, 97, 98
Andrew Ross, 3rd laird, 98
Robert Ross, 4th laird, 98, 100
William Ross, 5th laird, 98, 100
Andrew Ross, 6th laird, 98, 101
Andrew Ross, 7th laird, 98, 101, 102
Hugh Ross of Kerse and Skeldon, 99, 102
Lt. Col. Hugh Ross, 99, 103
Sir Campbell Ross, 99, 104, 105
Sir Ronald Ross, 99, 105, 106, 107
Charles Campbell Ross, Q.C., 64, 99, 108-10
Sheep, Cheviot, 84, 123
Sheriff or Ross, 75
Skye, Island of, 5, 9, 39, 41, 128, 129, 145
Skye, Lordship of, 39, 45
Skye and Lewis, Lord of, 39, 41
Sleat, house of, 59
Sleat, Sound of, 128
Smerte tribe, 4
Solway Firth, 131
Somerled, King of the Isles, 36, 44, 49, 50
South Sea Company, 81
Spey River, 17
Standing Stones, 19, 20
Clach an Truseil, 19
Clach a Charridh, 20
Cloch a Mhearlich, 20
Blar a Charaidh, 20
St. Andrews, 70
St. Columba, 15
Stornaway, 125
St. Duthac, 11, 18, 42, 43, 68, 173, 180
St. Duthac, shirt of, 43
Stirling, Earl of, 113, 114
St. Maelrubha, 39
St. Johnsbury V, 115
Sterling, U.S.A., 115
Stewart, Francis, 76, 77
Stewart, Lady Ann, 76
Stewart, Sir John, 47, 49
Stewart, Alexander (The Wolf), 46, 48
Strathgarvie, 2, 61
Strathglass, 128
Stromness, 129
Sudbury Mass, 139
Sutherland, Earl, 17
Sutherland, Robert, 65
Sutherlands, 66

T

Tacksmen, 8
Taggart, 3
Tain, 2, 16, 18, 68, 69, 70, 80, 88, 89, 94, 164, 169, 170, 173
Tain, Burgh of, 96, 173
Tain Historical Documents, 88, 89
Tain Tolbooth, 9, 89, 126
Tanistry, 8, 110, 111
Tantalon Castle, 55, 69
Tarantual, ship, 141
Tarbat, 16, 92, 164
Tarie, 8
Tarrell, 3
Terror, The ship, 157
Tolbooth of Tain, 9, 89, 126
Tarie, 8, 128
Tulloch, Earl of, 79

U

United Empire Loyalists, 127, 130, 131
Upper Canada, 128
Urquhart, 3, 10, 12, 56, 125
Urquhart Castle, 12, 56
Usher's Well, the wife of, 30

V

Van Gesel, Cornelius, 118
Van Gesel, Catherine, 118
Vass, 3, 65
Vicount of Canada, 114
Victory, The, 156, 157
Vitrified forts, 20
Voyageurs, 133

W

Wass, 3

Walter de Ross, Sir, 36, 42
Wife of Usher's Well, 30
William, Earl of Ross, 19
William of Orange, 17, 75
William the Lion, 6, 12, 184
Williams, Joanna, 117
Witchcraft, 70, 83
Witherspoon, 124
Wolf of Badenoch (Alexander Stewart), 13, 14, 46, 48, 178, 182
Wolfe, General, 169
Worcester, battle of, 75, 115, 134, 139

Y

York boats, 130
York Factory, 129, 130

# ABOUT THE AUTHOR

John Robert Ross, son of William Ross and Margaret Helena Shields, was born in Toronto, Canada. He took his medical education at University of Toronto and graduated with M.B. degree in 1926. After graduation he was a member of the Research team under the direction of Sir Frederick Banting, from whom he obtained a B.Sc. degree in the department of Medical Research at the Banting Institute. After further research at the Hospital for Sick Children, Toronto, where he was director of the Allergy Service, he commenced his medical practice in the specialties of Paediatrics and Allergy.

Dr. Ross enlisted as major and 2 I.C. in the Second Field Ambulance in 1940, and later received promotion to Lt.-Col. and Officer Commanding the Twenty Sixth Field Ambulance in the Second World War.

In the summer of 1936, when visiting in Scotland, he journeyed to Balnagowan Castle where he became very impressed with the ancient and noble history of the Earls of Ross and the later history of the Clan Ross. Since that time he has taken a particular interest in obtaining references to all available documents relating to Clan history from the late Chief of Clan, Miss Rosa R. Williamson Ross, from the late Charles Campbell Ross, Chief designate, and from many other sources for which grateful acknowledgement is given.

Dr. Ross is married to Eila Isobel, daughter of the late Dr. D. A. Hopper of Waterdown, Ontario. They have three children, Gordon David, John Donaldson, and Eila Marian.